MicroPython Cookbook

Over 110 practical recipes for programming embedded systems and microcontrollers with Python

Marwan Alsabbagh

BIRMINGHAM - MUMBAI

MicroPython Cookbook

Commissioning Editor: Richa Tripathi
Acquisition Editor: Chaitanya Nair
Content Development Editor: Ruvika Rao
Technical Editor: Romy Dias
Copy Editor: Safis Editing
Project Coordinator: Vaidehi Sawant
Proofreader: Safis Editing
Indexer: Darshana Jain
Graphics: Alishon Mendonsa
Production Coordinator: Alishon Mendonsa

First published: May 2019

Production reference: 1170519

Published by Packt Publishing Ltd.
Livery Place
35 Livery Street
Birmingham
B3 2PB, UK.

ISBN 978-1-83864-995-1

www.packtpub.com

`mapt.io`

Mapt is an online digital library that gives you full access to over 5,000 books and videos, as well as industry leading tools to help you plan your personal development and advance your career. For more information, please visit our website.

Why subscribe?

- Spend less time learning and more time coding with practical eBooks and Videos from over 4,000 industry professionals

- Improve your learning with Skill Plans built especially for you

- Get a free eBook or video every month

- Mapt is fully searchable

- Copy and paste, print, and bookmark content

Packt.com

Did you know that Packt offers eBook versions of every book published, with PDF and ePub files available? You can upgrade to the eBook version at `www.packt.com` and as a print book customer, you are entitled to a discount on the eBook copy. Get in touch with us at `customercare@packtpub.com` for more details.

At `www.packt.com`, you can also read a collection of free technical articles, sign up for a range of free newsletters, and receive exclusive discounts and offers on Packt books and eBooks.

Contributors

About the author

Marwan Alsabbagh has been coding in some form or other since before the web existed and has continued to develop software, with a particular passion for Python, his preferred programming language, for over a decade. He has been a speaker at a number of global Python conferences, where he has been known to present microcontroller projects with a healthy dose of humor and stage theatrics. The snow globe intruder alert system, which he created with his creative and curious daughters, was one of his favorite MicroPython projects. His research interests include software engineering, microcontrollers, and 3D printing.

I could not have reached this far in my life or in creating this book if it was not for the support of my loving family. Thank you for putting up with all the bananas I stole to make a whole chapter on programming microcontrollers with bananas.

About the reviewers

Arunkumar NT is 43 years of age, has completed his M.Sc. (Phy) and MBA (Finance), and is currently pursuing his CMA and CS qualifications. He has over 20 years' corporate experience and 2 years' experience of teaching MBA students. He is an entrepreneur and has previously worked for Airtel, Citi Finance, and ICICI Bank. He has also worked on the *Python for Finance* book.

I would like to thank my parents (my father for his support as a backup and filtering system, and my mother for her trust despite my repeated failures), my brothers (Anand NT for his critical acknowledgement and Prabhanjan NT for his love and support), my wife (Bharathi K), and my children (Vardhini AT and Charvangi AT). I would also like to thank my gurus (Prof. Badwe (deceased) and Prof. Sundararajan) and, of course, not forgetting my friends—Dr. Sreepathi B and Anand Karnawat.

Bhaumik Vaidya is an experienced computer vision engineer and mentor. He has worked extensively on OpenCV and the TensorFlow library to solve computer vision problems. He is a University gold medalist at the master's level, and is now doing his PhD on the acceleration of computer vision algorithms built using OpenCV and deep learning libraries, such as TensorFlow and Keras, on GPUs. He, along with his PhD mentor, has also received an NVIDIA Jetson TX1, which is an embedded development platform, as a research grant from NVIDIA. He has previously worked in the VLSI domain as an ASIC verification engineer. He has published numerous research papers in reputable journals, has filed two provisional patents, and has written one book on computer vision and GPU programming.

Packt is searching for authors like you

If you're interested in becoming an author for Packt, please visit authors.packtpub.com and apply today. We have worked with thousands of developers and tech professionals, just like you, to help them share their insight with the global tech community. You can make a general application, apply for a specific hot topic that we are recruiting an author for, or submit your own idea.

Table of Contents

Preface

MicroPython is a lean implementation of the Python 3 programming language that is capable of running on a wide range of microcontrollers. It provides the majority of features in the Python programming language, such as functions, classes, lists, dictionaries, strings, reading and writing files, list comprehensions, and exception handling to these microcontrollers.

Microcontrollers are tiny computers that usually include a CPU, memory, and input/output peripherals. Even though they will have more limited resources compared to a PC, they can be made to a much smaller dimension, with less power consumption and at a lower cost. These strengths make it possible to use them in a wide range of new applications that weren't possible before.

This book will cover a number of different features in the MicroPython language, as well as a number of different microcontroller boards. The initial chapters will provide simple and easy to understand recipes to get these boards to interact with people and their environment. Topics ranging from reading temperature, light, and motion data from sensors to interacting with push buttons, slide switches, and touchpads will also be covered. Producing output on these boards with audio playback and LED animations will also be covered in the early chapters. Once this foundation is in place, we will build more involved projects, such as interactive two-player games, electronic musical instruments, and an **Internet of Things** (**IoT**) weather machine. You will be able to take the skills you learn from these recipes and directly apply them to your own embedded projects.

Who this book is for

This book aims to help people apply the power and ease of use of the Python language to the versatility of microcontrollers. Prior knowledge of Python is expected in order to understand this book.

What this book covers

Chapter 1, *Getting Started with MicroPython*, introduces the Adafruit Circuit Playground Express microcontroller and teaches the core skills for using MicroPython on this hardware.

Chapter 2, *Controlling LEDs*, covers methods of controlling NeoPixel LEDs, the color of the lights, and how to create animated light shows by controlling the timing of light changes on the board.

Chapter 3, *Creating Sound and Music*, discusses methods of how to make sounds and playmusic on the Adafruit Circuit Playground Express. Topics such as making the board beep at a certain sound frequency and playing music files using the WAV file format and the board's built-in speakers will be covered.

Chapter 4, *Interacting with Buttons*, shows methods of interacting with the buttons and touch pads that come on board with the Adafruit Circuit Playground Express. The basics of detecting when a button is pressed or not, as well as advanced topics, such as fine tuning the touch threshold of the capacitive touch pads, will be discussed.

Chapter 5, *Reading Sensor Data*, introduces methods of reading sensor data from a number of different types of sensors, such as temperature, light, and motion sensors.

Chapter 6, *Button Bash Game*, guides us to create a two-player game called *Button Bash* that you can play directly on the Circuit Playground Express using the push buttons, NeoPixels, and built-in speakers.

Chapter 7, *Fruity Tunes*, explains how to create a musical instrument with the Adafruit Circuit Playground Express and some bananas. Touchpads will be used to interact with the bananas and play different musical sounds each time you touch a different banana.

Chapter 8, *Let's Move It, Move It*, introduces the Adafruit CRICKIT hardware add-on that will help control motors and servos through our Python scripts; in particular, their speed, rotational direction, and angle will be controlled through these scripts.

Chapter 9, *Coding on the micro:bit*, covers methods of interacting with the micro:bit platform. How to control its LED grid display and interact with the buttons that come on board will be discussed.

Chapter 10, *Controlling the ESP8266*, introduces the Adafruit Feather HUZZAH ESP8266 microcontroller, and discusses its features and strengths compared to other microcontrollers. Topics such as connecting to Wi-Fi networks, using the WebREPL, and transferring files over Wi-Fi will be covered.

Chapter 11, *Interacting with the Filesystem*, discusses a number of topics related to the **operating system (OS)**, such as listing files, removing files, creating directories, and calculating disk usage.

Chapter 12, *Networking*, discusses how to perform a number of different network operations, such as DNS lookups, implementing an HTTP client, and HTTP servers.

Chapter 13, *Interacting with the Adafruit FeatherWing OLED*, introduces the Adafruit FeatherWing OLED hardware add-on, which can be attached to the ESP8266 to add a display to an internet-connected microcontroller, to display display text graphics and interact with the user using the included three hardware push buttons.

Chapter 14, *Building an IoT Weather Machine*, explains how to create an IoT device that will retrieve weather data and show it to the user at the press of a button from the IoT device itself.

Chapter 15, *Coding on the Adafruit HalloWing*, introduces the Adafruit HalloWing microcontroller, which comes with a 128x128 full-color **Thin-Film Transistor (TFT)** display built into it, providing the ability to display rich graphical images on the microcontroller.

To get the most out of this book

Readers are expected to have a basic knowledge of the Python programming language. It would be beneficial for readers to have a basic understanding of importing packages and working with the REPL to get the most out of this book.

Download the example code files

You can download the example code files for this book from your account at www.packtpub.com. If you purchased this book elsewhere, you can visit www.packtpub.com/support and register to have the files emailed directly to you.

You can download the code files by following these steps:

1. Log in or register at www.packtpub.com.
2. Select the **SUPPORT** tab.
3. Click on **Code Downloads & Errata**.
4. Enter the name of the book in the **Search** box and follow the onscreen instructions.

Once the file is downloaded, please make sure that you unzip or extract the folder using the latest version of:

- WinRAR/7-Zip for Windows
- Zipeg/iZip/UnRarX for Mac
- 7-Zip/PeaZip for Linux

The code bundle for the book is also hosted on GitHub at `https://github.com/PacktPublishing/MicroPython-Cookbook`. We also have other code bundles from our rich catalog of books and videos available at `https://github.com/PacktPublishing/`. Check them out!

Download the color images

We also provide a PDF file that has color images of the screenshots/diagrams used in this book. You can download it here: `https://www.packtpub.com/sites/default/files/downloads/9781838649951_ColorImages.pdf`.

Conventions used

There are a number of text conventions used throughout this book.

`CodeInText`: Indicates code words in text, database table names, folder names, filenames, file extensions, pathnames, dummy URLs, user input, and Twitter handles. Here is an example: "This recipe requires Python and `pip` to be installed on the computer."

A block of code is set as follows:

```
from adafruit_circuitplayground.express import cpx
import time

cpx.pixels[0] = (255, 0, 0) # set first NeoPixel to the color red
time.sleep(60)
```

When we wish to draw your attention to a particular part of a code block, the relevant lines or items are set in bold:

```
from adafruit_circuitplayground.express import cpx
import time

RAINBOW = [
 0xFF0000, # red
 0xFFA500, # orange
```

Any command-line input or output is written as follows:

```
>>> 1+1
2
```

Bold: Indicates a new term, an important word, or words that you see onscreen. For example, words in menus or dialog boxes appear in the text like this. Here is an example: "Click the **Serial** button on the toolbar to open a REPL session with the device."

 Warnings or important notes appear like this.

 Tips and tricks appear like this.

Sections

In this book, you will find several headings that appear frequently (*Getting ready, How to do it..., How it works..., There's more...*, and *See also*).

To give clear instructions on how to complete a recipe, use these sections as follows:

Getting ready

This section tells you what to expect in the recipe and describes how to set up any software or any preliminary settings required for the recipe.

How to do it...

This section contains the steps required to follow the recipe.

How it works...

This section usually consists of a detailed explanation of what happened in the previous section.

There's more...

This section consists of additional information about the recipe in order to make you more knowledgeable about the recipe.

See also

This section provides helpful links to other useful information for the recipe.

Get in touch

Feedback from our readers is always welcome.

General feedback: Email feedback@packtpub.com and mention the book title in the subject of your message. If you have questions about any aspect of this book, please email us at questions@packtpub.com.

Errata: Although we have taken every care to ensure the accuracy of our content, mistakes do happen. If you have found a mistake in this book, we would be grateful if you would report this to us. Please visit www.packtpub.com/submit-errata, selecting your book, clicking on the Errata Submission Form link, and entering the details.

Piracy: If you come across any illegal copies of our works in any form on the internet, we would be grateful if you would provide us with the location address or website name. Please contact us at copyright@packtpub.com with a link to the material.

If you are interested in becoming an author: If there is a topic that you have expertise in and you are interested in either writing or contributing to a book, please visit authors.packtpub.com.

Reviews

Please leave a review. Once you have read and used this book, why not leave a review on the site that you purchased it from? Potential readers can then see and use your unbiased opinion to make purchase decisions, we at Packt can understand what you think about our products, and our authors can see your feedback on their book. Thank you!

For more information about Packt, please visit packtpub.com.

1
Getting started with MicroPython

It's an exciting time to work with technologies such as MicroPython. They make tiny and inexpensive hardware devices more accessible, as you can use a high-level language such as Python to code on them. Tasks such as retrieving data from web services can easily be done in a few lines of code, compared to other microcontroller languages that would require many more steps, because they operate at such a low level compared to Python. This is very empowering, as you will get results faster and be able to iterate through different designs and prototypes in a shorter amount of time.

In this chapter, we will provide you with the essential skills to get started and be productive with the software and hardware needed to run MicroPython. You'll learn how to update the firmware and libraries on the device. Recipes to load your first program on the board and use advanced features, such as auto-reloading your code, will also be covered. Finally, a number of recipes will cover the usage of the REPL that is a powerful way to quickly interact and experiment with the available components on MicroPython devices.

In this chapter, we will be covering the following recipes:

- Flashing the microcontroller firmware
- Executing your first program
- Using screen to access the REPL
- Using Mu to access the REPL
- Executing commands in the REPL
- Using the auto-reload feature
- Updating the CircuitPython Library

What is MicroPython?

MicroPython is the creation of the Australian programmer and physicist Damien George, who launched a Kickstarter campaign in 2013 to support the development of the language and the initial microcontroller hardware that it would run on. After the success of the project, more and more devices (which have a variety of chipsets from different manufactures) have become supported by MicroPython, creating a wide range of devices from which to choose when you make a project using MicroPython.

MicroPython is a lean implementation of the Python 3 programming language that is capable of running on hardware with very limited resources, such as microcontrollers. MicroPython has implemented the majority of features in the Python programming language, such as functions, classes, lists, dictionaries, strings, reading and writing files, list comprehensions, and exception handling.

The REPL is also implemented and can be interacted with using a serial connection. A selection of the core Python libraries is provided, which allows a range of applications to be implemented. The JSON and `socket` libraries allow web client and server implementations, making Python-based **Internet of Things (IoT)** projects on microcontrollers a reality.

By bringing one of the most popular and easy to use programming languages to the exciting world of embedded computing, MicroPython opens up new doors for makers and entrepreneurs to bring their creations to life. This book will explore the different ways to leverage the MicroPython language with a variety of unique microcontroller devices that each bring a different set of capabilities to the table.

One of the unique and fascinating aspects of running MicroPython on microcontrollers is that it does not run on an **operating system (OS)**, but instead runs directly on bare metal. These unique characteristics manifest themselves in many ways, such as the ability to run your Python code at the instant the hardware is powered on, as there is no OS that needs to boot up.

The other aspect of this is that the Python code has direct access to control and interact with the hardware, creating hardware possibilities that would not be possible with a typical Python application running on an OS.

As we know now that MicroPython runs on a microcontroller, let's see what microcontrollers are all about.

What is a microcontroller?

Microcontrollers are small computers on a single chip. They usually include a CPU, memory, and input/output peripherals. They will have more limited computing resources than what might be found on a modern PC.

Compared to a PC, however, they can be made to a much smaller dimension, allowing them to be embedded in all sorts of electronic and mechanical devices. Their power consumption is often far less in orders of magnitude, thus providing battery life for days. They have a much lower cost per unit, which opens up possibilities of having hundreds of such devices to collect sensor data across a broad geographical area and still be financially feasible.

Traditionally, it was a difficult process to create applications on microcontrollers because you would have to write very low-level code that took time and was difficult to debug. MicroPython brings the ease of use of Python to microcontroller. It's able to provide this easier interaction with the hardware, and yet still work in such a resource constrained environment and provide a wide range of functionality with a strong level of responsiveness.

What is CircuitPython?

CircuitPython is a branch of MicroPython created by Adafruit Industries that makes working with microcontrollers simpler. It has excellent support for many of the sensors and components that come with Adafruit devices through its Python libraries. It also allows code to be easily loaded and run without having to install any additional software applications by exposing the microcontroller's storage as a disk drive.

Generally, the differences between MicroPython and CircuitPython are minor, and, in many instances, code will run the same on both implementations.

What is the Circuit Playground Express?

The Adafruit Circuit Playground Express is an inexpensive, yet versatile microcontroller with a rich set of input and output devices that comes built-in with the device. The following are some of the main hardware features present in this device:

- 10 mini NeoPixels, each with the ability to display a full range of colors
- As motion sensor (triple-axis accelerometer with tap detection and free-fall detection)
- A temperature sensor
- A light sensor
- A sound sensor
- A mini speaker
- Two push buttons, which are labeled A and B
- A slide switch
- An infrared receiver and transmitter
- Eight alligator-clip friendly input/output pins
- Supports I2C and PWM output
- Seven capacitive touch inputs
- A red LED
- A reset button
- An ATSAMD21 ARM Cortex M0 processor, running at 3.3 V and 48 MHz
- 2 MB of flash storage
- A micro USB port for connecting to a PC

These will be the only required devices for eight chapters. Later chapters will introduce a different set of devices.

 Please refer to `https://learn.adafruit.com/welcome-to-circuitpython?view=all` for more information.

Where to buy

The Adafruit Circuit Playground Express can be purchased directly from Adafruit (`https:/ /www.adafruit.com/product/3333`). It can also be purchased from online retailers, such as Amazon and Pimoroni.

For the purpose of this book, we recommend buying the Circuit Playground Express – Base Kit (`https://www.adafruit.com/product/3517`) and also includes a USB cable and battery pack so that projects can easily be made portable.

References

Here are a few references:

- The MicroPython web page at `http://micropython.org`
- The MicroPython project on Kickstarter at `https://www.kickstarter.com/ projects/214379695/micro-python-python-for-microcontrollers`
- An article in microcontrollers on PC Mag at `https://www.pcmag.com/ encyclopedia/term/46924/microcontroller`
- The Adafruit learning guide on CircuitPython at `https://learn.adafruit.com/ welcome-to-circuitpython/what-is-circuitpython`
- The CircuitPython official documentation at `https://circuitpython. readthedocs.io`

Flashing the microcontroller firmware

In this recipe, we will show how to flash the firmware on the Circuit Playground Express with the latest CircuitPython firmware. There are two reasons to this before you start working with this device. First, the device also supports the Microsoft MakeCode programming environment and flashing the device with the CircuitPython firmware prepares it for use with the Python language.

Second, the CircuitPython language is under constant development, with a release every few months, so it is a good idea to update the firmware from time to time to load the latest release of the language onto the board.

Getting ready

This chapter's introduction gives us directions on how to buy the Circuit Playground Express, which will be required for all the recipes in this chapter. A USB micro B cable and a computer running macOS, Windows, or Linux will also be required.

How to do it...

Let's look at the following steps:

1. Download the latest CircuitPython Circuit Playground Express UF2 file (`https:/ /github.com/adafruit/circuitpython/releases/latest`). The name of the UF2 file for version 3.1.2 of CircuitPython is `adafruit-circuitpython-circuitplayground_express-3.1.2.uf2`. For each release of CircuitPython, there are many different `uf2` files for different supported microcontrollers. Make sure that you download the file for the Circuit Playground Express device.

> We will use the latest stable version of CircuitPython in this recipe, which is currently 3.1.2.

2. Connect the USB cable to the Circuit Playground Express and the computer.
3. Double-click the reset button located at the center of the board. If all goes well, you will see all the LEDs turn green; otherwise, there is most likely an issue with the USB cable being used. In some instances, if a double-click doesn't work, try a single click of the reset button.

4. You will see a new disk appear called **CPLAYBOOT**:

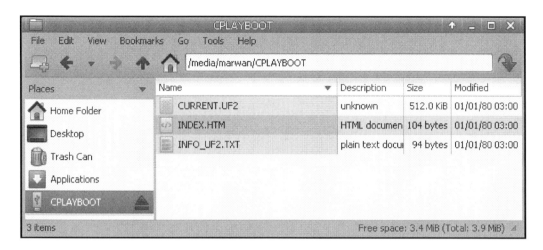

5. Copy the UF2 file into this drive.
6. Once the UF2 file has been fully written to the device, the firmware will be updated and a new drive will appear, called **CIRCUITPY**:

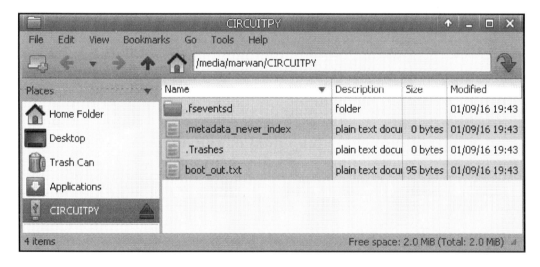

Now, our Circuit Playground Express can be used.

How it works...

Traditionally, special software has had to be installed and used to handle the delicate process of flashing a microcontroller. Microsoft developed the UF2 method, which greatly simplifies the process by not requiring any special software or command-line execution to flash the microcontroller.

Once the board is placed into the bootloader mode, it will then expect a UF2 file to be saved to it. When the UF2 is copied to the drive, the microcontroller will detect that the file copy has been completed and then automatically proceed to flash the microcontroller and restart the device, at which point the device is reattached and ready to be used.

 The UF2 file format can be found at`https://github.com/Microsoft/uf2`.

There's more...

The UF2 approach to flashing microcontroller firmware makes the process easier and faster compared to previous approaches. Not all MicroPython boards support the UF2 method and so require the more involved approach of installing special software to do the firmware flashing. The exact process and software required varies between different boards and manufactures.

When you use this flashing software, it will frequently require that you know the exact name of the serial device that the device appears as on your computer. The naming of these devices varies between Windows, Linux, and macOS. This type of software is usually required to be run in the Terminal, so you'll have to have some command-line knowledge to inter with it. For all these reasons, the use of UF2 with supported devices such as the Circuit Playground Express is the preferred way of starting your experimentation with MicroPython.

See also

There are a number of resources, both on the Adafruit and Microsoft websites, relating to the process described in this recipe. Here are a few references:

- Documentation of updating CircuitPython can be found at `https://learn.adafruit.com/adafruit-circuit-playground-express/circuitpython-quickstart`.
- The UF2 process is explained in more detail at `https://makecode.com/blog/one-chip-to-flash-them-all`.

Executing your first program

In this recipe, we will show you how to load your first program on the Circuit Playground Express and how to modify the program and reload it. The program will then light one of the ten NeoPixels that come available on the board.

Getting ready

Once the Circuit Playground Express has had the CircuitPython firmware flashed, you may load Python scripts onto the board and run them.

How to do it...

Let's have a look at how to do this:

1. Make sure that the board is connected to your computer with a USB cable and that the CIRCUITPY drive appears.
2. Save a text file on the drive with the following contents and name it main.py:

```
from adafruit_circuitplayground.express import cpx
import time

cpx.pixels[0] = (255, 0, 0)  # set first NeoPixel to the color red
time.sleep(60)
```

3. Once the file has been saved, eject the drive, and remove and reconnect the USB cable from the computer.
4. The first NeoPixel on the drive should light up with a red color.
5. Open the `main.py` file in your text editor of choice and change the `cpx.pixels[0]` line to `cpx.pixels[1]`. Save the file. This change will make the second NeoPixel light up instead of the first.
6. Eject the drive, remove, and then reconnect the USB cable to see the change take effect.

How it works...

When the device is turned on it looks for certain files, such as `code.py` or `main.py`, that, if found, will be executed as part of the startup process. In this way, you can specify the code you want run when the device is powered on. The script first imports the `adafruit_circuitplayground.express` library so that it can control the NeoPixels. The first NeoPixel is set to the color red by giving it a set of appropriate RGB values.

Finally, the script will sleep for 60 seconds so that the LED remains lit for one minute before the script ends execution.

There's more...

Now that the board has been loaded with a Python script, it can be disconnected from the computer and have the battery pack attached to it. Once the battery pack is powered on by the script, it should run and light up the selected NeoPixel.

This is a simple way to create portable and inexpensive projects that can have a code running directly from the board with no need for a connected PC and can be powered simply by three AAA batteries.

See also

There are a number of files that CircuitPython looks for when it boots up, which are described at `https://learn.adafruit.com/welcome-to-circuitpython?view=all#naming-your-program-file-7-30`.

Using screen to access the REPL

Linux and macOS have powerful Terminal emulators, such as `screen`, that can be used to directly connect to the device's **Read-Eval-Print Loop** (**REPL**) over a serial (USB) connection. This recipe will show how to connect to the REPL and start running a Python code interactively.

Getting ready

Either macOS or a Linux computer may be used for this recipe and may require the `screen` command to be available. On macOS, the Screen application is built-in and so requires no installation. On Ubuntu, the Linux Screen can be installed with the `apt install screen` command.

How to do it...

Let's have a look at how to connect the REPL and run the code:

1. Open the computer's Terminal application.
2. List device names before plugging in device by running `ls /dev/ttyACM*` on Linux or `ls /dev/tty.*` on macOS.
3. Connect the board to your computer with a USB cable.
4. List the device names again with the same command to discover the device name of the board.
5. If the device name is `/dev/ttyACM0`, then the `screen` command would be `screen /dev/ttyACM0 115200`.
6. Enter the command in the Terminal and start the Screen application.
7. If Screen is able to connect successfully, the Python REPL should appear on the Terminal with output similar to the following text:

   ```
   Adafruit CircuitPython 3.1.2 on 2019-01-07; Adafruit
   CircuitPlayground Express with samd21g18
   >>>
   ```

8. If the prompt doesn't appear, you can try pressing *Ctrl* + *C* and then press *Enter*, which will stop the currently running Python script and run the REPL with the following message:

   ```
   Press any key to enter the REPL. Use CTRL-D to reload.
   ```

9. Once the REPL prompt appears, we will have to test if the prompt is working by evaluating the 1+1 expression. It should produce the following output:

```
>>> 1+1
2
```

How it works...

The Circuit Playground Express exposes a serial device over the USB connection, which can be accessed by a number of different Terminal emulator programs. Besides `screen`, there are other programs, such as `picocom` and `minicom`, that may also be used.

The last parameter that was set as 115,200 in the command sets the baud rate of the connection, which should be set at that speed. Once the connection is successfully established, an interactive session is commenced that allows expressions to be directly evaluated on the device and the output is directly displayed on the Terminal.

There's more...

Many of the recipes in the book will introduce the different parts of a script using the REPL. This will give you a chance to get immediate feedback as you run each snippet of code. Once you've entered the different snippets in the REPL you can also use REPL features to assist in your experimentation with the code. You can use the *up* and *down* arrow keys to move through the history of commands that have been entered in the REPL. For example, if you had just executed a line of code in the REPL that turned on a specific pixel on the board, you could press the *up* key and change which pixel is lit up by editing the line and pressing *Enter* again.

See also

Here are a few references:

- The use of the REPL on CircuitPython boards is discussed in detail at `https://learn.adafruit.com/welcome-to-circuitpython/the-repl`.
- Details on using the REPL to access MicroPython can be found at `https://learn.adafruit.com/micropython-basics-how-to-load-micropython-on-a-board/serial-terminal`.

Using Mu to access the REPL

Mu is an easy-to-use graphical code editor written in Python that runs on Windows, macOS, Linux, and the Raspberry Pi. In this recipe, we will learn how to install Mu and use it to access the REPL on the Circuit Playground Express.

Getting ready

This recipe requires Python and `pip` to be installed on the computer. The Mu editor will be installed using the `pip` command, so this recipe can optionally be run within `virtualenv`.

How to do it...

Let's have a look at how to do this:

1. Execute the following `pip3 install mu-editor` command to install the Mu editor.
2. Run the `mu-editor` command to start the editor.
3. The first time you run the editor, it will ask which mode it should run in. On the following screenshot, select the **Adafruit CircuitPython** mode:

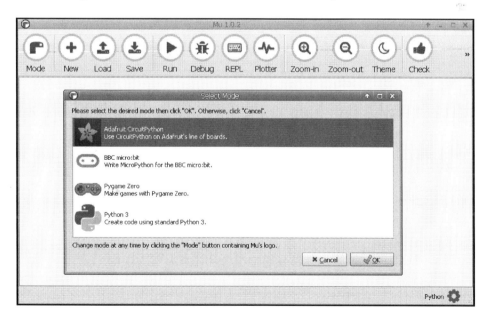

4. Click the **Serial** button on the toolbar to open a REPL session with the device.

5. On Linux systems, if a **Cannot connect to device** error appears, then exit the editor and start it again with the `sudo /full/path/to/mu-editor` command, where the absolute path to the editor is given.

6. Once a connection is successfully made to the device, you can test the REPL by evaluating the `1+1` expression, which should produce output like the following screenshot:

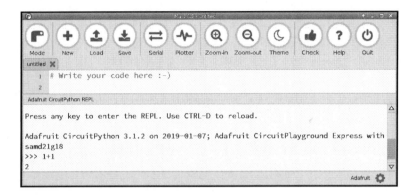

How it works...

When you click on the **Serial** button in the Mu editor, it will attempt to open a serial connection to the board. If successful, it captures your input, sends it the device, and displays the output just as a typical Terminal emulator would.

The beauty of this application is that it works on all the major desktop OSes and automatically finds the correct device address without the need to manually specify it, as is required by your typical Terminal emulators. It also has a very simple and approachable layout, making it easy to use for first-time users to connect to microcontrollers.

There's more...

The Mu editor is a great graphical application to begin with when you first start working with MicroPython. Its simple and intuitive design makes it easy to get productive fast and makes it fun to explore its different features. Beyond its REPL features, it also has the main part of the Screen, which can be used to edit and save Python scripts. It has code-editing features such as code completion and will show helpful popups with details on a function's accepted arguments and documentation on what the function does.

See also

Here are a few references:

- The GitHub repository for the project can be found at `https://github.com/mu-editor/mu`.
- The projects homepage can be found at`https://codewith.mu/`.

Executing commands in the REPL

The following recipe shows different ways that the REPL can be used.

Getting ready

Any one method can be used from the preceding two recipes here to obtain a REPL.

How to do it...

1. Open the REPL through your preferred application.
2. Many of the same capabilities provided by the REPL in CPython also work in the MicroPython implementation. The last returned value can be accessed with _:

```
>>> 2 + 2
4
>>> _ + 2
6
```

3. Continuation lines are also supported, making it possible to define functions or `for` loops through the REPL, as shown in the following output:

```
>>> def add(a, b):
...     return a + b
...
...
...
>>> add(2, 2)
4
>>>
```

4. Arbitrary precision integers are also supported, even on constrained microcontroller hardware. The following code shows arithmetic with integers beyond the limit of a 64-bit integer value:

```
>>> 2**100 + 2**101
3802951800684688204490109616128
```

How it works...

The REPL implementation has most of the features that we've come to know and love in the CPython implementation. The MicroPython implementation has to deal with tough hardware constraints so that it can run on a microcontroller. But, even with these constraints, the end user experience of the REPL in both implementations is almost identical, making it an easy transition for Python developers.

There's more...

The REPL can be an invaluable tool when you want to experiment with certain MicroPython libraries or certain features on a device. It lets you easily import different Python modules and call functions provided by those libraries in a more direct fashion to discover how they will actually interact with the hardware. Many components on these microcontrollers can be fine-tuned for different project needs. The REPL frequently ends up being an ideal place to do this fine-tuning.

See also

Here are a few references:

- The MicroPython Interactive Interpreter Mode (REPL) is documented at `http://docs.micropython.org/en/latest/reference/repl.html`.
- Documentation on the MicroPython built-in types can be found at `http://docs.micropython.org/en/latest/genrst/builtin_types.html`.

Using the auto-reload feature

The following recipe shows how to use auto-reload so that the cycle of editing and running code can become much faster and more fun.

Getting ready

Any of the methods used in the previous recipes can be used here to obtain a REPL.

How to do it...

Let's have a look at how to do this:

1. Open the `main.py` file and save the `print('hi there')` statement in the file.
2. Open the REPL through your preferred application. With the REPL open, press *Ctrl + D*. The following output should appear:

```
Adafruit CircuitPython 3.1.2 on 2019-01-07; Adafruit
CircuitPlayground Express with samd21g18
>>>
>>>
soft reboot

Auto-reload is on. Simply save files over USB to run them or enter
REPL to disable.
main.py output:
hi there

Press any key to enter the REPL. Use CTRL-D to reload.
```

3. Edit the `main.py` file and change the contents to `print('hi there again')`. The following output should be automatically displayed:

```
soft reboot

Auto-reload is on. Simply save files over USB to run them or enter
REPL to disable.
main.py output:
hi there again

Press any key to enter the REPL. Use CTRL-D to reload.
```

How it works...

By pressing *Ctrl + D*, the board will enter into auto-reload mode. In this mode, you can open the `main.py` file in your text editor of choice, and, the moment you save the file, the board detects that a change has happened and performs a soft reboot.

The soft reboot can be seen in the Screen output and then the new version of the code is executed with its output displayed immediately.

There's more...

It is quite common to start a script with a few basic lines of code to get the initial part of a script functioning. Once you have your first basic version running, you will go through many iterations to tweak and enhance it so that it behaves just the way you want it to. Beyond these tweaks, the inevitable bugs will appear in your code as you wrangle it into submission. The auto-reload feature will become your best friend during these intensive coding sessions as it will let you get results much faster and in an intuitive way.

See also

Here are a few references:

- The soft reset features of MicroPython are described at `http://docs.micropython.org/en/v1.8.6/wipy/wipy/tutorial/reset.html`.
- Documentation on leaving the REPL can be found at `https://learn.adafruit.com/welcome-to-circuitpython?view=all#returning-to-the-serial-console-10-24`.

Updating the CircuitPython Library

In addition to updating the firmware, there is also a rich set of Python libraries called the CircuitPython Library that can also be updated with the latest supported features.

Getting ready

Any of themethods used in the previous recipes can be used hereto obtain a REPL.

How to do it...

Let's have a look at how to do this:

1. Open the REPL through your preferred application.
2. Download the latest CircuitPython Library Bundle release (`https://github.com/adafruit/Adafruit_CircuitPython_Bundle/releases/latest`). The name of the bundle file is `adafruit-circuitpython-bundle-3.x-mpy-20190212.zip`. Since our firmware is using the 3.x release, we must select the bundle that is also for the 3.x release. Always use the `mpy` version, as this is optimized to use less disk space and has reduced memory usage.

> We are using the latest auto-release version of the CircuitPython Library Bundle in this recipe, which is version 20190212 of the 3.x series.

3. Extract the `.zip` file to a location on your computer.
4. If the `CIRCUITPY` drive does not contain a `lib` folder, then create one now.
5. Copy the contents of the extracted `lib` folder into the `lib` folder on the device.
6. Perform a soft reboot in the REPL by pressing *Ctrl + D*.
7. Run `import simpleio` in the REPL.
8. If it has executed successfully, then the libraries have been successfully loaded, as the `simpleio` module is not part of the firmware and was imported from the library folder.

How it works...

The `lib` path that was created is one of the standard paths the CircuitPython will look in when importing Python packages. By adding Python packages to this folder, this makes it available for import by any scripts running on the device.

The `mpy` files are built from the original source `py` files and bundled all together in one package to make it easier to install.

There's more...

The CircuitPython Library is under constant development, so it's important to know how to update the library on the board so that you can get the latest features. As you experiment with code from projects you find on the internet, you might occasionally find examples that don't work on your board because you are running an outdated version of the CircuitPython Library. Keep your board to the latest version, as this can help prevent this from happening.

See also

Here are a few references:

- For more details on how the `mpy` files are created, check out the `mpy-cross` command at `https://learn.adafruit.com/building-circuitpython/build-circuitpython`.
- Information on installing the CircuitPython Library Bundle is available at `https://learn.adafruit.com/adafruit-circuit-playground-express?view=all#installing-the-circuitpython-library-bundle-12-5`.

Controlling LEDs 2

In this chapter, we will introduce several methods of controlling the range of NeoPixel LEDs that come with the Adafruit Circuit Playground Express. In these recipes, we will examine various ways of setting the colors of the pixels, each with its own trade-off.

We will also demonstrate how to time operations so that fades and other light animation effects can be created. NeoPixels are a powerful way of allowing a richer visual interaction with your projects. These recipes will provide you with the necessary building blocks to incorporate these visual concepts into your own projects.

In this chapter, we will cover the following recipes:

- Turning on the pin 13 LED
- Setting the brightness of the NeoPixel
- Controlling the color of a single NeoPixel
- Displaying an LED color using the RGB and hex code
- Setting an LED color using color names
- Setting all NeoPixels to the same color
- Setting a range of NeoPixels to one color
- Generating random NeoPixel LED colors
- Creating LED animations with random colors
- Creating LED animations with rainbow colors

The Adafruit Circuit Playground Express layout

The following diagram shows the locations of the LEDs that will be used in this chapter:

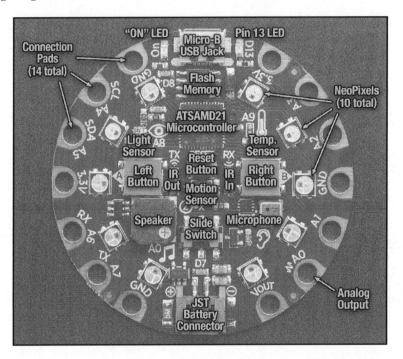

Courtesy of adafruit.com

The pin 13 LED is a simple single red LED that will be used in the first recipe. There are a total of 10 NeoPixels on the board. Each NeoPixel is made up of a red, green, and blue LED. By controlling the individual brightness of each of these LEDs, you will be able to set any NeoPixel to a specific color.

Turning on the pin 13 LED

In this recipe, we will learn how to turn the pin 13 LED on and off. This is the simplest LED available on the board as it has only one color, and interacting with it in Python is also very straightforward. For these reasons, the pin 13 LED is a good starting point.

Getting ready

You will need access to the REPL on the Circuit Playground Express to run the code presented in this recipe.

How to do it...

To do this, perform the following steps:

1. Run the following lines of code in the REPL:

```
>>> from adafruit_circuitplayground.express import cpx
>>> cpx.red_led = True
```

2. You should see the pin 13 LED turn red at this stage.
3. Check the current state of the LED using the following code:

```
>>> cpx.red_led
True
```

4. To turn off the LED, run the following code in the REPL:

```
>>> cpx.red_led = False
```

5. The light of the pin 13 LED will now be switched off.

How it works...

The first line of code imports the Circuit Playground Express library. This library contains an object class called `express`, which is the main class that we will use to interact with the hardware on this board. When the library is imported, it creates an instance of this class called `cpx`.

The `cpx` object exposes a property called `red_led`. This property can be used to retrieve the current value of the LED. If the LED is on, it will return the `True` value; otherwise, if the LED is off, it will return the `False` value. Setting the value of this property will turn the LED on or off depending on whether a `True` or `False` value is set.

There's more...

This is one of the simplest LED lights on the board to deal with, because it is controlled by setting a value to either `True` or `False`. You cannot control the color or the brightness of this LED. The other recipes in this book will control the NeoPixel lights on the board, which have a richer range of functionality and as a result, a more complicated API is needed to control them.

See also

You can find out more information using the following references:

- Documentation on the `red_led` property can be found at `https://circuitpython.readthedocs.io/projects/circuitplayground/en/latest/api.html#adafruit_circuitplayground.express.Express.red_led`.
- Details on importing the `cpx` variable can be found at `https://circuitpython.readthedocs.io/projects/circuitplayground/en/latest/#usage-example`.

Setting the brightness of the NeoPixel

Controlling the brightness of the pixels will be the theme of this recipe. It is important to be able to set the brightness of the pixels depending on the need of the project. Note that you will have to change the brightness to a level that is bright enough so that the pixels are clearly visible, but not so bright that it causes discomfort.

Getting ready

You will need access to the REPL on the Circuit Playground Express to run the code presented in this recipe.

How to do it...

To do this, perform the following steps:

1. Run the following lines of code in the REPL:

```
>>> from adafruit_circuitplayground.express import cpx
>>> cpx.pixels.brightness = 1.0
>>> cpx.pixels[0] = (255, 0, 0)
```

2. At this point, the first pixel should be the color red with full brightness. Run the following line of code to set the brightness level to 50%:

```
>>> cpx.pixels.brightness = 0.5
```

3. The brightness level can be brought further down to 10% and still be comfortably visible. You can do this by running the following line of code:

```
>>> cpx.pixels.brightness = 0.10
```

How it works...

The `brightness` property accepts a value from 0 to 1.0, which goes from least bright to most bright. Note that the NeoPixels on this board can be very bright, and they can strain your eyes if you look at them directly at the highest level of brightness.

I recommend that you set the brightness level to 10%, as this makes viewing the pixels more comfortable. Then, depending on the project, you can tweak the brightness to the most appropriate level.

There are times when the pixels will be underneath a thin covering of plastic and you will want to increase the brightness level. On the other hand, there will be times when you will be directly looking at them and you will want to decrease the brightness level.

There's more...

It is important to note that the way the brightness levels are implemented means that you can only change all the NeoPixels at one time. That is, with the brightness property, you cannot make some pixels brighter and some pixels darker. So, whatever value you set for brightness will apply to all the pixels on the board.

The pixels have the capability of being very bright when they are left at the maximum level of 100% brightness. An example of where this setting is more suitable is when you embed your device in a plastic container. The following photograph is taken from a NeoPixel project, where the Circuit Playground Express board was placed inside the base of a snow globe:

In this project, the base is made of white plastic. So, even though the board is not directly visible, the pixels are bright enough to shine through the white plastic and fill the whole globe with light.

 The DIY snow globe kit shown in this project can be found at `https://www.adafruit.com/product/3722`.

See also

You can find out more information using the following references:

- The brightness property is documented at `https://circuitpython.readthedocs.io/projects/NeoPixel/en/latest/api.html#NeoPixel.NeoPixel.brightness`.
- Examples of changing the brightness level can be found at `https://learn.adafruit.com/circuitpython-made-easy-on-circuit-playground-express/NeoPixels`.

Controlling the color of a single NeoPixel

This recipe will show you how to set the a specific NeoPixel to different colors. It will then show you how to change the color of any of the 10 NeoPixels that come with the board. This will be a useful recipe to follow so that you can start unleashing the power and flexibility of these onboard pixels.

Getting ready

You will need access to the REPL on the Circuit Playground Express to run the code presented in this recipe.

How to do it...

To do this, perform the following steps:

1. Run the following lines of code in the REPL:

```
>>> from adafruit_circuitplayground.express import cpx
>>> cpx.pixels[0] = (255, 0, 0)
```

2. Now, you should see the first NeoPixel turn red.
3. When you run the following code, you should see the first NeoPixel turn green:

```
>>> cpx.pixels[0] = (0, 255, 0)
```

4. When you run the following code, you should see the first NeoPixel turn blue:

```
>>> cpx.pixels[0] = (0, 0, 255)
```

5. The following code should retrieve the current color value of the first NeoPixel:

```
>>> cpx.pixels[0]
(0, 0, 255)
```

6. Run the following code to turn off the first NeoPixel:

```
>>> cpx.pixels[0] = (0, 0, 0)
```

7. Run the following code and the second NeoPixel should turn red:

```
>>> cpx.pixels[1] = (255, 0, 0)
```

How it works...

The first line of code imports the `cpx` object that will be used to control the NeoPixels. This object has an attribute called `pixels`, which can be accessed like a list. The index that is used indicates which of the 10 NeoPixels is to be manipulated.

In the first code snippet, we set the value to a tuple that represents the desired color—it is comprised of red, green, and blue values. Each value should be represented as an integer from 0 to 255. By setting the value to (255, 0, 0), the red LED will be at its highest value and the green and blue LEDs will be switched off. This will create the color red.

Following the same approach, the NeoPixel is then set to green and blue by providing the correct values for each of those colors. The current RGB values of a specific pixel can also be easily retrieved by simply accessing the value of any specific example.

A pixel can be switched off by setting all the RGB components to a value of 0, as shown in the preceding code in this recipe. The final preceding code snippet just gives an example of setting the second pixel to the color red by referring to the correct index value.

There's more...

In older versions of the library, you could provide the colors as a list of three integers, instead of a tuple of three integers. It is best to avoid doing this and stick to using tuples instead of lists. This is because your code will work in both the newer and older versions of the library.

Each NeoPixel is made up of a red, green, and blue LED. When you set the strength of each color in this recipe, it directly changes the brightness levels of these individual LEDs. It is a possible to use a consumer microscope to view each of the three individual LED lights that make up each NeoPixel. The following photograph is taken from one of these consumer grade microscopes with a magnification of 200x. As you can see, the separate red, green, and blue LEDs are clearly visible:

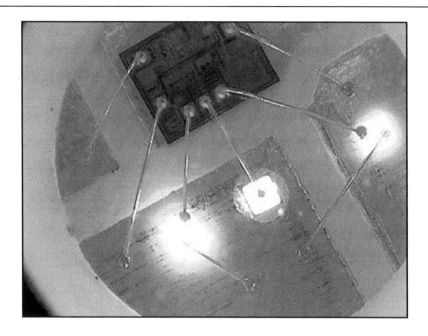

See also

You can find out more information using the following references:

- Documentation on the pixels attribute can be found at `https://circuitpython.readthedocs.io/projects/circuitplayground/en/latest/api.html#adafruit_circuitplayground.express.Express.pixels`.
- Details on the NeoPixel can be found at `https://learn.adafruit.com/adafruit-NeoPixel-uberguide/the-magic-of-NeoPixels`.

Displaying an LED color using the RGB and hex code

There is a common convention to express any color using the hex code, which works by representing the red, green, and blue components of the color. This recipe demonstrates how to set the color of a NeoPixel using this hex code convention. Using such a popular convention will be useful when you want to apply specific color settings from other applications on the web or your desktop.

Getting ready

You will need access to the REPL on the Circuit Playground Express to run the code presented in this recipe.

How to do it...

To do this, perform the following steps:

1. Run the following lines of code in the REPL:

```
>>> from adafruit_circuitplayground.express import cpx
>>> cpx.pixels[0] = 0xFF0000
```

2. You should see the first NeoPixel turn red. Run the following code to retrieve the color value of the first NeoPixel:

```
>>> cpx.pixels[0]
(0, 0, 255)
```

3. Run the following code to set the next two pixels to green and blue:

```
>>> cpx.pixels[1] = 0x00FF00
>>> cpx.pixels[2] = 0x0000FF
```

4. Use the following code to set the fourth pixel to yellow:

```
>>> cpx.pixels[3] = 0xFFFF00
```

5. Use the following code to display the integer value for the color blue, and then set the next pixel to the color blue using this integer value:

```
>>> 0x0000FF
255
>>> cpx.pixels[4] = 255
```

How it works...

The first code snippet sets the first pixel on the board to the color red using the hex notation for colors. The pixel's interface accepts color values to be given as either a tuple of three integers or as a hex value, which, in Python, correlates to an integer value.

Depending on the type of value given, the library extracts the correct values of the red, green, and blue components of the color and sets the pixel to that color. The second code snippet indicates that when reading back the values, they will always be retrieved as a tuple of the three color components.

The final code snippet demonstrates that the hex notation being used is a standard feature of the Python language, which is used to specify the value of an integer in terms of its hex values. The equivalent integer value can also be used to set a color.

There's more...

The hex code notation system to describe a color's red, green, and blue components is extremely popular. Due to its popularity, it is easy to find a variety of online tools and desktop applications that provide color pickers and color wheels, which represent colors as hex codes. You can simply choose you desired color in these programs and then copy and paste the hex values into your scripts. The following screenshot is taken from the popular open source image editor, GIMP:

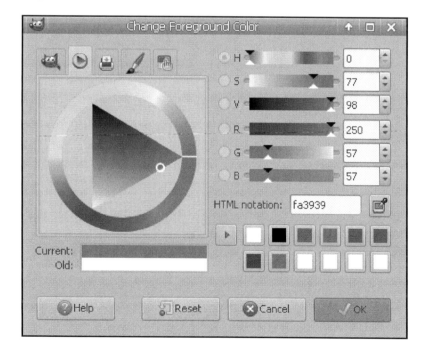

In the preceding screenshot, you can see the color wheel that is available in the application. This rich interface easily allows you to find the color that you are looking for by changing its hue or saturation. Once you have picked the color that you want, you can copy the hex code value, which is labeled as **HTML notation** in this application. This value can then be used in your script using the same technique shown in this recipe.

 GIMP is available on Linux, macOS, and Windows and can be downloaded for free from `https://www.gimp.org`.

See also

You can find out more information using the following references:

- Documentation on integer literals in the Python language can be found at `https://docs.python.org/3/reference/lexical_analysis.html#integer-literals`.
- An interactive color wheel can be found at `https://www.sessions.edu/color-calculator/`.

Setting an LED color using color names

Using human-readable color names can make it much easier to keep track of what colors are in use in your application. This recipe demonstrates a technique that allows you to set pixel colors using regular color names. This feature of referring to colors by a standard set of color names is available in popular languages, including CSS. This recipe shows you how to bring this feature to your MicroPython scripts.

Getting ready

You will need access to the REPL on the Circuit Playground Express to run the code presented in this recipe.

How to do it...

To do this, perform the following steps:

1. Run the following lines of code in the REPL:

```
>>> from adafruit_circuitplayground.express import cpx
>>> RGB = dict(black=0x000000, blue=0x0000FF, green=0x00FF00,
... cyan=0x00FFFF,
... red=0xFF0000, magenta=0xFF00FF, yellow=0xFFFF00,
... white=0xFFFFFF)
>>> cpx.pixels[0] = RGB['red']
```

2. You should see the first NeoPixel turn red.
3. Use the following code to set the first eight pixels to one of the named colors in alphabetical order:

```
>>> for i, name in enumerate(sorted(RGB)):
...     cpx.pixels[i] = RGB[name]
```

How it works...

A global variable called RGB is created; this is a dictionary that is used for matching color names to their RGB color codes. This allows the color values to be retrieved by their names, instead of directly specifying their hex codes every time they need to be used. The first snippet uses the RGB code to set the first pixel to the color red.

The second block of code loops through each color name in alphabetical order and sets a pixel to that color. Since there are eight colors defined in the color lookup dictionary, the first eight pixels will have their colors set—each pixel will have its own color from the list of colors.

There's more...

Using human-readable color names can improve code readability. The technique described in this recipe, however, requires you to specify each color name and its associated hex code manually. This is fine if you are only using a small number of colors, but if you want to support a large number of colors, then this can become very tedious. Another factor to bear in mind is that many of these boards have limited memory capacity, so creating very large dictionaries can cause the board to run out of memory. A small color lookup table, such as the one shown in this example, shouldn't cause these sorts of issues.

When you are looking for color names and their associated hex codes, there are a number of standard sources that can be used. One popular list of color names is the **World Wide Web Consortium (W3C)**, which is used in CSS. There is also a standard color list provided with the open source text editor, Vim. This list of color names is stored in a file called `rgb.txt`, which comes with each Vim installation.

The benefit of using this color listing is that it comes in a machine-readable format, where each line represents one color and the color components and names are whitespace-delimited. This makes parsing and using these color names a relatively trivial process. The following screenshot shows the output of a useful Vim script that parses this file and presents each color name and its applied color for easy selection:

50	176 196 222	#b0c4de	LightSteelBlue		LightSteelBlue_fg
51	173 216 230	#add8e6	LightBlue		LightBlue_fg
52	176 224 230	#b0e0e6	PowderBlue		PowderBlue_fg
53	175 238 238	#afeeee	PaleTurquoise		PaleTurquoise_fg
54	0 206 209	#00ced1	DarkTurquoise		DarkTurquoise_fg
55	72 209 204	#48d1cc	MediumTurquoise		MediumTurquoise_fg
56	64 224 208	#40e0d0	turquoise		turquoise_fg
57	0 255 255	#00ffff	cyan		cyan_fg
58	224 255 255	#e0ffff	LightCyan		
59	95 158 160	#5f9ea0	CadetBlue		CadetBlue_fg
60	102 205 170	#66cdaa	MediumAquamarine		MediumAquamarine_fg
61	127 255 212	#7fffd4	aquamarine		
62	0 100 0	#006400	DarkGreen		DarkGreen_fg
63	85 107 47	#556b2f	DarkOliveGreen		DarkOliveGreen_fg
64	143 188 143	#8fbc8f	DarkSeaGreen		DarkSeaGreen_fg
65	46 139 87	#2e8b57	SeaGreen		SeaGreen_fg
66	60 179 113	#3cb371	MediumSeaGreen		MediumSeaGreen_fg
67	32 178 170	#20b2aa	LightSeaGreen		LightSeaGreen_fg
68	152 251 152	#98fb98	PaleGreen		PaleGreen_fg
69	0 255 127	#00ff7f	SpringGreen		SpringGreen_fg
70	124 252 0	#7cfc00	LawnGreen		LawnGreen_fg
71	0 255 0	#00ff00	green		green_fg
72	127 255 0	#7fff00	chartreuse		chartreuse_fg
73	0 250 154	#00fa9a	MediumSpringGreen		MediumSpringGreen_fg
74	173 255 47	#adff2f	GreenYellow		GreenYellow_fg
75	50 205 50	#32cd32	LimeGreen		LimeGreen_fg
76	154 205 50	#9acd32	YellowGreen		YellowGreen_fg
77	34 139 34	#228b22	ForestGreen		ForestGreen_fg
78	107 142 35	#6b8e23	OliveDrab		OliveDrab_fg
79	189 183 107	#bdb76b	DarkKhaki		DarkKhaki_fg
80	240 230 140	#f0e68c	khaki		khaki_fg
81	238 232 170	#eee8aa	PaleGoldenrod		PaleGoldenrod_fg
82	250 250 210	#fafad2	LightGoldenrodYellow		
83	255 255 224	#ffffe0	LightYellow		
84	255 255 0	#ffff00	yellow		
85	255 215 0	#ffd700	gold		gold_fg

 This Vim color script can be found at `https://vim.fandom.com/wiki/View_all_colors_available_to_gvim`.

See also

You can find out more information using the following references:

- The W3C color names can be found at `https://www.w3.org/TR/css-color-3/`.
- An explanation of additive color theory can be found at `https://study.com/academy/lesson/additive-color-theory-definition.html`.

Setting all NeoPixels to the same color

This recipe explains how you can set all the pixels to one color through a single call, instead of looping through all the NeoPixels and setting their colors individually. You can use this technique to create a nice effect to set all 10 NeoPixels to the same color. They are arranged in a perfect circle, so it creates a ring of color when they are all set to the same color. It is also an easy way to turn all the NeoPixels off in one call.

Getting ready

You will need access to the REPL on the Circuit Playground Express to run the code presented in this recipe.

How to do it...

To do this, perform the following steps:

1. Run the following lines of code in the REPL:

```
>>> from adafruit_circuitplayground.express import cpx
>>> cpx.pixels.fill(0x0000FF)
```

2. You should see all 10 NeoPixels turn blue.
3. Use the following code to turn off all 10 NeoPixels:

```
>>> cpx.pixels.fill(0x000000)
```

How it works...

In the first code snippet, the `fill` method is called and the color value is provided as the first argument. The `fill` method will loop through all the pixels and set them to the desired color, which, in this case, is the color blue. This method accepts both the hex color notation and tuples of three integer values.

There's more...

This operation of setting all the pixels to the same color is relatively popular, and the method has been provided for your convenience. However, it is important to note that the implementation of this method doesn't just take a simple loop and set the color for each pixel. Instead, it uses a feature where you can set all the color values before displaying them.

The advantage of this feature is that you can first set all the colors, and then make a single call to display them all at once. This is a better way of setting the pixels rather than with a simple `for` loop, so it provides another good reason to use the `fill` method.

See also

You can find out more information using the following references:

- Documentation on the `fill` method can be found at `https://circuitpython.readthedocs.io/projects/NeoPixel/en/latest/api.html#NeoPixel.NeoPixel.fill`.
- A list of products that work with the NeoPixel library can be found at `https://www.adafruit.com/category/168`.

Setting a range of NeoPixels to one color

This recipe will explore how the slicing feature can be used to set a specific range of pixels to a specific color. This can be quite useful when you want to turn the ring of pixels into a gauge to show the level of a value from 1 to 10. Essentially, it provides a clearer and simpler way of setting a range of pixels to a particular color.

Getting ready

You will need access to the REPL on the Circuit Playground Express to run the code presented in this recipe.

How to do it...

To do this, perform the following steps:

1. Run the following lines of code in the REPL:

```
>>> from adafruit_circuitplayground.express import cpx
>>> cpx.pixels[0:2] = [0xFF0000, 0xFF0000]
```

2. You should see the first two NeoPixels light up as red.
3. Turn the next three pixels to green and the last five pixels to blue using the following code:

```
>>> cpx.pixels[2:5] = [0x00FF00] * 3
>>> cpx.pixels[5:10] = [0x0000FF] * 5
```

How it works...

The `pixels` attribute understands when you set values using the `slice` method. However, it expects that if you set the color for two pixels, then you should provide a list of two color values, as was done in the first example.

In Python, we can reduce this repetition by taking a list of the color values and multiplying it by the required number of values. This is the approach that is used to set the three pixels to the color green.

There's more...

The slicing notation that is used in Python is concise and powerful. It is a very smart way to change the colors on a range of pixels in one line of code. This very much embraces the Python approach of keeping code short and concise without compromising on readability.

See also

You can find out more information using the following references:

- Further details on using the * operator to repeat values in Python's lists can be found at http://interactivepython.org/runestone/static/CS152f17/Lists/ ConcatenationandRepetition.html.
- Documentation on Python string slicing can be found at https://docs.python. org/3/tutorial/introduction.html#lists.

Generating random NeoPixel LED colors

This recipe demonstrates a technique that can be used to endlessly generate random colors. We will then use these random colors on a specific NeoPixel. Adding randomness to the color section can make projects more interesting, as you can never predict the exact sequence of colors that will appear as your script executes.

Getting ready

You will need access to the REPL on the Circuit Playground Express to run the code presented in this recipe.

How to do it...

To do this, perform the following steps:

1. Run the following lines of code in the REPL:

```
>>> from adafruit_circuitplayground.express import cpx
>>> from random import randint
>>> randint(0, 255)
186
>>> randint(0, 255)
84
```

2. Each time you run the previous lines of code, you should get a random integer between the values of 0 and 255.

3. Use the following code to define a function, and then call the function to confirm that it is working correctly:

```
>>> def get_random_color():
...         return (randint(0, 255), randint(0, 255), randint(0, 255))
...
...
...
>>> get_random_color()
(208, 161, 71)
>>> get_random_color()
(96, 126, 158)
```

4. Call the following code repeatedly; the first NeoPixel should change to a random color on each call:

```
>>> cpx.pixels[0] = get_random_color()
```

5. Set all the pixels to the same random color on each call using the following code:

```
>>> cpx.pixels.fill(get_random_color())
```

How it works...

In this recipe, we use the `random` module, which is part of the Python standard library and CircuitPython. Calling `randint` and providing a range from 0 to 255 will give us a random integer for each color component.

We then define the `get_random_color` function to randomly select each of the three color components and, therefore, make a random color. Now that we have this function, we can call it to set the color of a single pixel or all the pixels, as demonstrated in the final two code snippets in this recipe.

There's more...

The use of the `random` module in MicroPython projects opens up a whole range of fun possibilities for unique and different projects. This recipe covered one example of combining the random library with code to specify a color so that random colors can be chosen. Over 16 million different colors might be randomly selected using this method.

See also

You can find out more information using the following references:

- Documentation on the CircuitPython random library can be found at `https://circuitpython.readthedocs.io/en/3.x/shared-bindings/random/__init__.html`.
- A project using the `random` library and Circuit Playground Express to create electronic dice can be found at `https://learn.adafruit.com/circuit-playground-d6-dice/`.

Creating LED animations with random colors

This recipe will combine some aspects of the previous recipes in this chapter to create an animation using randomly selected colors. This recipe builds on the techniques of other recipes to create your first animation. With 10 pixels on the board, there are a lot of options for creating engaging visual animations on the board—this is just one of those.

Getting ready

You will need access to the REPL on the Circuit Playground Express to run the code presented in this recipe.

How to do it...

To do this, perform the following steps:

1. Run the following lines of code in the REPL:

```
>>> from adafruit_circuitplayground.express import cpx
>>> from random import randint
>>> import time
>>> def get_random_color():
...     return (randint(0, 255), randint(0, 255), randint(0, 255))
...
...
>>> get_random_color()
(10, 41, 10)
```

2. Run the following block of code and a 10 second animation of colors should appear around the ring of pixels on the board:

```
>>> for i in range(10):
...        cpx.pixels[i] = get_random_color()
...        time.sleep(1)
...
...
...
>>>
```

3. Next, run the animation for 30 seconds and cycle through all the pixels three times, with a 1-second delay between each light change:

```
>>> cpx.pixels.fill(0x000000)
>>> for cycle in range(3):
...        for i in range(10):
...            cpx.pixels[i] = get_random_color()
...            time.sleep(1)
...
...
...
>>>
```

4. For this final animation, run the animation for five seconds and change all the pixel colors once a second:

```
>>> cpx.pixels.fill(0x000000)
>>> for i in range(5):
...        cpx.pixels.fill(get_random_color())
...        time.sleep(1)
...
...
...
>>>
```

How it works...

Three different animations are presented in this recipe. When it comes to light animations, the sky's the limit. There are so many different ways to control color change and timing and each different approach will create a slightly different visual effect. However, a key aspect of all animation is timing; we can control the pace of the animation by using the `sleep` call, which is part of the `time` module. In this way, we can slow down or speed up the animations we create.

The first animation in this recipe is a simple `for` loop, which sets the color of each pixel to a random color and pauses for one second between these color changes. The second animation builds on the first one by having an outer loop that loops 3 times and so changes the pixels 30 times.

Finally, the last animation takes a different approach by setting all the pixels to the same color and then changing them together during each loop.

There's more...

The animations in this recipe can be tweaked to create a variety of different animations. For instance, you could change the speed of the animation or the number of times the animation loops around the pixels. The preceding code can be used in a function that receives these two parameters as arguments. This can then be used in a larger program, which will call the function to make animations with different settings.

See also

You can find out more information using the following references:

- Documentation on the CircuitPython time library can be found at `https://circuitpython.readthedocs.io/en/3.x/shared-bindings/time/__init__.html`.
- A project using the Circuit Playground Express to create an animated bike light can be found at `https://learn.adafruit.com/circuit-playground-bike-light`.

Creating LED animations with rainbow colors

This recipe will produce a ring of colors following the same sequence of colors found in a rainbow. These colors will each appear after a certain delay, creating a rainbow animation effect. Using a sequence of colors that naturally fits together, like the ones found in the rainbow, can be both pleasing and engaging. The strength of this animation is in learning how to control the exact sequence of colors being animated, whether they be in a rainbow sequence or another sequence of your choosing.

Getting ready

You will need access to the REPL on the Circuit Playground Express to run the code presented in this recipe.

How to do it...

To do this, perform the following steps:

1. Run the following lines of code in the REPL:

```
>>> from adafruit_circuitplayground.express import cpx
>>> import time
```

2. The following block of code defines a list of color values that have the same values and sequence as that which appears in a rainbow:

```
>>> RAINBOW = [
... 0xFF0000,    # red
... 0xFFA500,    # orange
... 0xFFFF00,    # yellow
... 0x00FF00,    # green
... 0x0000FF,    # blue
... 0x4b0082,    # indigo
... 0xEE82EE,    # violet
... ]
>>>
```

3. Then, set a more comfortable level of brightness and turn off all the pixels before starting the animation:

```
>>> cpx.pixels.brightness = 0.10
>>> cpx.pixels.fill(0x000000)
>>>
```

4. Using the following block of code, loop through the seven colors in the rainbow and set one pixel to each color, with a brief delay of 0.2 seconds between each light change:

```
>>> for i, color in enumerate(RAINBOW):
...         cpx.pixels[i] = color
...         time.sleep(0.2)
...
...
...
>>>
```

5. Use the following animation to go back to each pixel and turn it off at the same rate of 0.2 seconds per light change:

```
>>> for i in range(len(RAINBOW)):
...         cpx.pixels[i] = 0x000000
...         time.sleep(0.2)
...
...
...
>>>
```

6. The following code combines all the steps described and wraps these into one infinite `while` loop. Add this section of code to the `main.py` file, and then create a continuous rainbow animation:

```
from adafruit_circuitplayground.express import cpx import time
RAINBOW = [ 0xFF0000, # red
  0xFFA500, # orange
  0xFFFF00, # yellow
  0x00FF00, # green
  0x0000FF, # blue
  0x4b0082, # indigo
  0xEE82EE, # violet
]

cpx.pixels.brightness = 0.10
cpx.pixels.fill(0x000000)
while True:
```

```
for i, color in enumerate(RAINBOW):
    cpx.pixels[i] = color
    time.sleep(0.2)
for i in range(len(RAINBOW)):
    cpx.pixels[i] = 0x000000
    time.sleep(0.2)
```

How it works...

A rainbow in nature is made up of seven colors: red, orange, yellow, green, blue, indigo, and violet. We store these colors' values, and their correct sequences as they appear in nature, in a list. The brightness level is set and then the `fill` method is called to turn off all the pixels on the board.

An infinite loop is started that contains two loops. The first inner loop will loop through each color in the rainbow and set one pixel to each color. The second inner loop will then go back to the seven pixels that were colored and turn each one off.

There's more...

The following photograph shows the rainbow animation from this recipe running on the Circuit Playground Express:

There are many ways to make further derivative animations from this rainbow animation. For instance, you could add more colors that are not part of the natural rainbow. We have defined 7 colors but there are 10 pixels on the board, so you could define another 3 different colors. You could also have the starting pixel be randomly selected in each loop, so that the animation starts at a different pixel in each loop.

See also

You can find out more information using the following references:

- The sequence and names of the seven colors of the rainbow can be found at `https://sciencetrends.com/7-colors-rainbow-order/`.
- A different implementation of a rainbow animation can be found at `https://learn.adafruit.com/adafruit-circuit-playground-express/circuitpython-NeoPixel`.

3
Creating Sound and Music

This chapter will introduce methods of making sounds and playing music using the hardware that comes on the Adafruit Circuit Playground Express. The chapter will first introduce the basics of making the board beep at a certain frequency of sound and will then move on to more advanced topics, such as playing music files using the WAV file format and the board's built-in sound speakers. The techniques in this chapter can be used directly in a wide array of MicroPython projects that you might make. The options for producing audio output in this chapter range from producing simple beeping sounds to playing songs in your embedded projects.

In this chapter, we will cover the following recipes:

- Making a beeping sound
- Controlling tone, frequency, and duration
- Playing a musical note
- Playing a melody
- Sounding the alarm
- Playing WAV files
- Converting MP3 files to WAV files
- Starting and stopping tones

The Adafruit Circuit Playground Express layout

The following photograph shows the locations of the speaker that is built into the board. All of the beeps and sounds covered in this chapter will use this speaker for playback:

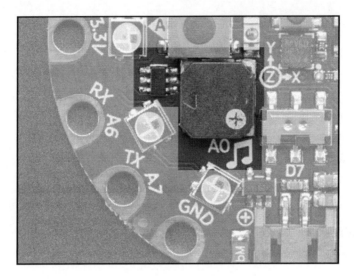

Courtesy of adafruit.com

Making a beeping sound

In this recipe, we will learn how to get the speakers to make a beeping sound at a specific sound frequency and for a specific duration of time. Audio output is a great way to get someone's attention; you can find it used everywhere from ringing phones to doorbells. This recipe will give you the skills that you need to add beeps to your embedded projects.

Getting ready

You will need access to the REPL on the Circuit Playground Express to run the code presented in this recipe.

How to do it...

Let's perform the following steps:

1. Run the following lines of code in the REPL. You should hear a beeping sound at a frequency of 900 Hz played for 0.2 seconds:

```
>>> from adafruit_circuitplayground.express import cpx
>>> cpx.play_tone(900, 0.2)
```

2. Execute the following code so that a lower frequency beep will be played for a longer duration:

```
>>> cpx.play_tone(500, 0.4)
```

How it works...

The first line of code imports the Circuit Playground Express library. The `cpx` object exposes a method called `play_tone`. This method accepts two arguments: frequency and duration. These arguments specify the frequency of the sound in Hz, and how long the sound will be played in seconds.

The duration can be given as a floating point number. This means that a value such as `0.2` will correlate to 200 milliseconds. This method call is a blocking call. So, calling the method will start playing the audio and it won't return anything until the specified time has elapsed.

There's more...

The technique presented in this chapter is a very straightforward way of generating a beeping sound from the speakers on the board. However, under the hood, a lot is happening. When you specify the frequency and duration of a sound, it will build the sound wave programmatically, and then feed the audio data into the speaker to play the sound. The audio data is created by building a sine wave in Python code.

The code that builds this audio data is part of the Circuit Playground Express library, which was imported in this recipe. You can download the code and read it to learn how this is done. It's a great way to understand the mathematics of sound waves and how they can be created through software. The following screenshot shows what a computer-generated tone playing at 500 Hz looks like:

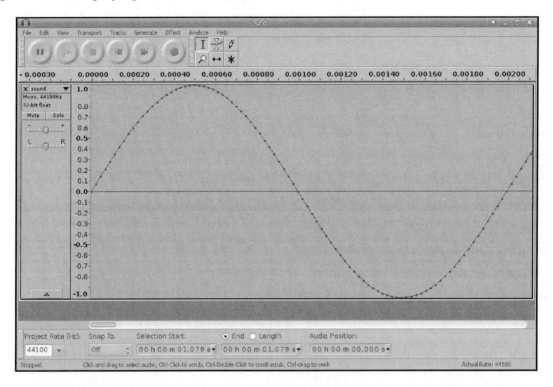

You can see clearly from the preceding screenshot that this looks just like a sine waveform. The screenshot was taken when we zoomed in to see an individual sound cycle. Since the sound is playing at 500 Hz, we would expect one cycle to be 1/500 of a second long. Here, we can see that this is where the first wave ends—at exactly 0.002 seconds.

See also

You can find out more information using the following references:

- Documentation on the play_tone method can be found at https://circuitpython.readthedocs.io/projects/circuitplayground/en/latest/api.html#adafruit_circuitplayground.express.Express.play_tone.

- More details on the audio spectrum that humans can hear can be found at https://www.teachmeaudio.com/mixing/techniques/audio-spectrum/.

Controlling tone, frequency, and duration

In this recipe, we will learn how to play tones with a varying frequency and duration. By playing different tones repeatedly with a different duration each time, we can learn how to go beyond individual beeps. These steps will eventually lead to us playing melodies or varying tones that can make the same sound as an alarm.

Getting ready

You will need access to the REPL on the Circuit Playground Express to run the code presented in this recipe.

How to do it...

Let's perform the following steps:

1. Run the following lines of code in the REPL. You should hear five separate tones playing for 0.2 seconds each. The sounds will start at a lower pitch and gradually get higher and higher. As each tone plays, the frequency of the tone will be printed to the output in the REPL:

```
>>> from adafruit_circuitplayground.express import cpx >>> for i in
range(500, 1000, 100): ... print(i) ... cpx.play_tone(i, 0.2)
...
...
...
500
600
700
800
900
>>>
```

2. Use the following code to play three different tones. The tones will increase in pitch and will also increase in terms of duration of the playback:

```
>>> from adafruit_circuitplayground.express import cpx
>>> for i in range(200, 500, 100):
```

```
...       print(i)
...       cpx.play_tone(i, i/1000)
...
...
...
200
300
400
>>>
```

How it works...

In the first block of code, the `for` loop will iterate over the frequency value, starting from 500 and raising the value in increments of 100 to end at 900. This range and these steps will be easily audible to the human ear. In each iteration, the frequency to be played will be printed out and then played using the `play_tone` method. Only the frequency of the sound changes in each iteration; they will all play for 200 milliseconds.

In the second block of code, the `for` loop will iterate over a lower sound pitch and through fewer tones. For each iteration, the frequency and duration of the tone increases. The frequency will be the exact value of the `i` variable, while the duration will be the value of `i` in terms of milliseconds. Since the `play_tone` method is expecting the value in seconds, we must divide it by 1,000.

There's more...

The two `for` loops presented in this chapter vary the way tones are played over a brief duration of time. In both examples, the tones play within one second but they have three or more different tones playing.

This is an excellent starting point to experiment with different variations of these loops. Because it only takes a second to play each loop, you can go through a fast cycle of experimentation and hear the results instantly. Try and experiment by changing the pitch or the pace at which the tones change.

In both loops, the pitch increased with each iteration. Try and experiment with a pitch that gets lower with each iteration.

See also

You can find out more information using the following references:

- Documentation on the Python range function can be found at `https://docs.python.org/3/library/functions.html#func-range`.
- An explanation of pitch and frequency can be found at `https://www.le.ac.uk/se/centres/sci/selfstudy/snd5.htm`.

Playing a musical note

In this recipe, we will learn how to define a number of global constants, each representing a specific musical note. Then, we can play these different musical notes by referring to their constants. Musical notes are the building blocks of melodies. This will be the first step toward playing a melody. Once we have learned how to play a musical note, we can then combine a number of notes in sequence to play a melody in future recipes.

Getting ready

You will need access to the REPL on the Circuit Playground Express to run the code presented in this recipe.

How to do it...

Let's perform the following steps:

1. Run the following lines of code in the REPL:

```
>>> from adafruit_circuitplayground.express import cpx
>>> E5 = 659
>>> C5 = 523
>>> G5 = 784
>>> cpx.play_tone(E5, 0.15)
```

You should hear the E5 musical note play on the speakers for 0.15 seconds.

2. Use the following code to play the C5 and G5 musical notes for 0.15 seconds:

```
cpx.play_tone(C5, 0.15)
cpx.play_tone(G5, 0.15)
```

How it works...

The first line of code in this recipe imports the Circuit Playground Express library. Then, three global constants are defined and are named after their associated musical notes. The **scientific pitch notation** (**SPN**) is used in this recipe. This notation works by combining the name of a musical note with the number specifying the pitch's octave. In the case of E5, the note will be E and the octave will be 5. Here, each note maps to a specific frequency of sound.

In the first block of code, the E5 note is played simply by referring to the E5 global constant when calling the play_tone method. Setting the duration to 0.15 allows each note play for 150 milliseconds, which creates a comfortable pace to the music. Reducing or increasing this value can increase or reduce the pace that the musical tone will play. The second block of code plays the remaining two notes defined at the same speed.

The frequencies used in this chapter follow the standard piano key frequencies. This is equivalent to the standard concert pitch and the 12-tone equal temperament.

There's more...

In this recipe, we used three musical notes to demonstrate the process of defining notes and then playing each note back. Of course, there are many more notes that can be defined.

A good learning exercise is to find the frequency of other popular notes and go through the process of defining them and playing them. Even though three notes seems like too few, they are enough to play a recognizable melody. We will see in the following recipe how these same three notes can be combined to play a popular melody.

See also

You can find out more information using the following references:

- An explanation of the octave notation can be found at http://www.flutopedia.com/octave_notation.html.
- A Python-based software synthesizer can be found at https://mdoege.github.io/PySynth/.

Playing a melody

In this recipe, we will learn how to play a melody by playing a sequence of musical notes. A single musical note on its own is rather boring. The real fun begins when you can combine a sequence of them and time them correctly to play a melody.

By following the standard musical notation, it will become possible to take popular melodies and specify them in Python in a way that the Circuit Playground Express will be able to play them back.

Getting ready

You will need access to the REPL on the Circuit Playground Express to run the code presented in this recipe.

How to do it...

Let's perform the following steps:

1. Run the following lines of code in the REPL. You should hear the E5 musical note play on the speakers for 0.15 seconds:

```
>>> import time
>>> from adafruit_circuitplayground.express import cpx
>>>
>>> E5 = 659
>>> C5 = 523
>>> G5 = 784
>>>
>>> def play_note(note, duration=0.15):
...     if note == 0:
...         time.sleep(duration)
...     else:
...         cpx.play_tone(note, duration)
...
>>> play_note(E5)
```

2. Use the following lines of code to play the same note at twice the speed, and then at half the speed:

```
>>> play_note(E5, 0.15 / 2)
>>> play_note(E5, 0.15 * 2)
```

3. Use the following line of code to play nothing and keep the speaker silent for the same period as one note playing at the normal speed:

```
>>> play_note(0)
```

4. Use the following lines of code to play the initial part of the *Super Mario Bros.* theme song:

```
>>> MELODY = (E5, E5, 0, E5, 0, C5, E5, 0, G5)
>>> for note in MELODY:
...         play_note(note)
...
>>>
```

5. The code that follows combines all the code shown in this recipe to make one complete program. Add this to the main.py file and it will play the start of the *Super Mario Bros.* theme song every time you reload the code:

```
import time
from adafruit_circuitplayground.express import cpx

E5 = 659
C5 = 523
G5 = 784

MELODY = (E5, E5, 0, E5, 0, C5, E5, 0, G5)

def play_note(note, duration=0.15):
    if note == 0:
        time.sleep(duration)
    else:
        cpx.play_tone(note, duration)

for note in MELODY:
    play_note(note)
```

How it works...

The initial lines of code import the necessary libraries and set up the constants that are required for the rest of the code in the program. The MELODY constant has the sequence of notes that make up the song. There are pauses of silence between certain notes; these are simply specified with a value of 0 to indicate that no notes should be played at this point. The play_note function expects to be given the frequency of the note to play and, optionally, the duration of time to play the note for. If a frequency of 0 is given, it will call the sleep function to stay silent; otherwise, it will play the note as a tone.

Finally, the for loop at the end of the program simply loops through each note defined in the melody and plays it by calling the play_note function. In this way, you can define many different melodies and songs, and play different songs depending on how the user interacts with the device.

There's more...

This recipe is written in a generic fashion: you take a popular melody, provide the sequence of notes and each note's associated frequency, and then add the melody to your project. The melody in this recipe has each note play for the same duration.

However, there are many melodies that might mix quarter notes and eighth notes. These melodies will require a different duration of time to be defined for each note. The recipe could be expanded so that we could keep track of each note to play and the duration that each note would need to play for.

See also

You can find out more information using the following references:

- The playback of the *Super Mario Bros.* theme song on an Arduino device can be found at https://www.princetronics.com/supermariothemesong/.
- A discussion on sound and music with the Circuit Playground can be found at https://learn.adafruit.com/circuit-playground-music.
- An example of playing a melody on the Circuit Playground can be found at https://learn.adafruit.com/circuit-playground-hot-potato/caternuson-playing-a-melody.

Sounding the alarm

In this recipe, we will learn how to play low and high frequency sounds to create the sound of an alarm. Alarm sounds are very useful for alerting people to get their attention. This recipe demonstrates a very simple, but effective, way to create an alarm sound, which can then be taken and adapted to the needs of your project.

Getting ready

You will need access to the REPL on the Circuit Playground Express to run the code presented in this recipe.

How to do it...

Let's perform the following steps for this recipe:

1. Run the following lines of code in the REPL. You should hear a high-pitched beeping sound for 0.5 seconds:

```
>>> from adafruit_circuitplayground.express import cpx
>>>
>>> BEEP_HIGH = 960
>>> BEEP_LOW = 800
>>>
>>> cpx.play_tone(BEEP_HIGH, 0.5)
```

2. Use the following code to play a low-pitched beeping sound for 0.5 seconds:

```
>>> cpx.play_tone(BEEP_LOW, 0.5)
```

3. Use the following code to play a siren that goes from a high to a low pitch through three cycles, playing for a total of three seconds:

```
>>> for i in range(3):
...     cpx.play_tone(BEEP_HIGH, 0.5)
...     cpx.play_tone(BEEP_LOW, 0.5)
...
>>>
```

4. The code that follows combines all the code shown in this recipe to make one complete program. Add this to the `main.py` file and it will play the siren alarm for three seconds every time you reload the code:

```
from adafruit_circuitplayground.express import cpx

BEEP_HIGH = 960
BEEP_LOW = 800

for i in range(3):
    cpx.play_tone(BEEP_HIGH, 0.5)
    cpx.play_tone(BEEP_LOW, 0.5)
```

How it works...

The initial lines of code import the necessary libraries and set up the constants that are required for the rest of the code in the program. The script then loops for a total of three iterations, with each iteration playing sounds for a total of one second.

In each iteration, a high-pitched tone will be played for a half a second, followed by a low-pitched tone for half a second. In this way, a siren sound effect is created, similar to an alarm.

There's more...

This code can be put into a function that receives an argument count, which specifies how many iterations or seconds the alarm is sounded for. Then, for any code in your project, you could call the function to make your board play an alarm for 10 seconds or 30 seconds. You could also combine this recipe with others in the book to make the pixels on the board flash red in the same way that an alarm would.

See also

You can find out more information using the following references:

- Examples of changing the frequency when calling the `play_tone` method can be found at `https://learn.adafruit.com/circuitpython-made-easy-on-circuit-playground-express/play-tone`.
- A microcontroller project that makes a siren alarm sound can be found at `https://www.instructables.com/id/How-to-Make-a-Siren-Using-Arduino/`.

Playing WAV files

In this recipe, we will learn how to use the speakers to play a WAV file of your choice. There is a good amount of storage on the Circuit Playground Express to store short audio clips, which can be played back at certain times.

Tones, beeps, alarms, and melodies are great; however, once you can play WAV files, then you can play any type of sound.

Getting ready

You will need access to the REPL on the Circuit Playground Express to run the code presented in this recipe.

How to do it...

Let's perform the following steps:

1. Copy the `hello.wav` file to the device in the same folder as the `main.py` file. Then, run the following lines of code in the REPL:

```
>>> from adafruit_circuitplayground.express import cpx
>>> cpx.play_file('hello.wav')
```

2. You should hear the board say *"Hello"* as it plays back the audio file.

How it works...

The first line of code imports the Circuit Playground Express library. The `cpx` object exposes a property method called `play_file`. This method accepts one argument in the `.wav` filename, which will be played on the onboard speaker.

The audio file should be in WAV file format; it should have a sample rate of 22,050 kHz, be 16-bit format, and have a mono channel of audio. This method will open the audio file and start the playback on the speaker. It will also keep polling the audio device until the playback is finished and will return once the audio playback has completed.

There's more...

Due to hardware constraints on the board, you won't be able to play compressed music formats such as MP3. The file will need to be in a specific uncompressed file format, which can be fed directly to the playback hardware that is on the board.

A consequence of this is that the uncompressed sound streams will be much larger, so only short audio clips will be able to be stored on the device. This still opens up a number of possibilities for playing sound effects or other short audio clips.

See also

You can find out more information using the following references:

- Documentation on the `play_file` method can be found at `https:// circuitpython.readthedocs.io/projects/circuitplayground/en/latest/api. html#adafruit_circuitplayground.express.Express.play_file`.
- Examples of calling the `play_file` method can be found at `https://learn. adafruit.com/circuitpython-made-easy-on-circuit-playground-express/ play-file`.

Converting MP3 files to WAV files

In this recipe, we will learn how to convert an MP3 file to a WAV file, which can then be played on the Circuit Playground Express. MP3 files are one of the most popular sound file formats around. This recipe is very useful for when you have an audio clip that you want to include in your embedded project, but need to get it in the right format so that it can play back correctly.

Getting ready

You will need to download and install the open source audio editing software, Audacity. It is available for Windows, macOS, and Linux.

> Audacity can be downloaded from the official website at https://www. audacityteam.org/.

How to do it...

Let's perform the following steps:

1. Start the Audacity software and select **File | Open**. Then, select the MP3 file and click on **Open**.
2. Details of the audio file should appear in the application, as shown in the following screenshot:

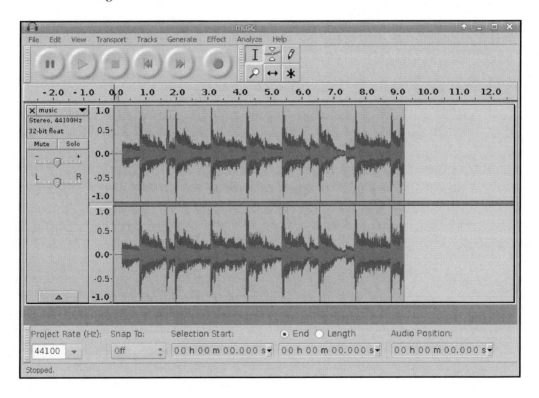

3. Select **Tracks** | **Resample** and the following dialog box should appear:

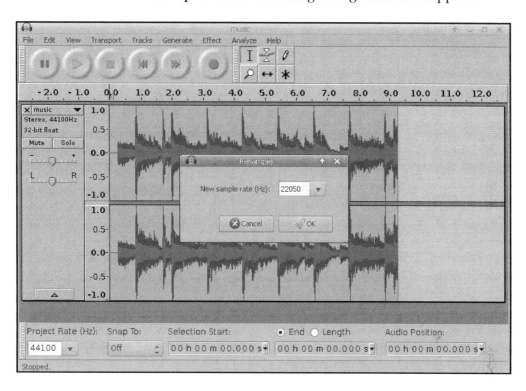

4. Set the new sample rate to 22050 and then click on **OK**.

5. Now, choose **Tracks | Stereo Track to Mono**. Instead of the stereo audio streams that were visible, there should only be one single mono channel on the screen:

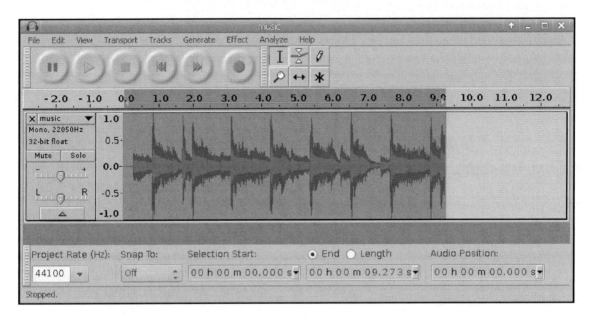

The audio data is now ready to be exported to the WAV format.

6. Next, choose **File | Export Audio**.
7. Set the file format drop-down menu to the value of WAV (Microsoft) signed 16-bit PCM.
8. Click on the **Save** button.
9. You can now copy the WAV file to the board and play it back on the device.

How it works...

The Circuit Playground Express board expects an audio file to be in the WAV file format and have a sample rate of 22,050 kHz, be in 16-bit format, and have a mono channel of audio data. Audacity is a versatile audio editor that can open any number of audio formats and perform the necessary changes to convert the audio data into the correct format.

The steps taken in this recipe resample the audio data and convert the audio channels to a single mono channel. Once that is done, the audio data can be exported to the correct WAV format. It is important to note that WAV files are not compressed like other audio formats, so they will take up much more space. This, combined with the storage constraints on this device, mean that only short audio clips should be used so that they can fit on the device.

There's more...

This recipe focused on the MP3 file format as the input format. However, Audacity supports a wide range of input formats, so you are not limited to only that input format for conversion. Audacity also has extensive editing capabilities that will come in very handy when you want to prepare a short audio clip from a much bigger audio stream.

A good example of this is when you have a song that might be five minutes long, but you only want a short five-second clip to be loaded on your board. You can then use the editing and conversion features of Audacity to achieve the final result.

See also

You can find out more information using the following references:

- More details on the WAV PCM soundfile format can be found at `http://soundfile.sapp.org/doc/WaveFormat/`.
- A guide to using Audacity for microcontroller audio projects can be found at `https://learn.adafruit.com/microcontroller-compatible-audio-file-conversion`.

Starting and stopping tones

In this recipe, we will learn how to use the `start_tone` and `stop_tone` calls to play tones in the background, and control other components on the board during the playback of the sound. The technique used in this recipe will essentially allow you to do more than one thing at an item when you play sounds.

One example of when you might want to implement this in a project is when you want to play an alarm sound and flash the lights at the same time.

Getting ready

You will need access to the REPL on the Circuit Playground Express to run the code presented in this recipe.

How to do it...

Let's perform the following steps:

1. Run the following lines of code in the REPL. You should hear a high-pitched beeping sound for 0.5 seconds:

    ```
    >>> from adafruit_circuitplayground.express import cpx
    >>> import time
    >>>
    >>> BEEP_HIGH = 960
    >>> BEEP_LOW = 800
    >>>
    >>> cpx.pixels.brightness = 0.10
    >>> cpx.start_tone(BEEP_HIGH)
    >>> time.sleep(0.5)
    >>> cpx.stop_tone()
    ```

2. Use the following code to play a beeping sound in the background while 10 pixels turn red at 0.1-second intervals. The beeping will then stop at the end of the animation:

    ```
    >>> cpx.start_tone(BEEP_HIGH)
    >>> for i in range(10):
    ...     cpx.pixels[i] = 0xFF0000
    ...     time.sleep(0.1)
    ...
    >>> cpx.stop_tone()
    >>>
    ```

3. Use the following block of code to perform a similar operation, but with a lower pitch. Here, the pixel animation will turn off each pixel one by one, ending the tone at the end of the animation:

    ```
    >>> cpx.start_tone(BEEP_LOW)
    >>> for i in range(10):
    ...     cpx.pixels[i] = 0x000000
    ...     time.sleep(0.1)
    ...
    ```

```
>>> cpx.stop_tone()
>>>
```

4. The code that follows combines all the code shown in this recipe to make one complete program. Add this to the `main.py` file and it will play a siren alarm and animate the pixels on and off with the siren:

```
from adafruit_circuitplayground.express import cpx
import time

BEEP_HIGH = 960
BEEP_LOW = 800

cpx.pixels.brightness = 0.10

cpx.start_tone(BEEP_HIGH)
for i in range(10):
    cpx.pixels[i] = 0xFF0000
    time.sleep(0.1)
cpx.stop_tone()

cpx.start_tone(BEEP_LOW)
for i in range(10):
    cpx.pixels[i] = 0x000000
    time.sleep(0.1)
cpx.stop_tone()
```

How it works...

The initial lines of code import the necessary libraries and set up the constants that are required for the rest of the code in the program. The brightness of the pixels is also set to a more comfortable level. The script then starts playing the high-pitched beeping tone in the background. It does so while looping through the 10 pixels and turning each one red, with a 0.1-second delay between each loop.

Once the animation is complete, the tone playback is stopped and a lower tone is played. The pixels are once again looped through; however, this time, they are shut off one by one. Finally, once the loop ends, the tone playback is stopped.

There's more...

Even though using `start_tone` and `stop_tone` requires more lines of code than simply calling `play_tone`, they allow you to do things that wouldn't be possible with just `play_tone`. For example, you can use your script to perform other tasks while audio is playing in the background.

In this recipe, the light and sound output were changed together. However, you could use the same technique to play a tone until someone presses a certain button. Alternatively, you could change the tones being played in reaction to different buttons being pressed.

See also

You can find out more information using the following references:

- Documentation on the `start_tone` method can be found at `https://circuitpython.readthedocs.io/projects/circuitplayground/en/latest/api.html#adafruit_circuitplayground.express.Express.start_tone`.
- Documentation on the `stop_tone` method can be found at `https://circuitpython.readthedocs.io/projects/circuitplayground/en/latest/api.html#adafruit_circuitplayground.express.Express.stop_tone`.

Interacting with Buttons

4

This chapter will introduce you to methods of interacting with the buttons and touchpads that come with the Adafruit Circuit Playground Express. You will learn how to detect whether a button is being pressed and you will also explore more advanced topics, such as fine tuning the sensitivity of capacitive touchpads.

In this chapter, we will cover the following recipes:

- Detecting push button presses
- Controlling LEDs with push buttons
- Reading a slide switch
- Calling functions on the button state change
- Moving active LEDs with push buttons
- Playing a beep on the button press
- Detecting touch on a touchpad
- Monitoring the touchpad raw measurements
- Adjusting the touch threshold

The Adafruit Circuit Playground Express layout

The following photograph displays the locations of the two push buttons, labeled **A** and **B**, that come with the board:

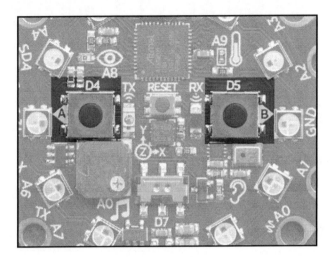

Courtesy of adafruit.com

The following photograph shows the location of the slide switch on the device:

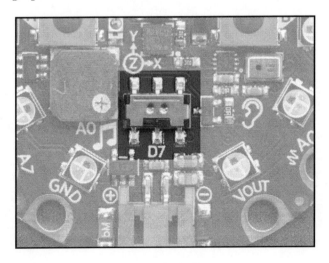

Courtesy of adafruit.com

The following photograph shows the location of the seven capacitive touchpads on the board:

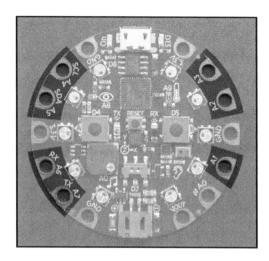

Courtesy of adafruit.com

Each touchpad contains a different material that can conduct electricity. Alligator clips can be used to connect these materials to the pads. Additionally, metals, water, and fruits can conduct electricity well enough to be used as connectors to the pads.

Now, let's take a look at how to detect the press of a button.

Detecting push button presses

In this recipe, we will learn how to create a program that will print a message when the push button is pressed. Push buttons are a great way to create user interaction on your devices. This board comes with two push buttons, A and B, so you can create all sorts of different interactions with your users by reading and responding to push button events.

Getting ready

You will need access to the REPL on the Circuit Playground Express to run the code presented in this recipe.

How to do it...

Let's perform the following steps:

1. First, run the following lines of code in the REPL. The value of `cpx.button_a` is `False` here because the button is not pressed:

```
>>> from adafruit_circuitplayground.express import cpx
>>> cpx.button_a
False
```

2. Keep push button A pressed while you run the following code block. This will change the value to `True`:

```
>>> cpx.button_a
True
```

3. Then, add the following code to the `main.py` file and this will repeatedly print the state of push button A on execution:

```
from adafruit_circuitplayground.express import cpx
import time

while True:
    print(cpx.button_a)
    time.sleep(0.05)
```

How it works...

The first line of code imports the Circuit Playground Express library. The `cpx` object exposes a property called `button_a`. This property will return `True` when the button is pressed, and it will return `False` when the button is not pressed.

The script loops forever with a 50 millisecond delay between each loop. The state of the button press is continually printed. When running this program, hold and release the push button to see the printed output change.

Note that there is another property called `button_b`, which serves the same function but for push button B instead.

There's more...

The interface for interacting with the push button in Python is very straightforward. Essentially, it translates to a Boolean value, which you can inspect at any time during your script execution in order to check the current state of the button.

This polling model of repeatedly checking the button state works well in simple scenarios. However, it proves to be problematic when you want to perform a single action for each button press, as opposed to continually pressing the button. This is similar to how you would expect to interact with a keyboard on a desktop. In this scenario, you expect that one physical key press will translate into an action being applied once. On the other hand, a physical key press that is held down for an extended period of time usually produces repeated key actions.

On most operating systems, a delay of 500 milliseconds or so is applied before the key is released, where it is considered as a **repeat key action**. It is important to bear these details in mind when you are trying to implement code that interacts with the push buttons in a natural and intuitive way.

See also

You can find out more information here:

- Further documentation on the `button_a` property can be found at `https://circuitpython.readthedocs.io/projects/circuitplayground/en/latest/api.html#adafruit_circuitplayground.cxpress.Express.button_a`.
- An example of interacting with push buttons can be found at `https://learn.adafruit.com/circuitpython-made-easy-on-circuit-playground-express/buttons`.

Controlling LEDs with push buttons

In this recipe, we will learn how to control two separate NeoPixels with two independent push buttons. This is a fun and simple way of creating interactivity with your device. Here, you will get immediate feedback from the board the moment you press each push button, as the pixels will light up in response.

Getting ready

You will need access to the REPL on the Circuit Playground Express to run the code presented in this recipe.

How to do it...

Let's perform the following steps:

1. First, run the following lines of code in the REPL:

```
>>> from adafruit_circuitplayground.express import cpx
>>>
>>> BLACK = 0x000000
>>> GREEN = 0x00FF00
>>>
>>> cpx.pixels.brightness = 0.10
```

2. Keep push button A pressed while you run the following code block. You should see pixel 2, which is located right next to the push button, light up green:

```
>>> cpx.pixels[2] = GREEN if cpx.button_a else BLACK
```

3. Release push button A and run the following code block; you should now see pixel 2 turn off:

```
>>> cpx.pixels[2] = GREEN if cpx.button_a else BLACK
```

4. Add the following code to the main.py file and it will turn pixel 2 and pixel 7 *on*, depending on whether push button A or push button B is being pressed:

```
from adafruit_circuitplayground.express import cpx

BLACK = 0x000000
GREEN = 0x00FF00

cpx.pixels.brightness = 0.10
while True:
    cpx.pixels[2] = GREEN if cpx.button_a else BLACK
    cpx.pixels[7] = GREEN if cpx.button_b else BLACK
```

How it works...

The first line of code imports the Circuit Playground Express library. The constants for the green and black color are defined and the pixel brightness is then set to a comfortable level.

Then, an infinite loop is started, which executes two lines of code on each iteration. The first line will set the color of pixel 2 to green if push button A is pressed, otherwise, it will set the pixel to off. The second line will set the color of pixel 7 to green if push button B is pressed, otherwise, it will set the pixel to off.

There's more...

In contrast to the first recipe in this chapter, there is no call to the `sleep` function to cause a delay between each loop. In this specific recipe, there is a reason why no delay is needed between each time the button state is polled. If one of the buttons is held down, then one of the lights will turn on and stay on without an issue.

In the case of the first recipe, a flood of print statements will occur while the button is being pressed. It is important to look at each scenario carefully to decide whether a delay is required between each poll.

See also

You can find out more information here:

- More documentation on conditional expressions can be found at `https://docs.python.org/3/reference/expressions.html#conditional-expressions`.
- Further details on how push buttons work can be found at `https://sciencing.com/push-switches-work-electrical-circuit-5030234.html`.

Reading a slide switch

In this recipe, we will learn how to create a program that will repeatedly print whether a slide switch is on or off. Slide switches have their own strengths, and this recipe will demonstrate how you can incorporate one into your project.

Getting ready

You will need access to the REPL on the Circuit Playground Express to run the code presented in this recipe.

How to do it...

Let's perform the following steps:

1. Ensure that the slide switch is flipped to the left-hand side. Run the following lines of code in the REPL:

```
>>> from adafruit_circuitplayground.express import cpx
>>> cpx.switch
True
```

2. Change the slide switch to be flipped to the right-hand side. Run the following code block:

```
>>> cpx.switch
False
```

3. Add the following code to the main.py file and it will repeatedly print the state of the slide switch on execution. Turn the slide switch to the left and right to observe the change in output:

```
from adafruit_circuitplayground.express import cpx
import time

while True:
    print(cpx.switch)
    time.sleep(0.05)
```

How it works...

The first line of code imports the Circuit Playground Express library. The cpx object exposes a property called switch. This property will return True when the switch is in the left position, and False when it is in the right position.

The script loops forever with a 50 millisecond delay between each loop. The state of the slide switch is continually printed.

There's more...

Push buttons are great for applying an action repeatedly, or when you want to register a single button press. Slide switches, however, are more suitable when you want people to be able to specify between two operating modes.

For instance, you might have a project that has two animation modes that can be selected with a slide switch. You could use the slide switch to enable or disable an alarm sound in your project. Depending on the user action, a slide switch or push button might be more appropriate.

The good thing about the Circuit Playground Express is that both options are available, so you can pick and choose which one works best for you.

See also

You can find out more information here:

- Further documentation on the switch property can be found at `https:// circuitpython.readthedocs.io/projects/circuitplayground/en/latest/api. html#adafruit_circuitplayground.express.Express.switch`.
- An explanation of how common types of switches work can be found at `https:/ /learn.sparkfun.com/tutorials/switch-basics/all`.

Calling functions on the button state change

In this recipe, we will learn how to call a function when the state of a button has changed. It is a common requirement that you only want an action to be performed when a button has a state change, as opposed to while the button is pushed down. This recipe demonstrates one technique that you can use to implement this requirement in your project.

Getting ready

You will need access to the REPL on the Circuit Playground Express to run the code presented in this recipe.

How to do it...

Let's perform the following steps:

1. First, run the following lines of code in the REPL:

```
>>> from adafruit_circuitplayground.express import cpx
>>> def button_change(pressed):
...     print('pressed:', pressed)
...
```

2. This will define the button_change function, which will be called each time a change has occurred in the button state. Run the following code and then repeatedly press and release push button A:

```
>>> last = cpx.button_a
>>> while True:
...     if cpx.button_a != last:
...         button_change(cpx.button_a)
...         last = cpx.button_a
...
pressed: True
pressed: False
pressed: True
pressed: False
pressed: True
pressed: False
```

3. The code that follows combines all the code shown in this recipe to make one complete program. Add this to the main.py file; it will print a message each time push button A is pressed or released:

```
from adafruit_circuitplayground.express import cpx

def button_change(pressed):
    print('pressed:', pressed)

last = cpx.button_a
while True:
    if cpx.button_a != last:
        button_change(cpx.button_a)
        last = cpx.button_a
```

How it works...

The button_change function is defined, which will be called each time the state of the button changes.

The last global variable will be used to keep track of the last state of the button. Then, an infinite loop is started, which will check whether the current state of the button differs from its last state. If it has detected a change, then it will call the button_change function.

Finally, the latest button state is saved in the last variable whenever it changes. This script essentially implements an event loop that detects button press events and calls the button_change event handler to handle these events whenever they are detected.

There's more...

Occasionally, you might want to register a button press as a single event regardless of whether the user holds the button down for a long or short period of time. This recipe achieves that goal by keeping track of the previous state of the button and only calling the event handler once, as the result of a button press.

Even though you have the extra step of tracking the last state of a button, the benefit of this approach is that you don't have to fiddle with the timing of delays between polling for key presses, or the timing of repeated keyboard delays. This recipe is just another viable approach to solve the problem of when and how to respond to physical button interactions.

See also

You can find out more information here:

- A good example of an event loop and event handlers can be found at https://docs.python.org/3/library/cmd.html.
- An example of responding to button presses can be found at https://learn.adafruit.com/sensor-plotting-with-mu-and-circuitpython/buttons-and-switch.

Moving active LEDs with push buttons

In this recipe, we will learn how to move the active NeoPixel clockwise and counterclockwise depending on whether the left or right push button is pressed. This recipe goes beyond the simpler button and LED interactions shown in previous recipes. This is a more involved recipe, which will create the impression that button presses are moving the light in a circular motion around the board.

Getting ready

You will need access to the REPL on the Circuit Playground Express to run the code presented in this recipe.

How to do it...

Let's perform the following steps:

1. Run the following lines of code in the REPL:

```
>>> from adafruit_circuitplayground.express import cpx
>>> import time
>>>
>>> BLACK = 0x000000
>>> BLUE = 0x0000FF
>>>
>>> cpx.pixels.brightness = 0.10
>>> i = 0
>>> direction = 1
>>>
>>>
```

2. Run the following code and press the push buttons to see the effect this has on the pixels:

```
>>> while True:
...     if cpx.button_a:
...         direction = 1
...     if cpx.button_b:
...         direction = -1
...     i += direction
...     i = i % 10
...     cpx.pixels.fill(BLACK)
...     cpx.pixels[i] = BLUE
```

```
...        time.sleep(0.05)
...
```

3. The code that follows combines all the code shown in this recipe to make one complete program. Add this block of code to the `main.py` file and it will change the direction of the lighted pixels from clockwise to counterclockwise each time push button A and push button B are pressed:

```
from adafruit_circuitplayground.express import cpx
import time

BLACK = 0x000000
BLUE = 0x0000FF

cpx.pixels.brightness = 0.10
i = 0
direction = 1
while True:
    if cpx.button_a:
        direction = 1
    if cpx.button_b:
        direction = -1
    i += direction
    i = i % 10
    cpx.pixels.fill(BLACK)
    cpx.pixels[i] = BLUE
    time.sleep(0.05)
```

How it works...

The first line of code imports the Circuit Playground Express library and the `time` library. Then, the color constants and brightness level are set. The `i` variable will keep track of which pixel is currently lit. The `direction` variable will either have the value of 1 or −1 and will control whether the pixel moves in a clockwise or counterclockwise direction.

In the infinite loop, the direction will be changed if either push button A or push button B is pressed. The direction is applied to the position and a modulus 10 operation is applied so that the position value rotates between the values of 0 and 10.

In each iteration, all the pixels are turned off and then the selected pixel is turned on. The speed of the light animation is controlled with a call to make the board sleep for 50 milliseconds between each loop iteration.

There's more...

This recipe combines a number of different techniques in order to produce the final result. It uses an animation effect where someone looking at the board thinks the light is moving around the board in a circle.

The animation effect has been implemented to support directional motion so that it will look as if the light is moving in either a clockwise or counterclockwise direction. Then, the push buttons are combined with this animation to change the direction of the animation.

You can take this base recipe and adapt it to different scenarios. For instance, you could replace the light show with a sound effect that goes from either quiet to loud, or loud to quiet, depending on which button is pressed. Additionally, you could use the two push buttons to increase or decrease the level of brightness. Having two push buttons opens many options to either increase or decrease a particular value depending on which button is being pressed.

See also

You can find out more information here:

- Details on a Circuit Playground project that uses the push buttons and pixels can be found at `https://learn.adafruit.com/circuit-playground-simple-simon`.
- Documentation on the modulo operator can be found at `https://docs.python.org/3.3/reference/expressions.html#binary-arithmetic-operations`.

Playing a beep on the button press

In this recipe, we will learn how to play a beeping tone when the button is pressed. The previous recipes allowed us to interact with light using the buttons. This recipe will show you how to introduce button and sound interactions in your projects.

Getting ready

You will need access to the REPL on the Circuit Playground Express to run the code presented in this recipe.

How to do it...

Let's perform the following steps:

1. Run the following lines of code in the REPL while keeping push button A
   pressed:

   ```
   >>> from adafruit_circuitplayground.express import cpx
   >>> if cpx.button_a:
   ...     cpx.play_tone(500, 0.2)
   ...
   ...
   ...
   >>>
   ```

2. The speaker should have given a low-pitch beep. Run the following code while
   keeping push button B pressed, and you should hear a high-pitch beep:

   ```
   >>> if cpx.button_b:
   ...     cpx.play_tone(900, 0.2)
   ...
   ...
   ...
   >>>
   ```

3. The code that follows combines all the code shown in this recipe and adds a
   while loop to it to make one complete program. Add this to the main.py file,
   and, when executed, it will produce either a high-or low-pitch beep each time
   either push button A or push button B is pressed:

   ```
   from adafruit_circuitplayground.express import cpx

   while True:
       if cpx.button_a:
           cpx.play_tone(500, 0.2)
       if cpx.button_b:
           cpx.play_tone(900, 0.2)
   ```

How it works...

The first line of code imports the Circuit Playground Express library. An infinite loop is
then entered that will check whether push button A or push button B is being pressed in
each loop iteration, and play a different pitched beep in each case for a duration of 0.2
seconds.

There's more...

This simple recipe demonstrates how you can make the board react to different button presses by playing different tones. Another way that you can make the script behave is by playing different audio .wav files depending on which push button is being pressed. The slide switch could also be incorporated into the recipe to set two different modes; one mode could play notes of a low pitch, and the other could play notes of a high pitch.

See also

You can find out more information here:

- Examples of how CircuitPython can read the input from push buttons can be found at https://learn.adafruit.com/circuitpython-essentials/circuitpython-digital-in-out.
- An example of a Circuit Playground project that reacts to inputs to play different tones can be found at https://learn.adafruit.com/dear-diary-alarm.

Detecting touch on a touchpad

In this recipe, we will learn how to detect when a touchpad is touched and to print a message each time this event occurs. The Circuit Playground Express comes with a number of touchpad connectors that can be attached to all sorts of objects.

Essentially, anything that can conduct electricity can be used as a way to interact with your device. You can use wires, conductive thread, fruit, water, or copper tape to interact with your device.

Getting ready

You will need access to the REPL on the Circuit Playground Express to run the code presented in this recipe.

How to do it...

Let's perform the following steps:

1. Run the following lines of code in the REPL. The value of `cpx.touch_A1` is
   `False` because touchpad A1 is not being touched:

```
>>> from adafruit_circuitplayground.express import cpx
>>> cpx.touch_A1
False
```

2. Keep your finger touching touchpad A1 while you run the following code block:

```
>>> cpx.touch_A1
True
```

3. The following code should be added to the `main.py` file. This will print a
   message every time you press touchpad A1:

```
from adafruit_circuitplayground.express import cpx
import time

while True:
    if cpx.touch_A1:
        print('detected touch')
    time.sleep(0.05)
```

How it works...

The first few lines of code import the Circuit Playground Express library and the `time`
library. The script then enters into an infinite loop where it checks the state of touchpad A1
in each loop iteration. If it has detected a touch occurring, then it will print a message.

There's more...

This recipe demonstrates a simple way to interact with touchpads. However, when it comes
to capacitive touch sensors, the devil is in the detail. Depending on how conductive the
material you attach to the touchpad is, you might find yourself in one of two extremes; that
is, the sensors might not detect some touch events at all, or if there is a lot of ambient noise,
which is being falsely detected as multiple touch events.

These devices aren't as simple as a mechanical push button. On the flip side, however, they will let you create projects where you can interact with your embedded device using bananas and oranges (as they are electrically conductive).

See also

You can find out more information here:

- Further documentation on the `touch_A1` property can be found at `https://circuitpython.readthedocs.io/projects/circuitplayground/en/latest/api.html#adafruit_circuitplayground.express.Express.touch_A1`.
- An example of interacting with capacitive touch sensors can be found at `https://learn.adafruit.com/adafruit-circuit-playground-express/adafruit2-circuitpython-cap-touch`.

Monitoring the touchpad raw measurements

In this recipe, we will learn how to monitor the touchpad raw measurements, which is a very useful way to verify how much the touch threshold should be adjusted. It is very important to be able to directly read the raw sensor values that are coming from the touch sensors.

This level of detail is necessary when you want to correctly set touch thresholds or when you want to find out why the touchpads aren't responding the way you expect them to.

Getting ready

You will need access to the REPL on the Circuit Playground Express to run the code presented in this recipe.

How to do it...

Let's perform the following steps:

1. Run the following lines of code in the REPL. The output shows the value taken from a raw touch measurement and the initial threshold value that was automatically set when the object was created:

```
>>> import time
>>> import touchio
>>> import board
>>> a1 = touchio.TouchIn(board.A1)
>>> a1.raw_value
1933
>>> a1.threshold
2050
>>>
```

2. Keep your finger touching touchpad A1 while you run the next block of code:

```
>>> a1.raw_value
4065
```

3. Release your finger from touchpad A1 while you run the next block of code:

```
>>> a1.raw_value
1839
```

4. The following code should be added to the `main.py` file and then run. While this code is executing, it will continually print the raw touch measurements and the current threshold, and determine whether the current reading is considered a touch event. This script can be used to get live sensor readings:

```
import time
import touchio
import board

a1 = touchio.TouchIn(board.A1)
while True:
    touch = a1.raw_value > a1.threshold
    print('raw:', a1.raw_value, 'threshold:', a1.threshold,
'touch:', touch)
    time.sleep(0.5)
```

How it works...

The first few lines of code import the different low-level libraries that are required to interact with the touchpad. A TouchIn object is created and connected to pad A1. Then, an infinite loop is run, which continually prints out a number of values relating to the sensor. It prints the current raw touch measurement of the threshold and whether the current measurement should be registered as a touch event.

The last value is simply True, but if the raw value exceeds the threshold, then it is False. The threshold is set when the TouchIn object is first instantiated by taking the initial raw value and adding 100 to this value.

There's more...

This script is very useful for verifying the actual values that are being read from the touch sensor and for deciding how low or high the touch threshold should be set. It's also a great way to connect different materials to your board and see how well they perform in conducting electricity and detecting touch events. Without these raw values, you can only guess at what is actually going on.

The higher-level properties used elsewhere in this chapter actually used a lot of the libraries introduced in this recipe under the hood. It is helpful to look at the source code of this higher-level code, as much of it is implemented in Python. Additionally, it gives you an insight into how the code is actually interacting with the hardware.

See also

You can find out more information here:

- Further documentation on the touchio module can be found at https:// circuitpython.readthedocs.io/en/3.x/shared-bindings/touchio/__init__. html.
- Further documentation on the board module can be found at https:// circuitpython.readthedocs.io/en/3.x/shared-bindings/board/__init__. html.

- A discussion on the capabilities of capacitive touch sensors on the Circuit Playground can be found at `https://learn.adafruit.com/circuit-playground-fruit-drums/hello-capacitive-touch`.
- An explanation of how capacitive touch sensors work can be found at `https://scienceline.org/2012/01/okay-but-how-do-touch-screens-actually-work/`.

Adjusting the touch threshold

In this recipe, we will learn how to adjust the sensitivity of the touchpad by changing the threshold value. This is used to decide whether a signal will be treated as a touch event not. This is an important setting to tweak and set to the correct value. If you don't, then a lot of your touch projects won't behave correctly.

Getting ready

You will need access to the REPL on the Circuit Playground Express to run the code presented in this recipe.

How to do it...

Let's perform the following steps:

1. Run the following lines of code in the REPL. The touch threshold will have been increased by 200 at this point:

```
>>> from adafruit_circuitplayground.express import cpx
>>> import time
>>>
>>> cpx.adjust_touch_threshold(200)
```

2. Keep your finger touching touchpad A1 while you run the next block of code:

```
>>> cpx.touch_A1
True
```

3. The following code should be added to the `main.py` file and run. The script will increase the touch threshold by `200` and print a message each time the sensor detects a touch event:

```python
from adafruit_circuitplayground.express import cpx
import time

cpx.adjust_touch_threshold(200)
while True:
    if cpx.touch_A1:
        print('detected touch')
    time.sleep(0.5)
```

How it works...

The first line of code imports the Circuit Playground Express library. The `cpx` object exposes a method called `adjust_touch_threshold`. This method can be used to change the configured threshold on the touchpads. When called, the threshold for all touchpads will be increased by the specified amount.

Increasing the threshold value makes the touchpad less sensitive, while decreasing this value will make the sensor more sensitive. If the threshold setting is set too low, then many sensor readings will be incorrectly detected as touch events. On the other hand, if the threshold is too high, then genuine touch events will not be detected. A sleep function of 500 milliseconds is applied between each loop iteration so that a flood of touch events isn't detected during each iteration.

There's more...

The best way to decide on what to set as the value for the threshold is through experimentation. Connect all the actual conductive materials to the touchpads before starting your threshold tuning. Then, use the *Monitoring the touchpad raw measurements* recipe in this chapter to get a live view of the sensor readings you are receiving.

You can also repeatedly touch the material in question to see how the readings vary when you touch and let go. Based on these readings, you can set the ideal threshold that will reliably read touch events. It is important to restart your script each time you change the materials as the initial threshold autoconfiguration occurs each time you run the code the first time.

See also

You can find out more information here:

- Further documentation on the `adjust_touch_threshold` method can be found at `https://circuitpython.readthedocs.io/projects/circuitplayground/en/latest/api.html#adafruit_circuitplayground.express.Express.adjust_touch_threshold`.
- An example of calling the `adjust_touch_threshold` method can be found at `https://learn.adafruit.com/make-it-sense/circuitpython-6`.

5
Reading Sensor Data

This chapter will introduce you to methods that you can use to read sensor data from a number of sensors that come onboard with Adafruit Circuit Playground Express. We will cover the temperature and light sensors, as well as the motion sensor, and you will also learn how to make the board react to sensor events, such as the board being shaken or the light levels changing. Having access to this rich sensor data can make all sorts of projects possible. For example, you could make a project that makes an alarm beep if the detected temperature has exceeded a certain level. By learning how to read and process this sensor data, you can make a wide array of embedded projects a reality.

In this chapter, we will be covering the following topics:

- Circuit Playground Express sensors
- Reading temperature readings
- Reading brightness levels from the light sensor
- Creating a light meter
- Reading data from the motion sensor
- Detecting a single or double tap
- Detecting a shake
- Beeping on a shake

Circuit Playground Express sensors

Three different hardware sensors will be used in this chapter to get sensor readings from the environment. The following photograph is of a thermistor, showing the location of the temperature sensor:

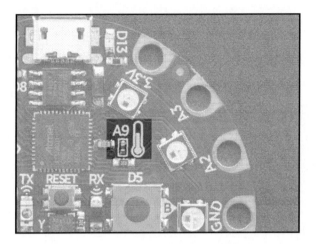

Courtesy of adafruit.com

The following photograph shows the light sensor that is available on the device:

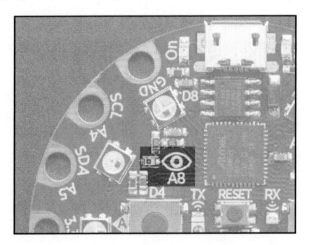

Courtesy of adafruit.com

The following photograph shows the accelerometer, which can be used to detect motion, as well as tap and double tap strikes on the board:

Courtesy of adafruit.com

Let's check our first recipe now.

Reading temperature readings

In this recipe, we will learn how to create a loop that repeatedly reads the current temperature from the temperature sensor and prints it out. This will let us experiment with the sensor and see how it reacts to changes in temperature. The methods in this recipe can be used whenever you need to incorporate temperature readings into your project.

Getting ready

You will need access to the REPL on Circuit Playground Express to run the code presented in this recipe.

How to do it...

Follow these steps to learn how to read temperature readings:

1. Run the following lines of code in the REPL. The output shows that the room temperature is around 25°C:

```
>>> from adafruit_circuitplayground.express import cpx
>>> import time
>>> cpx.temperature
25.7499
```

2. Now, use your body temperature to increase the temperature sensor readings by pressing your finger on the temperature sensor while you take the next reading:

```
>>> cpx.temperature
30.031
```

3. The temperature should have increased by a number of degrees. If you run the following code, a floating-point number should be returned:

```
>>> start = time.monotonic()
>>> start
27.409
```

4. Wait for a few seconds before executing the following line of code. It will calculate the number of seconds since you assigned the value to the start variable:

```
>>> time.monotonic() - start
11.37
```

5. If you run the following code, a list of all the local variables and their values should be displayed as a dictionary:

```
>>> locals()
{'time': <module 'time'>, 'start': 60.659, '__name__': '__main__'}
>>>
```

6. The following code should be put into the `main.py` file and, when executed, will repeatedly print the current elapsed time and current temperature reading:

```
from adafruit_circuitplayground.express import cpx
import time

start = time.monotonic()
while True:
    elapsed = time.monotonic() - start
    temp = cpx.temperature
    print('{elapsed:.2f}\t{temp}'.format(**locals()))
    time.sleep(0.1)
```

How it works...

The first lines of code import the Circuit Playground Express library and the `time` module. The `cpx` object exposes a property called `temperature`—this property returns the current temperature reading from the thermistor as a floating-point number whenever the value is accessed.

This value is expressed on the Celsius temperature scale. The start time is recorded so that the elapsed time can be calculated for each temperature reading. The script then goes into an infinite loop, calculating the elapsed time and getting a temperature reading for each loop iteration.

The elapsed time and temperature are printed with a tab delimiter. A 0.1-second delay is applied before the next iteration of the loop is started.

There's more...

The temperature sensor on this device is a **negative temperature coefficient** (**NTC**) thermistor. This component is a resistor that changes resistance with a change in temperature. By measuring its resistance, we can get a reading for the temperature. In the case of NTC thermistors, the resistance will decrease as the temperature increases.

In this recipe, the time and temperature data was output in a tab-delimited format. This format makes it easy to move the data into other applications for analysis. The following graph was generated using data that was output from the main script in this recipe:

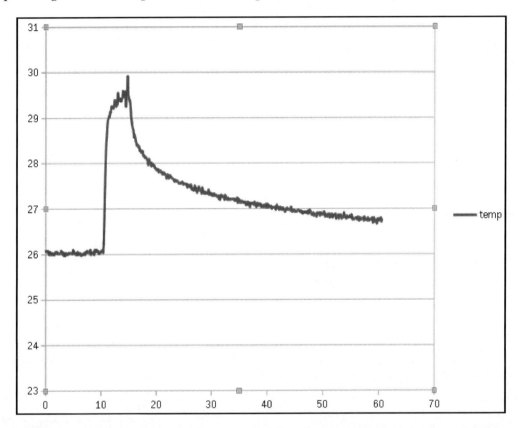

After the script was run for 60 seconds, the output from the REPL was taken and copy-pasted into our spreadsheet program, LibreOffice Calc. The tab delimiter separates the time and temperature data into their own columns by default. Then, using this table of data, the *x-y* scatter graph was generated.

Graphing sensor data like this makes it very easy to visualize what is happening to the temperature readings over time. In this specific dataset (at the start of script execution), the temperature sensor was reading the ambient room temperature as being around 26°C. Around 10 seconds into the script execution, the sensor was touched to heat it up to almost 30°C.

This can be seen in the sharp increase in temperature in the preceding diagram, which occurs at the 10-second mark. After letting go of the sensor, it starts the slow process of cooling down, until the sensor cools down past the 27°C mark over a 40-second period.

See also

Here are a few references regarding this recipe:

- Documentation on the temperature property can be found at `https://circuitpython.readthedocs.io/projects/circuitplayground/en/latest/api.html#adafruit_circuitplayground.express.Express.temperature`.
- Documentation on the CircuitPython `time` module can be found at `https://circuitpython.readthedocs.io/en/3.x/shared-bindings/time/__init__.html`.
- Documentation on the built-in `locals` function can be found at `https://docs.python.org/3/library/functions.html#locals`.
- Details on how thermistors work can be found at `https://www.omega.com/prodinfo/thermistor.html`.
- The project page and the application download for the LibreOffice Calc application can be found at `https://www.libreoffice.org/`.

Reading brightness levels from the light sensor

In this recipe, we will learn how to create a loop that will repeatedly read the current light brightness from the light sensor. Getting live readings from the sensor can be a fun way to experiment with the sensor to see how sensitive it is to different light sources.

Ultimately, the techniques in this recipe can help you build projects that interact with their environment, depending on the presence or absence of light.

Getting ready

You will need access to the REPL on Circuit Playground Express to run the code presented in this recipe.

How to do it...

Follow these steps to learn how to read brightness levels from the light sensor:

1. Execute the following block of code in the REPL:

```
>>> from adafruit_circuitplayground.express import cpx
>>> cpx.light
5
```

2. The number that's output is the light level of the room. Under normal lighting conditions, this should be a low number.

3. Now, shine a flashlight on the light sensor while you run the following block of code:

```
>>> cpx.light
308
```

4. You should see the value shoot up to a much higher value. The following code should be put into the `main.py` file and, when executed, will repeatedly print the current light levels that are being read from the light sensor:

```
from adafruit_circuitplayground.express import cpx
import time

while True:
    print(cpx.light)
    time.sleep(0.1)
```

How it works...

The first lines of code import the Circuit Playground Express library and the `time` module. The `cpx` object exposes a property called `light`. This property will return the current light level reading from the light sensor. This value is expressed using lux units, which is a unit for measuring illuminance.

In this script, an infinite loop is run, which prints the current lights levels and then sleeps for 0.1 seconds before the next iteration starts.

There's more...

A convenient way to experiment with the light sensor is to use the flashlight found on most smartphones. This flashlight is bright enough to create dramatic differences in the light readings on Circuit Playground Express. While running the main script in this recipe, watch how the values change as you bring the flashlight closer and farther away from the sensor.

The light sensor on this device is a phototransistor. This type of device is a transistor that, when exposed to different light levels, will cause a difference in the flow of current to its circuits. These electrical changes can be read to then calculate the light level.

See also

Here are a couple of references regarding this recipe:

- Documentation on the `light` property can be found at `https://circuitpython.readthedocs.io/projects/circuitplayground/en/latest/api.html#adafruit_circuitplayground.express.Express.light`.
- More details on how phototransistors work can be found at `https://www.elprocus.com/phototransistor-basics-circuit-diagram-advantages-applications/`.

Creating a light meter

In this recipe, we will use 10 NeoPixels to create a ring that will show the current light level. The ring will get smaller and bigger as the light level increases and decreases. This recipe will show you one way you can make your projects interact with light. It will also show a generic technique for turning the ring of pixels into a 10-level gauge that you can use in all sorts of projects.

Getting ready

You will need access to the REPL on Circuit Playground Express to run the code presented in this recipe.

How to do it...

Follow these steps to learn how to create a light meter:

1. Use the REPL to run the following lines of code:

```
>>> from adafruit_circuitplayground.express import cpx
>>> import time
>>>
>>> BLACK = 0x000000
>>> BLUE = 0x0000FF
>>> MAX_LUX = 330
>>> cpx.pixels.brightness = 0.10
>>>
>>> def gauge(level):
...     cpx.pixels[0:level] = [BLUE] * level
...
...
...
>>> gauge(2)
```

2. At this point, you should see the first two pixels turn blue. Run the following line of code to see the first five pixels turn blue:

```
>>> gauge(5)
```

3. The following code should be put into the main.py file and, when executed, it will create a light meter that gets bigger and smaller as the light levels get brighter and darker:

```
from adafruit_circuitplayground.express import cpx
import time

BLACK = 0x000000
BLUE = 0x0000FF
MAX_LUX = 330
cpx.pixels.brightness = 0.10

def gauge(level):
    cpx.pixels[0:level] = [BLUE] * level

last = 0
while True:
    level = int((cpx.light / MAX_LUX) * 10)
    if level != last:
        cpx.pixels.fill(BLACK)
        gauge(level)
```

```
        last = level
time.sleep(0.05)
```

How it works...

The first lines of code import the Circuit Playground Express library and the `time` module. The color codes are defined for the colors blue and black. The brightness is then set to a comfortable level. The `gauge` function is then defined. This function receives a single integer argument, which should range its value from 0 to 10. This value will be used to determine how many pixels will be turned blue in the ring of pixels. This function creates a visual display similar to a classic gauge, which shows a smaller or larger ring depending on the level of the value.

Then, the `last` variable is initialized. This variable is used to keep track of whether the gauge level has changed since the last loop. This extra step is needed to prevent the pixels from flickering because of unnecessarily turning them off and on in each loop. The gauge level is calculated by taking the current light level and dividing it by its maximum possible value, which happens to be 330 on this board.

This value is then multiplied by 10, which is the number of levels in the gauge. If the gauge level has changed, all the pixels are turned off and then the correct gauge level is displayed. This process is done during each iteration of the infinite loop with a delay of 50 milliseconds between each loop to create a responsive feeling when interacting with the light sensor.

There's more...

In this recipe, the functionality to display the gauge was intentionally kept in its own function to encourage reusability. It can be used in other projects or kept in its own module, which can be imported and used whenever you have the need to display information as a gauge using the pixels that come with the board.

Another aspect of this recipe is the extra work that had to be done to address the light flickering issue that occurs when you unnecessarily turn pixels on and off repeatedly. When you change the state of many pixels all at once, flickering issues can occur if you don't do your implementation carefully. This is not a major issue in terms of the functionality of the light meter; it is more about creating a more pleasant visual experience when people use the light meter.

See also

Here are a couple of references regarding this recipe:

- A project that uses Circuit Playground Express pixels to create a sound meter can be found at `https://learn.adafruit.com/adafruit-circuit-playground-express/playground-sound-meter`.
- More details on what a light meter is and their uses can be found at `https://shuttermuse.com/glossary/light-meter/`.

Reading data from the motion sensor

In this recipe, we will create a loop that continually reads from the accelerometer and prints the *x*, *y*, and *z* axes' data. Printing output will help us experiment with how the sensor will react to shaking the board or tilting it in different directions. Once you get a sense of how the sensor works, you can start incorporating it into projects to have your board react to tilt or acceleration.

Getting ready

You will need access to the REPL on Circuit Playground Express to run the code presented in this recipe.

How to do it...

Follow these steps to learn how to read data from the motion sensor:

1. Run the following lines of code in the REPL while the board is placed on a level surface with its buttons facing upward:

```
>>> from adafruit_circuitplayground.express import cpx
>>> cpx.acceleration.z
9.46126
```

2. Run the following block of code while the board is placed with its buttons facing downward:

```
>>> cpx.acceleration.z
-9.30804
```

3. The following code should be put into the `main.py` file and, when executed, will continually print the current *x*, *y*, and *z* axes' data from the accelerometer:

```
from adafruit_circuitplayground.express import cpx
import time

while True:
    x, y, z = cpx.acceleration
    print('x: {x:.2f} y: {y:.2f} z: {z:.2f}'.format(**locals()))
    time.sleep(0.1)
```

How it works...

The first lines of code import the Circuit Playground Express library and the `time` module. An infinite loop is started, which will get readings from the accelerometer during each loop. The readings are unpacked into the *x*, *y*, and *z* variables. Then, the value of each axis is printed before the script goes to sleep for 0.1 seconds and starts the next iteration.

There's more...

While this script is running, experiment with tilting the board in different directions. This sensor is quite sensitive and can give you a pretty accurate reading that's related to the tilt of the board. Beyond detecting the orientation of the board, it can also be used to detect acceleration on any of the three axes. As the script is running, also shake the board in different directions—you should see the readings related to acceleration shoot up. Depending on the direction you shake the board, different axes should react accordingly.

See also

Here are a couple of references regarding this recipe:

- Documentation on the `acceleration` property can be found at `https://circuitpython.readthedocs.io/projects/circuitplayground/en/latest/api.html#adafruit_circuitplayground.express.Express.acceleration`.
- More details on the accelerometer that comes with Circuit Playground Express can be found at `https://learn.adafruit.com/circuit-playground-lesson-number-0/accelerometer`.

Detecting a single or double tap

In this recipe, we will learn how to configure the board to detect single or double taps. Sensor data from the accelerometer will be used to detect these tap events. This recipe shows you how to create applications that can react to people tapping the board.

Getting ready

You will need access to the REPL on Circuit Playground Express to run the code presented in this recipe.

How to do it...

Follow these steps to learn how to detect a single or double tap:

1. Execute the following block of code in the REPL:

    ```
    >>> from adafruit_circuitplayground.express import cpx
    >>> cpx.detect_taps = 1
    >>> cpx.tapped
    False
    ```

2. Tap the board once and then run the following block of code. You should get a True value for the first value, indicating that a tap was detected, and then a False value on the next check, which indicates that no new taps have been detected since the last check:

    ```
    >>> cpx.tapped
    True
    >>> cpx.tapped
    False
    ```

3. The following code should be put into the main.py file and, when executed, will continually print whether or not a tap has been detected since the last check:

    ```
    from adafruit_circuitplayground.express import cpx
    import time

    cpx.detect_taps = 1
    while True:
        print('tap detected:', cpx.tapped)
        time.sleep(0.1)
    ```

How it works...

The first lines of code import the Circuit Playground Express library and the `time` module. The tap detection algorithm is configured to detect single taps by setting `detect_taps` to 1.

An infinite loop is started, which will retrieve the value of the `tapped` property on each loop. This property will return `True` only if a single tap has been detected by the accelerometer since the last time taps were checked. The `sleep` function is then called to cause a 0.1-second delay before starting the next iteration.

There's more...

Modify the script by setting `detect_taps` to 2. When you run it again, try and perform some single taps on the board. It shouldn't register anything.

Now try performing some double taps. You should see them being detected. Try varying the amount of force you use to tap the board to see what level of force is required before a tap can be detected.

See also

Here are a few references regarding this recipe:

- Documentation on the `detect_taps` property can be found at https:// circuitpython.readthedocs.io/projects/circuitplayground/en/latest/api. html#adafruit_circuitplayground.express.Express.detect_taps.
- Documentation on the `tapped` property can be found at https:// circuitpython.readthedocs.io/projects/circuitplayground/en/latest/api. html#adafruit_circuitplayground.express.Express.tapped.
- More details on the board's tap detection abilities can be found at https:// learn.adafruit.com/circuitpython-made-easy-on-circuit-playground-express/tap.

Detecting a shake

In this recipe, we will learn how to poll the shake method and print it whenever the board has been shaken. Creating projects that can respond to the device being shaken can be really fun. The board can also be configured so that you can specify whether a light or heavy shake is required before it registers as a shake. This can open up new and creative ways to make people interact with your devices.

Getting ready

You will need access to the REPL on Circuit Playground Express to run the code presented in this recipe.

How to do it...

Follow these steps to learn how to detect a shake:

1. Use the REPL to run the following lines of code:

```
>>> from adafruit_circuitplayground.express import cpx
>>> cpx.shake(20)
False
```

2. Shake the board repeatedly while you run the following block of code:

```
>>> cpx.shake(20)
True
```

3. The following code should be put into the main.py file and, when executed, will continually print whether or not the board is currently being shaken:

```
from adafruit_circuitplayground.express import cpx
import time

while True:
    print('shake detected:', cpx.shake())
    time.sleep(0.1)
```

How it works...

The first lines of code import the Circuit Playground Express library and the `time` module. An infinite loop is started, which will print the result of the `shake` method on each loop. This method will return `True` or `False`, depending on whether or not the board is currently being shaken. The `sleep` function is then called to cause a 0.1-second delay before starting the next iteration.

There's more...

Modify the script and give the `shake` function the value `20` as the first argument. Now, run the script and try and shake it. You should find that less force is needed for the board to register a shake event. The default value for the first argument, `shake_threshold`, is `30`, and the lower the value, the more sensitive the board will be to detecting shakes. Do not set the value to `10` or lower, otherwise it will be too sensitive and will continuously think that it has detected shakes.

See also

Here are a couple of references regarding this recipe:

- Documentation on the `shake` method can be found at `https://circuitpython.readthedocs.io/projects/circuitplayground/en/latest/api.html#adafruit_circuitplayground.express.Express.shake`.
- Examples of using the `shake` method can be found at `https://learn.adafruit.com/circuitpython-made-easy-on-circuit-playground-express/shake`.

Beeping on a shake

In this recipe, we will learn how to make the board beep every time you give it a shake. This is an interesting way to make the board respond to motion. The same approach can be used to make pixels respond to shakes instead of just beeps.

Getting ready

You will need access to the REPL on Circuit Playground Express to run the code presented in this recipe.

How to do it...

Follow these steps to learn how to make the board beep every time you shake it:

1. Run the following lines of code in the REPL; you should hear a beep:

```
>>> from adafruit_circuitplayground.express import cpx
>>> cpx.play_tone(900, 0.2)
```

2. The following code should be put into the main.py file and, when executed, will beep every time the board is shaken:

```
from adafruit_circuitplayground.express import cpx
import time

while True:
    if cpx.shake(20):
        cpx.play_tone(900, 0.2)
    time.sleep(0.1)
```

How it works...

The first lines of code import the Circuit Playground Express library and the time module. An infinite loop is started, which will check to see whether the board is currently being shaken. If a shake event is detected, a short beep is played for 0.2 seconds. After this, check that the board then sleeps for 0.1 seconds before starting the process again.

There's more...

You could incorporate the slide switch into this recipe so that people can choose a high or low shake threshold, depending on what position the slide switch is in. In this way, the slide switch can be used to make it easy or difficult for a shake to be detected. You could create a game where each shake increments a counter and plays a beep.

When the counter reaches 10, you could play a victory melody. Then, whoever achieves 10 shakes first wins. Interacting with devices using shakes instead of push-button presses can be a fun way to vary how people interact with your projects.

See also

Here are a couple of references regarding this recipe:

- A guide to how accelerometers work can be found at `https://www.dimensionengineering.com/info/accelerometers`.
- Documentation on the Python library being used to interact with the onboard accelerometer can be found at `https://circuitpython.readthedocs.io/projects/lis3dh/en/latest/api.html`.

6
Button Bash Game

In this chapter, we will create a two-player game called Button Bash that you can play directly on Circuit Playground Express without a computer. Each player must press their push button as fast as they can. Each press of the button increases that player's score by one point. The players' current scores will be shown visually with the NeoPixels. The first player that reaches a score of 20 points wins the game.

To create this game, we will combine button input with light output through the NeoPixels and with audio output through the built-in speakers. This chapter contains a number of recipes, each showing different parts of the game, and we combine all of these pieces in the final recipe to produce the complete game.

In this chapter, we will cover the following topics:

- Creating a class to detect a button state change
- Creating your own Python modules
- Adding button interactions to the event loop
- Creating a generator to get pixel colors
- Showing scores with the ScoreBoard class
- Detecting winners with the ScoreBoard class
- Adding the ScoreBoard class to the event loop

Technical requirements

The code files for this chapter can be found in the `Chapter06` folder in the GitHub repository, at `https://github.com/PacktPublishing/MicroPython-Cookbook`.

Many of the recipes in this chapter require three audio files to be transferred to the Circuit Playground Express board. These files are called `start.wav`, `win1.wav`, and `win2.wav`. They can all be downloaded from the `Chapter06` folder in the GitHub repository. They should be saved in the top-level folder with your `main.py` file.

Many of the recipes in this chapter make use of the Circuit Playground Express library, which will typically get imported in the first line of the script, with the following line of code:

```
from adafruit_circuitplayground.express import cpx
```

This library will help us interact with the buttons, pixels, and speaker that come with the board.

Circuit Playground Express power

The game that will be presented in this chapter can run directly on Circuit Playground Express, without a need for a connected computer. This is an excellent opportunity to introduce the options you have to make your project portable on this type of board. The board can receive power from a number of different portable sources.

We'll explore two different approaches to solving the problem of portable power. Each approach uses a different connector on the board. The first connector we will look at is the Micro B USB connector, which appears in the following image:

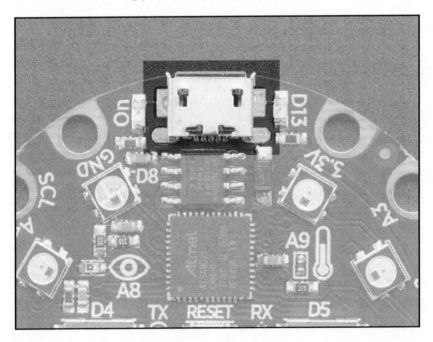

Courtesy of adafruit.com

This connector can be used to connect the board to a computer for power and to transfer your code and audio files onto the board. One approach is to attach a portable power bank to the board via USB. The following photograph shows the board being powered by one of these power banks:

The benefit of this approach is that these power banks come in all different sizes and capacities, so you have plenty of options to choose the one that best meets your needs. They are rechargeable, making them reusable, and they can easily be purchased at most electronics retailers.

The second connector that we will look at is the JST battery input, which appears in the next photograph:

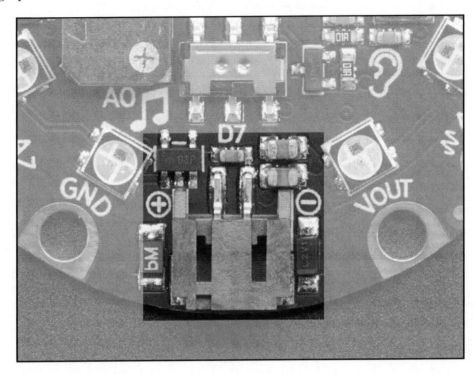

Courtesy of adafruit.com

There are a number of portable battery sources that can be attached to this connector. Many of these battery holders are quite inexpensive, and they often support popular battery sizes, such as AAA batteries. Because the board has no built-in battery charging, you can safely use regular batteries or rechargeable batteries. The following photograph shows a battery holder with an on/off switch:

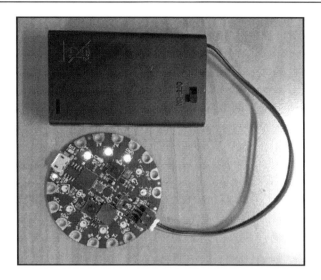

The next photograph shows the same holder with the cover open, to provide a view of the three AAA batteries it uses:

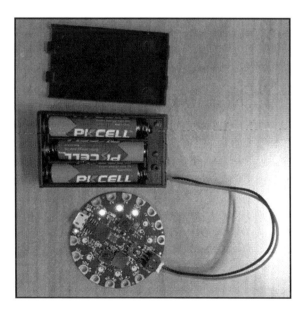

The battery holder shown in the previous photograph can be purchased for around $2 USD from https://www.adafruit.com/product/727.

Creating a class to detect a button state change

In this recipe, you will learn how to define a class that, when instantiated, can keep track of the button press events of a specific button on the board. We will use this class in later recipes in this chapter, in order to create objects that will keep track of button presses on push buttons A and B.

You will learn how to put common chunks of code into functions and classes, which will improve the code reuse in your projects. It can also help with large projects, in order to break up a lot of the logic into smaller, independent chunks of functions and classes. The implementation of this button event class will be kept generic on purpose, so that it can easily be reused in different projects.

Getting ready

You will need access to the REPL on Circuit Playground Express to run the code that will be presented in this recipe.

How to do it...

Let's go over the steps required in this recipe:

1. Run the following lines of code in the REPL:

```
>>> from adafruit_circuitplayground.express import cpx
>>> class ButtonEvent:
...     def __init__(self, name):
...         self.name = name
...         self.last = False
...
...
...
>>> button = ButtonEvent('button_a')
```

2. At this stage, we have defined our class and have given it a constructor. Run the next block of code to create your first instance of this class and to inspect its name attribute:

```
>>> button = ButtonEvent('button_a')
>>> button
```

```
<ButtonEvent object at 20003410>
>>> button.name
'button_a'
```

3. The following block of code will access the attribute from the `cpx` library that will indicate whether the push button was pressed:

```
>>> pressed = getattr(cpx, button.name)
>>> pressed
False
```

4. Run the following block of code while holding down push button A. It should show the state of the push button as `pressed`:

```
>>> pressed = getattr(cpx, button.name)
>>> pressed
True
```

5. The following code should be put into the `main.py` file, and, when executed, it will repeatedly print a message whenever push button A is pressed:

```python
from adafruit_circuitplayground.express import cpx


class ButtonEvent:
    def __init__(self, name):
        self.name = name
        self.last = False

    def is_pressed(self):
        pressed = getattr(cpx, self.name)
        changed = (pressed != self.last)
        self.last = pressed
        return (pressed and changed)


button = ButtonEvent('button_a')
while True:
    if button.is_pressed():
        print('button A pressed')
```

That's it for the coding part; now, let's see how this works.

How it works...

The `ButtonEvent` class is defined to help us keep track of button presses with either push button A or push button B. When you instantiate the class, it expects one argument, which specifies the name of the button we are tracking. The name is saved to an attribute on the instance called `name`, and then the last variable is initialized with the value `False`. This variable will keep track of the last known value of the button state each time we check for a new event.

The `is_pressed` method is called each time we want to check whether a new button press event has occurred since the last time we checked. It first retrieves the current state of the physical push button, to find out whether it is pushed down. We check the value with its last known value to calculate whether a change has occurred; we keep this result in a variable called `changed`. We then save the current value for future reference. The method will then return a `True` value if the button state has changed and if it is currently being pushed down.

After the class definition, we create one instance of this class that will keep track of push button A. Then, an infinite loop is started that keeps checking for new button press events and prints a message each time one of them is detected.

There's more...

In this recipe, we used the class once, to keep track of a single button; but because we haven't hardcoded any specific button values in the class definition itself, we can reuse this code to keep track of a number of different buttons. We can just as easily watch both push buttons for button press events. Many MicroPython boards let you attach many extra push buttons. This approach of making a generic class to watch buttons can be very useful in these scenarios.

There is also a bit of logic involved in keeping track of the previous button state, so that we can detect what we are interested in, which is new button press events. By keeping all this code in one contained class, we can make our code more readable and more manageable.

See also

Here are a few references:

- Documentation for creating classes in Python can be found at `https://docs.python.org/3/tutorial/classes.html`.
- Documentation on the built-in `getattr` function can be found at `https://docs.python.org/3/library/functions.html#getattr`.

Creating your own Python modules

In this recipe, you will learn how to take the code you create and put it into its own Python modules. We will take the code from the previous recipe, which helped us track button press events, and place it into its own dedicated module.

We will then import this newly created module into our main Python script and use its class definition to track button presses. This can be a very useful approach when you start working on large projects and want to split up your code into different modules. It can also be helpful when you find a useful module that you would like to incorporate into your own project.

Getting ready

You will need access to the REPL on Circuit Playground Express to run the code presented in this recipe.

How to do it...

Let's go over the steps required for this recipe:

1. The following code should be put into a new file called `button.py`; this will become the Python module that we can import in later steps:

```python
from adafruit_circuitplayground.express import cpx


class ButtonEvent:
    def __init__(self, name):
        self.name = name
        self.last = False
```

```
        def is_pressed(self):
            pressed = getattr(cpx, self.name)
            changed = (pressed != self.last)
            self.last = pressed
            return (pressed and changed)
```

2. Run the following lines of code in the REPL:

```
>>> from button import ButtonEvent
>>> ButtonEvent
<class 'ButtonEvent'>
>>>
```

3. At this stage, we have been able to import a class from our new Python module. The next line of code will create a new object that we can use to detect new button press events:

```
>>> button = ButtonEvent('button_a')
>>> button.is_pressed()
False
```

4. Run the following block of code while you hold down push button A, and it should detect a button press event:

```
>>> button = ButtonEvent('button_a')
>>> button.is_pressed()
```

5. The following code should be put into the main.py file and, when executed, it will repeatedly print a message whenever push button A is pressed:

```
from button import ButtonEvent

button = ButtonEvent('button_a')
while True:
    if button.is_pressed():
        print('button A pressed')
```

How it works...

In our previous recipes, we got accustomed to working with the main.py file. Creating a new Python module is as simple as creating a new file and placing our code in it. We have taken the ButtonEvent class and placed it into its own Python module, called button.

Now, we can import the class and create objects using that class. The rest of the code creates an object to monitor button presses and prints a message whenever they are detected.

There's more...

When you create your own custom Python module, it is important to be mindful of the name you give the module. The same naming restrictions for any Python module also apply to your MicroPython code. For example, you can't create a module that has space characters in it. You should also make sure not to name your module the same name as an existing MicroPython or CircuitPython module. Hence, you shouldn't call your module `board` or `math`, as these names are already taken.

The simplest way to prevent this is by going into the REPL before you create your new module and trying to import a module by that name. If you get an `ImportError`, then you know that name is not in use.

See also

Here are a few references:

- Documentation for creating Python modules can be found at `https://docs.python.org/3/tutorial/modules.html`.
- A discussion on the benefits of using Python modules can be found at `https://realpython.com/python-modules-packages/`.

Adding button interactions to the event loop

In this recipe, we will start to build our main event loop. Each player will be assigned a single push button to press during the game. Player 1 will be assigned push button A, and player 2 will be assigned push button B. The event loop will continually check each of these buttons, looking for new button press events. When a new push button event is detected, it will print a message.

This will be further expanded in the next recipes in this chapter, in order to add the rest of the Button Bash game's functionality. Event loops can be found in many types of software applications. Exploring their usage can help you whenever you have to make your own, or when you have to interact with a built-in event loop.

Getting ready

You will need access to the REPL on Circuit Playground Express to run the code presented in this recipe.

How to do it...

Let's go over the steps required for this recipe:

1. Execute the next block of code in the REPL:

```
>>> from button import ButtonEvent
>>>
>>> buttons = {}
>>> buttons[1] = ButtonEvent('button_a')
>>> buttons[2] = ButtonEvent('button_b')
>>> buttons[1].is_pressed()
False
```

2. At this stage, we have created two objects to monitor the two push buttons. Hold down push button A while you run the next block of code:

```
>>> buttons[1].is_pressed()
True
```

3. The following code should be put into the `main.py` file and, when executed, it will repeatedly print a message whenever push button A or push button B is pressed:

```
from button import ButtonEvent

def main():
    buttons = {1: ButtonEvent('button_a'), 2:
ButtonEvent('button_b')}
    while True:
        for player, button in buttons.items():
            if button.is_pressed():
                print('button pressed for player', player)

main()
```

How it works...

First of all, the `ButtonEvent` class is imported from the `button` module. A function called `main` is defined, which will contain the code for our main event loop. The last line of code calls the `main` function to start the execution of the main event loop. The main event loop first defines a dictionary that keeps track of each player's push button. It defines a mapping that player 1 will be assigned push button A and player 2 will be assigned push button B.

An infinite loop is started, which will loop through each of the `ButtonEvent` objects and check if a button press event has occurred. If a button press is detected, it will then print which player pressed a button.

There's more...

As your code gets bigger, it's a good idea to put your main block of code into its own function, which you can call to start execution. As your program grows in size, it will make it easier to keep track of variables, as they will all be in the scope of this main function, instead of residing in the global namespace. This helps to reduce some ugly bugs that can appear with large blocks of code all sharing the same big global namespace.

Another thing to note in this recipe is the use of a dictionary to maintain the association of players and their buttons. The dictionary data structure is a very natural choice for this type of requirement. If we were using hardware that had more push buttons, we could just keep adding an item for each player to our data structure. It's always a good idea to make good use of data structures in your code; it makes debugging and software design much easier.

See also

Here are a few references:

- Documentation on the `tkinter` library that makes use of an event loop to respond to button press events can be found at `https://docs.python.org/3/library/tkinter.html#a-simple-hello-world-program`.
- A discussion on the main event loop of `tkinter` can be found at `https://gordonlesti.com/use-tkinter-without-mainloop/`.

Creating a generator to get pixel colors

In this recipe, we will prepare the code that will be used to control the pixels in the game. There are 10 pixels on the board, so each player will be given 5, to indicate how many points they have so far. Now, each player gets a point each time they press their button and a score of 20 is needed to win the game. So, we have to present a score of 0 to 20, but with only 5 pixels.

The way we will do that is to have the score on each pixel be represented by four colors. So, for the first four points, the first pixel would go through the colors yellow, dark orange, red, and magenta. Then, when you reach the score 5, the second pixel would light up yellow and go through the same cycle.

A generator will be used to get the list of colors and pixel positions that relate to each score for each player. Player 1 will use push button A and will have the five pixels next to this push button. These are pixels 0 to 4. Player 2 will use push button B and will have the five pixels next to that push button. These are pixels 5 to 9.

Both sets of pixels will start lighting up near the USB connector and will race towards the finish line, which will be the JST battery input. This makes the sequence 0 to 4 for player 1 and 9 to 5 for player 2. This recipe will cover an interesting use case for generators, which can come in handy in some projects, when you need to generate a sequence of values based on some involved logic.

Getting ready

You will need access to the REPL on Circuit Playground Express to run the code presented in this recipe.

How to do it...

Let's go over the steps required for this recipe:

1. Use the REPL to run the following lines of code:

```
>>> from adafruit_circuitplayground.express import cpx
>>> BLACK = 0x000000
>>> SEQUENCE = [
...     0xFFFF00,    # Yellow
...     0xFF8C00,    # DarkOrange
...     0xFF0000,    # Red
...     0xFF00FF,    # Magenta
```

```
...          ]
>>> cpx.pixels.brightness = 0.02
>>> cpx.pixels[0] = SEQUENCE[0]
```

2. At this stage, the first pixel should be lit up with the color yellow. In the next block of code, we will define the generator and call it to generate the list of positions and colors for both player 1 and player 2. There are 21 items in the list. The first item, which represents score 0, is a special case where we want all the pixels to be off if no one has scored any points yet. The remaining 20 items represent the scores 1 to 20:

```
>>> PLAYER_PIXELS1 = [0, 1, 2, 3, 4]
>>> PLAYER_PIXELS2 = [9, 8, 7, 6, 5]
>>>
>>> def generate_colors(positions):
...         yield 0, BLACK
...         for i in positions:
...             for color in SEQUENCE:
...                 yield i, color
...
...
...
>>> COLORS = dict()
>>> COLORS[1] = list(generate_colors(PLAYER_PIXELS1))
>>> COLORS[2] = list(generate_colors(PLAYER_PIXELS2))
>>>
>>> COLORS[1]
[(0, 0), (0, 16776960), (0, 16747520), (0, 16711680), (0,
16711935), (1, 16776960), (1, 16747520), (1, 16711680), (1,
16711935), (2, 16776960), (2, 16747520), (2, 16711680), (2,
16711935), (3, 16776960), (3, 16747520), (3, 16711680), (3,
16711935), (4, 16776960), (4, 16747520), (4, 16711680), (4,
16711935)]
>>> len(COLORS[1])
21
```

3. The following code should be put into the colors.py file and can then be imported in the next recipes, in order to access the color data for the game:

```
BLACK = 0x000000
SEQUENCE = [
    0xFFFF00,    # Yellow
    0xFF8C00,    # DarkOrange
    0xFF0000,    # Red
    0xFF00FF,    # Magenta
]
PLAYER_PIXELS1 = [0, 1, 2, 3, 4]
```

```
PLAYER_PIXELS2 = [9, 8, 7, 6, 5]


def generate_colors(positions):
    yield 0, BLACK
    for i in positions:
        for color in SEQUENCE:
            yield i, color


COLORS = dict()
COLORS[1] = list(generate_colors(PLAYER_PIXELS1))
COLORS[2] = list(generate_colors(PLAYER_PIXELS2))
```

How it works...

First of all, the SEQUENCE list represents the four colors that will be shown on each pixel to represent the player's score. The position and order of the five pixels that will be lit up for each player is then defined. The generate_colors generator is then defined. When called, it will produce a sequence of tuples, each containing the position and color of a specific score representation. This will be converted into a list for each player.

In this way, we can take any score and immediately look up its associated color and pixel position. These colors and position values for each player and each score are stored in a dictionary called COLORS that can be used to look up these values by player, number, and score.

There's more...

Python **iterators** are a very powerful feature of the language. Generators are a type of iterator that let you implement some powerful solutions in a concise way. They are used in this recipe as a way to assist in building a list that has a special first case and two levels of nesting for the remaining values.

By putting all this logic in a generator, we can contain it in one place and then use it as a building block to make more complicated structures. In the case of this recipe, the single generator is being used to build the color lookup data for player 1 and player 2.

See also

Here are a few references:

- Documentation on iterators can be found at `https://docs.python.org/3/tutorial/classes.html#iterators`.
- Documentation on generators can be found at `https://docs.python.org/3/tutorial/classes.html#generators`.

Showing scores with the ScoreBoard class

In this recipe, we will prepare the code that will be used to keep track of each player's score and show their current score on the pixels. We will create a new class called `ScoreBoard` and put it into a new module called `score`.

This recipe will show you one way to implement a scoreboard functionality in a MicroPython-based game. This recipe will start with the initial logic of starting the game, keeping track of the score and then displaying the score on the pixels. In the next recipes, we will add more functionality to deal with incrementing the score and detecting when one of the players has won the game.

Getting ready

You will need access to the REPL on Circuit Playground Express to run the code presented in this recipe.

How to do it...

Let's go over the steps required for this recipe:

1. Run the following lines of code in the REPL:

```
>>> from adafruit_circuitplayground.express import cpx
>>> from colors import COLORS
>>>
>>> class ScoreBoard:
...     def __init__(self):
...         self.score = {1: 0, 2: 0}
...         cpx.pixels.brightness = 0.02
...         cpx.play_file('start.wav')
```

```
. . .
. . .
. . .
>>> board = ScoreBoard()
>>> board.score[1]
0
```

2. After running the previous code, you should hear the board play the game startup audio, which says 1 2 3 Go!. Then, you should see the current score of player 1 as the value 0.

3. The following code should be put into the score.py file, and then we can import it and use it elsewhere:

```python
from adafruit_circuitplayground.express import cpx
from colors import COLORS


class ScoreBoard:
    def __init__(self):
        self.score = {1: 0, 2: 0}
        cpx.pixels.brightness = 0.02
        cpx.play_file('start.wav')

    def show(self, player):
        score = self.score[player]
        pos, color = COLORS[player][score]
        cpx.pixels[pos] = color
```

4. The following code will import the ScoreBoard class from the score module, set the score of the first player to the value 3, and then show this score on the pixels. The first pixel should turn on with the color red:

```
>>> from score import ScoreBoard
>>>
>>> board = ScoreBoard()
>>> board.score[1] = 3
>>> board.show(1)
```

How it works...

The ScoreBoard class is defined in the score module. When the class is first instantiated, it prepares the board to start a match of the game. It initializes the scores for players 1 and 2 to 0. Then, it sets the brightness of the pixels and plays the audio clip to announce the start of the match to the players.

The `show` method expects one argument, which will be the number of the player to show the score for. Then, it gets the value of the player's score and uses it with the player number to look up the color and position of the pixel that must be set. This pixel then has its color set to the correct color.

There's more...

We have started to build the logic for showing the current scoreboard to our players. It's important to make a fun and responsive scoreboard in competitive games in which you want to keep the two players engaged in trying to beat one another.

The code to update the scoreboard has to be implemented in a fashion that performs well. If each update to the scoreboard is a sluggish process, the players will feel it and get frustrated at an application that doesn't feel responsive. All the code to get the color and position of the pixel to set is implemented in an efficient fashion to ensure its performance.

See also

Here are a few references:

- An example of a MicroPython project that shows the scores of players in a game can be found at `https://tinkercademy.com/tutorials/flappy-bird/`.
- An example of a battery operated MicroPython project to control NeoPixels can be found at `https://learn.adafruit.com/neopixel-coat-buttons`.

Detecting winners with the ScoreBoard class

In this recipe, we will extend the `ScoreBoard` class to be able to update player scores and to detect when a player has won the game. Once one of the players has won the game, the board will announce which player has won the game by playing an audio clip with the announcement.

This recipe is the last piece to complete the logic in the `ScoreBoard` class. Once it's completed, we can combine it into the main event loop and complete the game in the next recipe.

Getting ready

You will need access to the REPL on Circuit Playground Express to run the code presented in this recipe.

How to do it...

Let's go over the steps required for this recipe:

1. The following code should be put into the `score.py` file, and then we can import it and use it elsewhere:

```python
from adafruit_circuitplayground.express import cpx
from colors import COLORS


class ScoreBoard:
    def __init__(self):
        self.score = {1: 0, 2: 0}
        cpx.pixels.brightness = 0.02
        cpx.play_file('start.wav')

    def scored(self, player):
        self.score[player] += 1
        self.show(player)
        if self.score[player] == 20:
            cpx.play_file('win%s.wav' % player)

    def show(self, player):
        score = self.score[player]
        pos, color = COLORS[player][score]
        cpx.pixels[pos] = color
```

2. The following code will import the `ScoreBoard` class from the `score` module and print out the current scores of the players:

```python
>>> from score import ScoreBoard
>>> board = ScoreBoard()
>>> board.score
{2: 0, 1: 0}
```

3. The next block of code will increment the score of player 1, causing the first pixel to light up yellow, and then print out the current score. The score should show that player 1 has a score of 1 point:

```
>>> board.scored(1)
>>> board.score
{2: 0, 1: 1}
```

How it works...

The `ScoreBoard` class has an additional method added to it that will increment in the `score` data structure whenever one of the players has scored. The `scored` method receives one argument, the player number, and increments that player's score.

It then updates the pixels to show the latest score of the player, and then checks whether the player's score has reached 20 points. If the player has reached 20 points, the board will then play an announcement announcing which player has won the game.

There's more...

Sound and light are a great way to interact with players in video games. Sound is used effectively in this class to both announce the start of the game and to announce its end. During the game play, light is used to motivate each player to bash their buttons faster, so that they can be the first to reach the finish line. Even though a lot is going on in this class, each method is only three to four lines long, making it easier to see what each piece is involved in. This is one way of breaking your code up into smaller chunks, by putting the different parts into different methods.

See also

Here are a few references:

- A multiplayer game that uses Circuit Playground Express can be found at https://learn.adafruit.com/circuit-playground-express-ir-zombie-game/.

- A game implemented in CircuitPython can be found at https://learn.adafruit.com/circuit-playground-treasure-hunt/.

Adding the ScoreBoard class to the event loop

This final recipe of this chapter combines all the previous recipes in this chapter to create the final Button Bash game. We will upgrade the event loop by adding the ScoreBoard class that we implemented in the previous recipe. This is the last piece of the puzzle.

The final result is a main loop with only six lines of code. We have been able to achieve this result by keeping a lot of the game logic in each of the three Python modules created in this chapter. You can use a similar approach in your own projects when you find the code base has become too big and concentrated in one file or one function.

Getting ready

You will need access to the REPL on Circuit Playground Express to run the code presented in this recipe.

How to do it...

Let's go over the steps required for this recipe:

1. The following code should be put into the main.py file, and then you can start to play the Button Bash game:

```
from button import ButtonEvent
from score import ScoreBoard


def main():
    buttons = {1: ButtonEvent('button_a'), 2:
ButtonEvent('button_b')}
    board = ScoreBoard()
    while True:
        for player, button in buttons.items():
            if button.is_pressed():
                board.scored(player)


main()
```

2. If you have one of the portable power supplies mentioned at the start of this chapter, then you can disconnect the board from your computer and connect that power supply.

3. You can now take the game anywhere you like and play rounds between each player. To start the next match, press the reset button at the center of the board for a new round to begin.

How it works...

We first import the ButtonEvent and ScoreBoard objects; they are the two main objects that we will need to implement the remainder of the event loop. After we have created our button dictionary, we instantiate a new ScoreBoard object called board.

This will announce that the game has started, and then we will enter into the infinite loop that will keep checking for button press events. The moment one of these events is detected, it will call the scored method on the board object to increment that specific player's score. If any player has reached the final score, they will then be announced as the winner.

There's more...

Now that we have the basic version of the game working, there are many ways to change it and enhance it. We could create two modes of the game that can be selected with the slide switch. There could be an easy and hard mode, where one needs a score of 10 and the other needs 20. When the board starts up, it checks the switch to load the correct parameters for colors and the final score.

You could make a best of three mode, where the two players have to fight it out repeatedly for three rounds, and the one who gets the best of three wins. To see the game in action, take a look at the next photograph to see two players intensely battling away at Button Bash:

See also

Here are a few references:

- A battery powered portable CircuitPython project that uses the NeoPixels can be found at https://learn.adafruit.com/ufo-circuit-playground-express.
- A basketball hoop game that uses the NeoPixels can be found at https://learn.adafruit.com/neopixel-mini-basketball-hoop.

Fruity Tunes 7

In this chapter, you will learn how to create a musical instrument with Circuit Playground Express and some bananas. We will connect four bananas to the touchpads on the board so that you can play a certain musical sound for each banana you touch. We'll add some visual feedback to the project by lighting up a pixel next to each touchpad each time you make contact with it. This project will show a creative, fun way to bring your capacitive touch projects to life.

By using unexpected objects such as bananas in your projects, you can add a unique twist to your mundane MicroPython projects.

In this chapter, we will be covering the following recipes:

- Creating a class to react to touch events
- Creating a function to enable speaker output
- Creating a function to play audio files
- Using the NeoPixel object to control pixels
- Creating a touch handler to play sounds
- Creating a touch handler to light up pixels
- Creating an event loop to handle all touch events

Technical requirements

The code files for this chapter can be found in the Chapter07 folder in the GitHub repository, at https://github.com/PacktPublishing/MicroPython-Cookbook.

Many of the recipes in this chapter require four audio files to be transferred to the Circuit Playground Express board. They can all be downloaded from the Chapter07 folder in the GitHub repository. They should be saved in the top-level folder with your main.py file.

Circuit Playground Express touchpads

Circuit Playground Express comes with seven capacitive touchpads. Each of them can be connected to any object that can conduct electricity, and touching that object will, in turn, trigger the sensor. You can use good electrical conductors, such as metal, and even weaker ones, such as a banana.

Water conducts electricity, and the surfaces of many fruits have enough moisture for the touchpads to detect a touch event. Many fruits, such as bananas, limes, oranges, and apples, will do the job. You can use alligator clips to connect the fruit to the touchpads. The following photograph shows a bundle of alligator clips:

These alligator clips come in a variety of different colors. It's a good idea to use a different color wire for each touchpad. It will make it easier to trace which fruit is connected to which touchpad. In this project, we will use green, red, yellow, and white wires. We'll set the color of the pixels next to each pad to also be green, red, yellow, and white. The next photograph shows a single banana connected to one of the touchpads:

The alligator clips work very well, as they don't require any soldering and can easily connect to both the board and a variety of objects. The teeth on the alligator clips will also create a good grip, so that a good electrical connection can be established between the board and the banana. The following photograph gives a closer view of the alligator teeth that are attached to the banana:

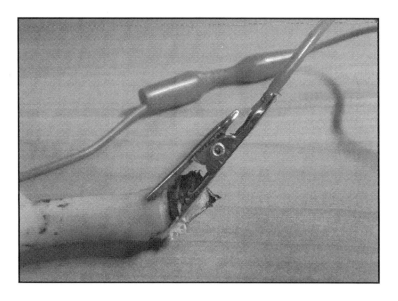

The next photograph shows a closer view of the alligator teeth that are attached to the touchpad:

In previous chapters, we used the Circuit Playground Express library to interact with the different components on the board. When you play audio files with this library, the library will block your code until the playback of the file is complete. In this project, we want the ability to respond to touch events immediately, and to play new sounds without waiting for the current audio file to finish playback.

This level of control can only be achieved if we use the CircuitPython libraries that control audio playback and the touchpads directly. For this reason, none of the code in this chapter will use the Circuit Playground Express library. By taking this approach, we will also get see how to get more fine-tuned control of the components on the board.

Creating a class to react to touch events

In this recipe, you will learn how to define a class that can help you use handle touch events on a particular touchpad. When you create an instance of this class, you specify the pad name and a callback function that will be called each time a touch event starts and ends. We can use this class as a building block to have a callback called for each of the four touchpads that will be connected to bananas. You can use this style of code in your own projects, whenever you want to handle a variety of events with a set of callback functions.

Getting ready

You will need access to the REPL on Circuit Playground Express to run the code presented in this recipe.

How to do it...

Let's go over the steps required for this recipe:

1. Run the following lines of code in the REPL:

```
>>> from touchio import TouchIn
>>> import board
>>>
>>> def handle(name, current):
...         print(name, current)
...
...
...
>>> handle('A1', True)
A1 True
>>> handle('A1', False)
A1 False
>>>
```

2. At this stage, we have defined a function that will handle touch events by printing the name of the touchpad and whether the pad is being touched.

3. Run the next block of code to create a class that will check for touch events. After defining the class, it will create one instance and then print out the current touch state of the pad:

```
>>> class TouchEvent:
...         THRESHOLD_ADJUSTMENT = 400
...
...         def __init__(self, name, onchange):
...             self.name = name
...             self.last = False
...             self.onchange = onchange
...             pin = getattr(board, name)
...             self.touch = TouchIn(pin)
...             self.touch.threshold += self.THRESHOLD_ADJUSTMENT
...
...
...
>>> event = TouchEvent('A1', handle)
```

```
>>> event.touch.value
False
```

4. Hold down your finger on touchpad A1 while running the next block of code:

```
>>> event.touch.value
True
```

5. Run the next block of code to create a class with a method to process touch events:

```
>>> class TouchEvent:
...         THRESHOLD_ADJUSTMENT = 400
...
...         def __init__(self, name, onchange):
...             self.name = name
...             self.last = False
...             self.onchange = onchange
...             pin = getattr(board, name)
...             self.touch = TouchIn(pin)
...             self.touch.threshold += self.THRESHOLD_ADJUSTMENT
...
...         def process(self):
...             current = self.touch.value
...             if current != self.last:
...                 self.onchange(self.name, current)
...                 self.last = current
...
...
...
>>> event = TouchEvent('A1', handle)
```

6. Hold down your finger on touchpad A1 while running the next block of code:

```
>>> event.process()
A1 True
```

7. The following code should be put into the main.py file:

```
from touchio import TouchIn
import board

class TouchEvent:
    THRESHOLD_ADJUSTMENT = 400

    def __init__(self, name, onchange):
        self.name = name
        self.last = False
```

```
        self.onchange = onchange
        pin = getattr(board, name)
        self.touch = TouchIn(pin)
        self.touch.threshold += self.THRESHOLD_ADJUSTMENT

    def process(self):
        current = self.touch.value
        if current != self.last:
            self.onchange(self.name, current)
            self.last = current


def handle(name, current):
    print(name, current)


event = TouchEvent('A1', handle)
while True:
    event.process()
```

When executed, this script will repeatedly print a message whenever a touch event starts or ends on touchpad A1.

How it works...

The `TouchEvent` class is defined to help us keep track of the last known state of the touchpad and to respond to a change in its state by making a call to the specified callback function. A default touch threshold of `400` is defined so that subclasses of this class can override the value. The constructor expects the first argument to be the name of the touchpad to monitor and the callback function that will be called when a state change is detected.

The name and callback function are saved with attributes on the instance. The last known state is initialized to the `False` value. Then, the pin value for the named touchpad is retrieved from the `board` Python module. This pin is used to create a `TouchIn` instance, which is also saved as an attribute on the object. Finally, the threshold is set on this touchpad as part of the initialization process.

The other method that is defined on the class will be called regularly, to check for any changes in the touchpad state and to process this state change by calling the defined callback function. This is done by getting the current touch state and comparing it to the last known value. If they differ, the callback is called and the value is saved for future reference.

A simple function is defined to handle any touch events by simply printing out the name of the touchpad that had a state change and what the current state is.

After these class and function definitions, we create one instance of this class that will watch touchpad A1. We then enter into an infinite loop that repeatedly checks for state changes and prints out a message each time one occurs.

There's more...

It's always a good idea to set a touch threshold on your touchpads. If you don't, you will get a lot of false positives when interacting with the touchpad. The value that has been chosen, `400`, is a value that is suitable to this specific setup of connecting bananas with alligator clips. It's best to connect the actual objects intended for use with your project, and then fine-tune this value to a suitable value.

In this recipe, we have mixed the uses of functions and classes. This approach is perfectly fine in Python, and it lets you have the best of both worlds. We needed to keep track of the state between each call to the process method, which is why we chose a class for that purpose. The callback doesn't need to keep track of any states between calls, so a simple function does the job just fine.

See also

Here are a few references:

- Documentation on the `TouchIn` class can be found at `https://circuitpython.readthedocs.io/en/3.x/shared-bindings/touchio/TouchIn.html`.
- Documentation on the `board` Python module can be found at `https://circuitpython.readthedocs.io/en/3.x/shared-bindings/board/__init__.html#module-board`.

Creating a function to enable speaker output

In this recipe, you will learn how to create a function that, when called, will enable the speaker. If you don't enable the speaker before audio playback, then it will be played through pin A0, which can have a headphone connected to it.

This project will use the speaker on the board instead of headphones, so we will need this function to enable the speaker at the start of our script. Beyond showing you how to enable the speaker, this recipe will also introduce you to ways of digitally controlling input/output pins.

Getting ready

You will need access to the REPL on Circuit Playground Express to run the code presented in this recipe.

How to do it...

Let's go over the steps required for this recipe:

1. Execute the next block of code in the REPL:

```
>>> from digitalio import DigitalInOut
>>> import board
>>>
>>>
>>> speaker_control = DigitalInOut(board.SPEAKER_ENABLE)
>>> speaker_control
<DigitalInOut>
```

2. At this stage, we have created an object that is connected to the pin, which will enable the speaker. Run the next block of code to enable the speaker:

```
>>> speaker_control.switch_to_output(value=True)
```

3. Reload the board and enter the REPL again. The next block of code will define the function to enable the speaker, and will call it:

```
>>> from digitalio import DigitalInOut
>>> import board
>>>
>>> def enable_speakers():
...     speaker_control = DigitalInOut(board.SPEAKER_ENABLE)
```

```
...         speaker_control.switch_to_output(value=True)
...
...
...
>>> enable_speakers()
```

How it works...

The `enable_speakers` function is defined first. It doesn't receive any arguments, as there is only one speaker on the board to enable, and it returns nothing, as once the speaker is enabled, its pin doesn't need to be interacted with again. The `DigitalInOut` object is used to interact with the pin that will enable the speaker. Once this object is created, the `switch_to_output` method is called to enable speaker output. After the function is defined, it is called to enable the speakers.

There's more...

The `DigitalInOut` object that is used in this recipe can be used to interact with a wide range of pins. On this board, for example, it can be used to connect the pins that read input from push button A and push button B. Once you connect and configure these push button pins correctly, you can start polling the pin's value to check whether the push button is pressed.

See also

Here are a few references:

- Example usage of the `DigitalInOut` object can be found at `https://learn.adafruit.com/adafruit-circuit-playground-express/circuitpython-digital-in-out`.
- Documentation on the `DigitalInOut` object can be found at `https://circuitpython.readthedocs.io/en/3.x/shared-bindings/digitalio/DigitalInOut.html`.

Creating a function to play audio files

In this recipe, you will learn how to create a function that, when called, will play a specific audio file on the built-in speakers. This recipe will illustrate how to get access to the audio output device, as well as how to read the contents of a .wav file, convert it to an audio stream, and feed that audio stream to the onboard audio playback device. The techniques shown in this recipe can be used in all sorts of projects that need more fine control over the way audio files are played back.

Getting ready

You will need access to the REPL on Circuit Playground Express to run the code presented in this recipe.

How to do it...

Let's go over the steps required for this recipe:

1. Use the REPL to run the following lines of code:

```
>>> from digitalio import DigitalInOut
>>> from audioio import WaveFile, AudioOut
>>> import board
>>> import time
>>>
>>> def enable_speakers():
...     speaker_control = DigitalInOut(board.SPEAKER_ENABLE)
...     speaker_control.switch_to_output(value=True)
...
...
...
>>> enable_speakers()
>>> speaker = AudioOut(board.SPEAKER)
>>> speaker
<AudioOut>
>>>
```

2. At this stage, we have enabled the speaker and have created an object to feed audio data to the speakers. When you run the next block of code, you should hear a piano note play on the speakers:

```
>>> file = open('piano.wav', "rb")
>>> audio = WaveFile(file)
>>> speaker.play(audio)
>>>
```

3. Run the next block of code to hear the same piano note again, but this time, played back through a function call:

```
>>> def play_file(speaker, path):
...      file = open(path, "rb")
...      audio = WaveFile(file)
...      speaker.play(audio)
...
...
...
>>> play_file(speaker, 'piano.wav')
```

4. The following code should be put into the main.py file and, when executed, it will play a single piano note each time the board is reloaded:

```
from digitalio import DigitalInOut
from audioio import WaveFile, AudioOut
import board
import time


def play_file(speaker, path):
    file = open(path, "rb")
    audio = WaveFile(file)
    speaker.play(audio)


def enable_speakers():
    speaker_control = DigitalInOut(board.SPEAKER_ENABLE)
    speaker_control.switch_to_output(value=True)


enable_speakers()
speaker = AudioOut(board.SPEAKER)
play_file(speaker, 'piano.wav')
time.sleep(100)
```

How it works...

First, the speakers are enabled so that we can hear the audio playback without headphones. The `AudioOut` class is then used to access the audio output device. The `play_file` function is then called with the speaker audio object and the path to the audio file that will be played. This function opens the file in binary mode.

This file object is then used to create a `WaveFile` object, which will return us the data as an audio stream. This audio data is then given to the `play` method on the `AudioOut` object to start playback. This method immediately returns, and doesn't wait for playback to complete. This is why the `sleep` method is called afterward, to give the board a chance to play the audio stream before the main script ends execution.

If you exclude this line of code from the file and reload the code, then the script will exit before the board has a chance to play the file, and you won't hear any audio being played back.

There's more...

Using this function, you can play any number of audio files by just passing the audio output object and the file path. You can also use this recipe as a starting point to experiment further with the audio playback library that comes with this board. For example, there's a method to poll and check whether the last provided stream is still playing, or if it has finished playback.

See also

Here are a few references:

- Documentation on the `AudioOut` object can be found at `https://circuitpython.readthedocs.io/en/3.x/shared-bindings/audioio/AudioOut.html`.
- Documentation on the `WaveFile` object can be found at `https://circuitpython.readthedocs.io/en/3.x/shared-bindings/audioio/WaveFile.html`.

Using the NeoPixel object to control pixels

In this recipe, you will learn how to control the pixels on the board using the NeoPixel object. We covered a lot of the methods in this object in previous chapters, but this is the first time we will directly create a NeoPixel object. It's useful to have the skills to directly use the NeoPixel object, instead of accessing it through another object. You will need these skills if you decide to add an additional ring or strip of pixels to your project. In those cases, you will need direct access to this object to control the pixels.

Getting ready

You will need access to the REPL on Circuit Playground Express to run the code presented in this recipe.

How to do it...

Let's go over the steps required for this recipe:

1. Run the following lines of code in the REPL:

```
>>> from neopixel import NeoPixel
>>> import board
>>>
>>> PIXEL_COUNT = 10
>>> pixels = NeoPixel(board.NEOPIXEL, PIXEL_COUNT)
>>> pixels.brightness = 0.05
>>> pixels[0] = 0xFF0000
```

2. After running the previous block of code, the first pixel should become the color red. Run the next block of code to make the second pixel green:

```
>>> RGB = dict(
...     black=0x000000,
...     white=0xFFFFFF,
...     green=0x00FF00,
...     red=0xFF0000,
...     yellow=0xFFFF00,
... )
>>> pixels[1] = RGB['green']
```

3. Run the next block of code to turn off the first pixel:

```
>>> pixels[0] = RGB['black']
```

4. The following code should be put into the `main.py` file and, when executed, it will color the first two pixels red and green:

```
from neopixel import NeoPixel
import board

PIXEL_COUNT = 10
RGB = dict(
    black=0x000000,
    white=0xFFFFFF,
    green=0x00FF00,
    red=0xFF0000,
    yellow=0xFFFF00,
)

pixels = NeoPixel(board.NEOPIXEL, PIXEL_COUNT)
pixels.brightness = 0.05
pixels[0] = RGB['red']
pixels[1] = RGB['green']

while True:
    pass
```

How it works...

The `NeoPixel` class is used to access the array of pixels on the board. When we create this object, we have to specify the pin on the board to connect to and the number of pixels connected to that pin.

In the case of Circuit Playground Express, there are 10 pixels on the board. We keep this value in a global constant to improve code readability. We then set the brightness of the pixels to 5%.

The names and hex codes for the five different colors we need in the project are defined in a global dictionary. The colors white, green, red, and yellow, each relate to the four colors of the attached wires. The color black is used to switch off a pixel. We then set the first and second pixels to the colors red and green. Finally, we run an infinite loop, so that we can see these colors and stop the script from exiting.

There's more...

This code has everything required to interact with any of the 10 pixels that come with the board. You can take this base code and start experimenting with the different methods available on the provided object. Using these different methods, you can change the color of all the pixels in one call. You can also turn off the default auto-write feature, and then have direct control over when the changes you make to colors get applied. This low-level control of the pixels is all available through this library.

See also

Here are a few references:

- Documentation on ways of testing the pixel features can be found at `https://circuitpython.readthedocs.io/projects/neopixel/en/latest/examples.html`.
- An overview of the NeoPixel driver can be found at `https://circuitpython.readthedocs.io/projects/neopixel/en/latest/`.

Creating a touch handler to play sounds

In this recipe, we will create the first version of our touch handler. This first version will play a specific audio file each time a touch event is detected. We can then use this handler in later recipes, in order to map each touchpad to a specific audio file. We will also expand the functionality of this handler in future recipes to add light, as well as sound, to the touch event. Event handlers are a common part of many software systems. This recipe will help you see how you can use this common approach with your MicroPython projects.

Getting ready

You will need access to the REPL on Circuit Playground Express to run the code presented in this recipe.

How to do it...

Let's go over the steps required for this recipe:

1. Execute the next block of code in the REPL:

```
>>> from touchio import TouchIn
>>> from digitalio import DigitalInOut
>>> from audioio import WaveFile, AudioOut
>>> import board
>>> def enable_speakers():
...     speaker_control = DigitalInOut(board.SPEAKER_ENABLE)
...     speaker_control.switch_to_output(value=True)
...
...
...
>>> def play_file(speaker, path):
...     file = open(path, "rb")
...     audio = WaveFile(file)
...     speaker.play(audio)
...
...
...
>>> enable_speakers()
>>> speaker = AudioOut(board.SPEAKER)
```

2. At this point, we have enabled the speakers and have set up an object to play audio files on the speaker. In the next block of code, we will define a `Handler` class and then create an instance of it that will use our `speaker` object:

```
>>> class Handler:
...     def __init__(self, speaker):
...         self.speaker = speaker
...
...     def handle(self, name, state):
...         if state:
...             play_file(self.speaker, 'piano.wav')
...
>>> handler = Handler(speaker)
```

3. When you run the next block of code, you should hear a piano sound on the speaker:

```
>>> handler.handle('A1', True)
```

4. The following code should be put into the `main.py` file and, when executed, it will play a piano sound each time the touchpad A1 is touched:

```python
from touchio import TouchIn
from digitalio import DigitalInOut
from audioio import WaveFile, AudioOut
import board

def enable_speakers():
    speaker_control = DigitalInOut(board.SPEAKER_ENABLE)
    speaker_control.switch_to_output(value=True)

def play_file(speaker, path):
    file = open(path, "rb")
    audio = WaveFile(file)
    speaker.play(audio)

class Handler:
    def __init__(self, speaker):
        self.speaker = speaker

    def handle(self, name, state):
        if state:
            play_file(self.speaker, 'piano.wav')

class TouchEvent:
    THRESHOLD_ADJUSTMENT = 400

    def __init__(self, name, onchange):
        self.name = name
        self.last = False
        self.onchange = onchange
        pin = getattr(board, name)
        self.touch = TouchIn(pin)
        self.touch.threshold += self.THRESHOLD_ADJUSTMENT

    def process(self):
        current = self.touch.value
        if current != self.last:
            self.onchange(self.name, current)
            self.last = current

enable_speakers()
speaker = AudioOut(board.SPEAKER)
handler = Handler(speaker)
event = TouchEvent('A1', handler.handle)
while True:
    event.process()
```

How it works...

The `Handler` class that is defined will be used to react to touch events. It expects one argument in the constructor, which is the `speaker` object that will handle audio playback. This object is saved to an attribute on the object instance. This class then defines a method that will be called each time a touch event has occurred. The method expects the first argument to be the name of the touchpad, and the second argument is a Boolean value that indicates the state of the touchpad.

When the method is called, it checks whether the pad is being touched; if so, it calls the `play_file` function to play the piano sound. The remainder of the code in the recipe supports the process of continually checking for new touch events and calls the defined handler.

There's more...

The recipe in this example only plays one sound as a single touchpad is pressed. However, it also creates the core structure for us to expand. You can experiment with this recipe and try two touchpads, each playing a different sound. You could do this by having multiple defined event objects connected to different handlers. In later recipes, you will see that a single event class definition and a single handler class definition can be used to connect to four different pads and play four different sounds.

See also

Here are a few references:

- The source code for the `AudioOut` class can be found at https://github.com/ adafruit/circuitpython/blob/3.x/shared-bindings/audioio/AudioOut.c.
- The source code for the `WaveFile` class can be found at https://github.com/ adafruit/circuitpython/blob/3.x/shared-bindings/audioio/WaveFile.c.

Creating a touch handler to light up pixels

In this recipe, we will create a touch handler that will react to touch events by playing sounds and lighting up pixels. When the touch sensor gets triggered, the handler will play a sound and light up a specific pixel. When the touch sensor detects that you have released your finger, the specific pixel that was lit up will turn off.

In this way, you can hear and see the board react to each of the configured touchpads uniquely. This recipe shows a useful way to create different types of output, based on different triggered input. Many projects can come to life when you add a mix of unique audio and visual output that will react to different types of human input.

Getting ready

You will need access to the REPL on Circuit Playground Express to run the code presented in this recipe.

How to do it...

Let's go over the steps required for this recipe:

1. Use the REPL to run the following lines of code. This will set up the speakers and create an object to interact with the pixels:

```
>>> from touchio import TouchIn
>>> from digitalio import DigitalInOut
>>> from audioio import WaveFile, AudioOut
>>> from neopixel import NeoPixel
>>> import board
>>>
>>> PIXEL_COUNT = 10
>>>
>>> def enable_speakers():
...     speaker_control = DigitalInOut(board.SPEAKER_ENABLE)
...     speaker_control.switch_to_output(value=True)
...
...
...
>>> def play_file(speaker, path):
...     file = open(path, "rb")
...     audio = WaveFile(file)
...     speaker.play(audio)
...
>>>
>>> enable_speakers()
>>> speaker = AudioOut(board.SPEAKER)
>>> pixels = NeoPixel(board.NEOPIXEL, PIXEL_COUNT)
>>> pixels.brightness = 0.05
```

2. In the next block of code, we will define a `Handler` class and then create an instance of it to which we will pass the objects to deal with the speaker and pixels:

```
>>> class Handler:
...     def __init__(self, speaker, pixels):
...         self.speaker = speaker
...         self.pixels = pixels
...
...     def handle(self, name, state):
...         if state:
...             play_file(self.speaker, 'piano.wav')
...             self.pixels[0] = 0xFF0000
...         else:
...             self.pixels[0] = 0x000000
...
...
>>> handler = Handler(speaker, pixels)
```

3. When you run the next block of code, you should hear a piano sound on the speaker, and the first pixel should turn red:

```
>>> handler.handle('A1', True)
```

4. Run the next block of code, and you should see the first pixel light switch off:

```
>>> handler.handle('A1', False)
```

5. The following code should be put into the `main.py` file:

```
from touchio import TouchIn
from digitalio import DigitalInOut
from audioio import WaveFile, AudioOut
from neopixel import NeoPixel
import board

PIXEL_COUNT = 10

def enable_speakers():
    speaker_control = DigitalInOut(board.SPEAKER_ENABLE)
    speaker_control.switch_to_output(value=True)

def play_file(speaker, path):
    file = open(path, "rb")
    audio = WaveFile(file)
    speaker.play(audio)

class Handler:
```

```
        def __init__(self, speaker, pixels):
            self.speaker = speaker
            self.pixels = pixels

        def handle(self, name, state):
            if state:
                play_file(self.speaker, 'piano.wav')
                self.pixels[0] = 0xFF0000
            else:
                self.pixels[0] = 0x000000

class TouchEvent:
    THRESHOLD_ADJUSTMENT = 400

    def __init__(self, name, onchange):
        self.name = name
        self.last = False
        self.onchange = onchange
        pin = getattr(board, name)
        self.touch = TouchIn(pin)
        self.touch.threshold += self.THRESHOLD_ADJUSTMENT

    def process(self):
        current = self.touch.value
        if current != self.last:
            self.onchange(self.name, current)
            self.last = current

enable_speakers()
speaker = AudioOut(board.SPEAKER)
pixels = NeoPixel(board.NEOPIXEL, PIXEL_COUNT)
pixels.brightness = 0.05
handler = Handler(speaker, pixels)
event = TouchEvent('A1', handler.handle)
while True:
    event.process()
```

When the script is executed, it will play a piano sound and light up a pixel each time touchpad A1 is touched.

How it works...

The Handler class that is defined will play sounds and light up pixels each time a touch event is detected. The constructor of this class takes the speaker and pixel objects and saves them to the instance for later use. Each time the handle method is called, it checks whether the touchpad is currently pressed.

If it is pressed, a pixel is lit up and a sound is played. If the pad is released, that same pixel is turned off. The remainder of the script is in charge of initializing the speaker and pixels so that they can be used by the handler, and for creating an infinite loop that will keep calling the handler each time an event is detected.

There's more...

The script in this recipe lights up a specific pixel each time. You can extend it to use a random color each time the touchpad is pressed. There are ways to light up more pixels the longer a touchpad is pressed. Another fun experiment to try would be to have the board play a random sound each time an event occurred. Now that we have added sound and light, there are more options to apply creativity to this project and to create a more unique project.

See also

Here are a few references:

- A project that connects limes to Circuit Playground Express can be found at `https://learn.adafruit.com/circuit-playground-express-piano-in-the-key-of-lime/`.
- The source code for the `TouchIn` class can be found at `https://github.com/adafruit/circuitpython/blob/3.x/shared-bindings/touchio/TouchIn.c`.

Creating an event loop to handle all touch events

This final recipe in this chapter takes all the previous recipes in this chapter and combines them to complete the banana power musical machine. Beyond the previous recipes, we will need to create an event loop that combines all this logic into one structure that can handle all the four touchpads and their related audio files and pixels. After going through this recipe, you will be able to create generic event loops and handlers that can be extended to meet the varying needs of the embedded projects you might create.

Getting ready

You will need access to the REPL on Circuit Playground Express to run the code presented in this recipe.

How to do it...

Let's go over the steps required for this recipe:

1. Run the following lines of code in the REPL:

```
>>> from touchio import TouchIn
>>> from digitalio import DigitalInOut
>>> from audioio import WaveFile, AudioOut
>>> from neopixel import NeoPixel
>>> import board
>>>
>>> PIXEL_COUNT = 10
>>> TOUCH_PADS = ['A1', 'A2', 'A5', 'A6']
>>> SOUND = dict(
...        A1='hit.wav',
...        A2='piano.wav',
...        A5='tin.wav',
...        A6='wood.wav',
... )
>>> RGB = dict(
...        black=0x000000,
...        white=0xFFFFFF,
...        green=0x00FF00,
...        red=0xFF0000,
...        yellow=0xFFFF00,
... )
>>> PIXELS = dict(
...        A1=(6, RGB['white']),
...        A2=(8, RGB['red']),
...        A5=(1, RGB['yellow']),
...        A6=(3, RGB['green']),
... )
```

2. We have now imported all the libraries we need and have created the main data structures that we need in our script. Run the next block of code, and the speakers should play a piano sound:

```
>>> def play_file(speaker, path):
...        file = open(path, "rb")
...        audio = WaveFile(file)
```

```
...         speaker.play(audio)
...
...
>>> def enable_speakers():
...         speaker_control = DigitalInOut(board.SPEAKER_ENABLE)
...         speaker_control.switch_to_output(value=True)
...
...
>>> enable_speakers()
>>> speaker = AudioOut(board.SPEAKER)
>>> play_file(speaker, SOUND['A2'])
```

3. Run the next block of code to create an instance of our event handler:

```
>>> class Handler:
...         def __init__(self, speaker, pixels):
...             self.speaker = speaker
...             self.pixels = pixels
...
...         def handle(self, name, state):
...             pos, color = PIXELS[name]
...             if state:
...                 play_file(self.speaker, SOUND[name])
...                 self.pixels[pos] = color
...             else:
...                 self.pixels[pos] = RGB['black']
...
...
>>> class TouchEvent:
...         THRESHOLD_ADJUSTMENT = 400
...
...         def __init__(self, name, onchange):
...             self.name = name
...             self.last = False
...             self.onchange = onchange
...             pin = getattr(board, name)
...             self.touch = TouchIn(pin)
...             self.touch.threshold += self.THRESHOLD_ADJUSTMENT
...
...         def process(self):
...             current = self.touch.value
...             if current != self.last:
...                 self.onchange(self.name, current)
...                 self.last = current
...
...
>>> pixels = NeoPixel(board.NEOPIXEL, PIXEL_COUNT)
>>> pixels.brightness = 0.05
```

```
>>> handler = Handler(speaker, pixels)
```

4. Run the next block of code to simulate a touch event on pad 2. You should hear a piano sound and see one of the pixels turn red:

```
>>> handler.handle('A2', True)
```

5. The following code should be put into the `main.py` file and, when executed, it will play different sounds and light up different pixels each time one of the four configured touchpads is pressed:

```python
from touchio import TouchIn
from digitalio import DigitalInOut
from audioio import WaveFile, AudioOut
from neopixel import NeoPixel
import board

PIXEL_COUNT = 10
TOUCH_PADS = ['A1', 'A2', 'A5', 'A6']
SOUND = dict(
    A1='hit.wav',
    A2='piano.wav',
    A5='tin.wav',
    A6='wood.wav',
)
RGB = dict(
    black=0x000000,
    white=0xFFFFFF,
    green=0x00FF00,
    red=0xFF0000,
    yellow=0xFFFF00,
)
PIXELS = dict(
    A1=(6, RGB['white']),
    A2=(8, RGB['red']),
    A5=(1, RGB['yellow']),
    A6=(3, RGB['green']),
)

def play_file(speaker, path):
    file = open(path, "rb")
    audio = WaveFile(file)
    speaker.play(audio)

def enable_speakers():
    speaker_control = DigitalInOut(board.SPEAKER_ENABLE)
    speaker_control.switch_to_output(value=True)
```

```
class Handler:
    def __init__(self, speaker, pixels):
        self.speaker = speaker
        self.pixels = pixels

    def handle(self, name, state):
        pos, color = PIXELS[name]
        if state:
            play_file(self.speaker, SOUND[name])
            self.pixels[pos] = color
        else:
            self.pixels[pos] = RGB['black']

class TouchEvent:
    THRESHOLD_ADJUSTMENT = 400

    def __init__(self, name, onchange):
        self.name = name
        self.last = False
        self.onchange = onchange
        pin = getattr(board, name)
        self.touch = TouchIn(pin)
        self.touch.threshold += self.THRESHOLD_ADJUSTMENT

    def process(self):
        current = self.touch.value
        if current != self.last:
            self.onchange(self.name, current)
            self.last = current

def main():
    enable_speakers()
    speaker = AudioOut(board.SPEAKER)
    pixels = NeoPixel(board.NEOPIXEL, PIXEL_COUNT)
    pixels.brightness = 0.05
    handler = Handler(speaker, pixels)
    events = [TouchEvent(i, handler.handle) for i in TOUCH_PADS]
    while True:
        for event in events:
            event.process()

main()
```

How it works...

The `main` function contains our event loop. This function first initializes the speakers and pixels. Then, it creates a single handler instance. This single handler instance is generic enough that it will be used as the handler for all four of the touchpads.

Then, a list of events is created, where each one is connected to one of the four pads. An infinite loop is started that loops through each event object and calls its `process` method to call the event handler whenever a change in the touchpad state is detected.

The constants at the top of the script are used to specify the names of the touchpads to use, which sound files to play for each pad, and the pixel position and color to set when a pad is pressed.

There's more...

This script makes heavy use of a number of data structures, so that values don't need to be hardcoded in the function and class definitions. Dictionaries are used as a natural structure to map each pad name to the audio filename that should be played. A list of data structures is used to define the names of the touchpads that will be connected. Finally, a dictionary of tuples is used to map the touchpad to its related pixel position and color. Python has a rich set of data structures that, when leveraged effectively, can make code much more readable and maintainable.

This project connects four bananas to the board, with each banana playing a different sound when touched. Because the code was constructed to respond to each touch immediately, you can even have two people play at the same time. The next photograph shows two people, each with a pair of bananas, creating music and controlling the pixels on the board:

See also

Here are a few references:

- Documentation on providing audio output with CircuitPython can be found at
  `https://learn.adafruit.com/adafruit-circuit-playground-express/`
  `circuitpython-audio-out`.
- The source code for the `NeoPixel` class can be found at `https://github.com/`
  `adafruit/Adafruit_CircuitPython_NeoPixel`.

8
Let's Move It, Move It

In this chapter, you will learn how to control motors and servos. Using DC motors will help with projects where you need to control the wheels on a vehicle. The servos can help in your projects that need to control robotic arms to move around. Both of these devices will give us a way to create mechanical motion. Depending on what motion you are trying to create in your project, you may want to choose one over the other. How each of them functions, and where they are best suited, will be covered in the following sections.

By the end of this chapter, you will be able to use what you have learned to create projects that move around in all sorts of interesting ways. This opens up a whole new set of possibilities in terms of the types of projects that you will be able to build.

In this chapter, we will cover the following topics:

- Tuning a servo to the correct pulse width
- Setting the actuation range of a servo
- Setting the angle of a servo
- Sweeping a servo
- Controlling a servo with buttons
- Controlling multiple servos
- Turning on a DC motor
- Setting the speed and direction of a DC motor
- Controlling a DC motor with buttons

Technical requirements

The code files from this chapter can be found in the `Chapter08` folder in the GitHub repository at `https://github.com/PacktPublishing/MicroPython-Cookbook`.

Many of the recipes in this chapter will make use of the Circuit Playground Express library, which will typically get imported in the first few lines of the script, with the following line of code:

```
from adafruit_circuitplayground.express import cpx
```

This library will help us to interact with the buttons and switches that come with the board. There is another library that will be imported in many of the recipes in this chapter, using the following statement:

```
from adafruit_crickit import crickit
```

This library will help us to interact with the CRICKIT board, so that we can control the servos and DC motors.

The recipes involving servos in this chapter expect the two servos to be connected to servo port 1 and servo port 2. When connecting the servo cables, make sure the yellow wire is facing outward from the board.

The recipes in the chapter involving a DC motor expect the motor to be attached to driver 1 of the motor connections. The two wires can be attached to the two connectors in either direction. All that will happen is the direction of rotation will be flipped, depending on which way the wires are connected.

DC motors

DC motors take DC electricity and turn that energy into rotational motion. This is usually achieved through the use of electromagnets that drive the motion as their magnetic fields change. The following illustration shows how the internals of this type of motor appear:

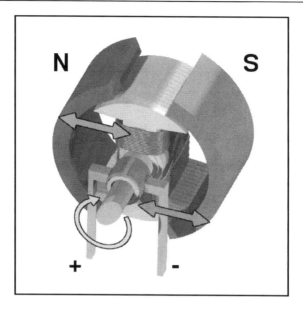

Source: https://commons.wikimedia.org/wiki/File:Ejs_Open_Source_Direct_Current_Electrical_Motor_Model_Java_Applet_(_DC_Motor_)_80_degree_split_ring.gif

DC motors work great in applications in which you need rotational motion at high speeds. They would be suitable for operating fans or wheels on a remote control car.

Servos

Servos are more complicated than DC motors and are more suitable for a situations in which you need more control over the exact position of something attached to the servo. A servo will usually contain a DC motor, gears, control circuits, and a sensor to detect the exact position of the servo. All these components come together in a device that lets you have more precise control over the exact angle that the servo is pointing at.

The following image shows a disassembled servo in which you can see the DC motor, gears, and circuitry:

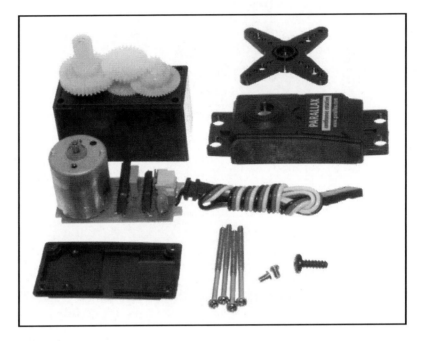

Servos work great in applications in which you need exact control over the angle of a certain part; for example, where you need to control the angle of a robotic arm or the angle of a rudder on a boat.

Adafruit CRICKIT

The Adafruit CRICKIT is a board that lets you control many different types of motors from a variety of hardware. Different CRICKIT models support the Raspberry Pi and the FeatherWing set of products.

In this chapter, we will be using the CRICKIT for Circuit Playground Express. The following image shows what the CRICKIT looks like before you attach the Circuit Playground Express:

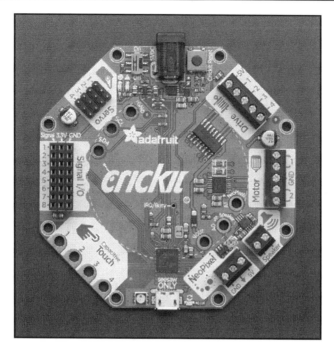

Courtesy of adafruit.com

To connect these 2 devices together, you will require 6 hexagonal brass standoffs that will each be screwed into both devices with 12 screws. The following image shows what these standoffs and screws look like:

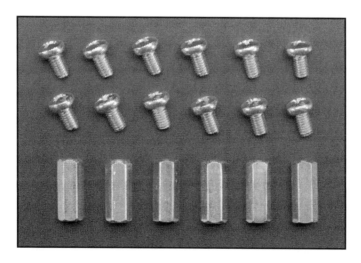

Courtesy of adafruit.com

Once you have connected the two boards using these screws and standoffs, your two boards should look like the following image:

Courtesy of adafruit.com

Up to four separate servos can be attached to the board. Micro, mini, and standard servos are all supported. The servo's three-pin connector should be connected to one of the available servo slots, as shown in the following image:

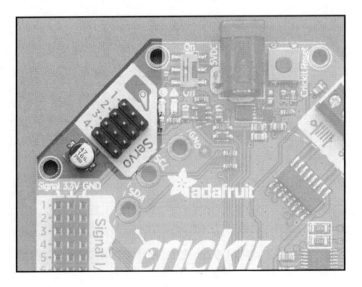

Courtesy of adafruit.com

Up to two DC motors can be attached to the board. Each motor will be connected to two pins. The pairs of pins for each of the two motor connections are shown in the following image:

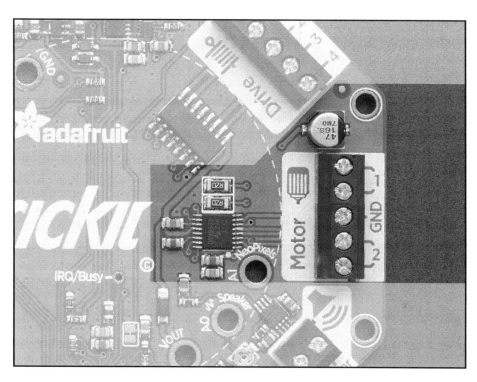

Courtesy of adafruit.com

Once the two devices are connected, you can power each one on and connect the Circuit Playground Express to your computer using a USB cable, in the same way that we did in the previous chapters of this book. Once connected, you will need to flash the firmware with an image that has support for the CRICKIT hardware.

The name of the UF2 file used in this chapter is for version 3.1.2 of CircuitPython that has CRICKIT support, and is called `adafruit-circuitpython-circuitplayground_express_crickit-3.1.2.uf2`.

 For details on how to flash the board with this firmware, please follow the instructions in `Chapter 1`, *Getting Started with MicroPython*, regarding how to flash the microcontroller firmware.

Where to buy

This chapter uses a number of components, which can all be purchased from the Adafruit online retailer.

The Adafruit CRICKIT for Circuit Playground Express can be purchased directly from Adafruit (`https://www.adafruit.com/product/3093`). It can also be purchased from other online retailers, such as Pimoroni.

The Circuit Playground Bolt-On Kit can be purchased directly from Adafruit (`https://www.adafruit.com/product/3816`). This kit includes the six hexagonal standoffs and 12 screws that are needed to attach the two boards together. The servo used in this chapter can be purchased directly from Adafruit (`https://www.adafruit.com/product/169`).

The DC motor used in this chapter can be purchased directly from Adafruit (`https://www.adafruit.com/product/3777`). Adafruit also sells a number of optional wheel attachments, but none are required to follow along with the recipes in this chapter.

The CRICKIT can be powered by a three-AA battery holder, which can be purchased directly from Adafruit (`https://www.adafruit.com/product/3842`). The benefit of this power supply, as compared to others, is its portability and low cost.

Tuning a servo to the correct pulse width

Servos can have their arms rotated to specific angles by sending them different electrical pulses. The angle that the arm moves to will be controlled by the width of the electrical pulse. Before setting these angles, each servo must first be configured with the correct minimum and maximum width settings.

This recipe will show you how to do that. This configuration will be required whenever you want to use servos in your projects.

Getting ready

You will need access to the REPL on the Circuit Playground Express to run the code presented in this recipe.

How to do it...

Let's go over the steps required for this recipe:

1. Run the following lines of code in the REPL:

```
>>> from adafruit_circuitplayground.express import cpx
>>> from adafruit_crickit import crickit
>>>
>>> MIN_PULSE=750
>>> MAX_PULSE=2250
```

2. At this stage, we have imported the necessary libraries and have defined the minimum and maximum pulse width values we want for this specific set of servos. The following block of code will configure the servo connected to the first port with these settings:

```
>>> crickit.servo_1.set_pulse_width_range(MIN_PULSE, MAX_PULSE)
```

3. Run the next block of code to move the servo to the lowest angle:

```
>>> crickit.servo_1.angle = 0
```

4. The following block of code will move the arm to the middle position, exactly between the lowest and highest values:

```
>>> crickit.servo_1.angle = 90
```

5. Hold down your finger on touch pad A1 while running the next block of code:

```
>>> event.process()
A1 True
```

6. The following code should be put into the `main.py` file, and, when executed, it will move servo 1 to the lowest angle for 3 seconds, and then move it to the middle range angle for 60 seconds:

```
import time
from adafruit_circuitplayground.express import cpx
from adafruit_crickit import crickit

MIN_PULSE = 750
MAX_PULSE = 2250

crickit.servo_1.set_pulse_width_range(MIN_PULSE, MAX_PULSE)
crickit.servo_1.angle = 0
time.sleep(3)
```

```
crickit.servo_1.angle = 90
time.sleep(60)
```

How it works...

The `crickit` object will be the way we can interact with all the servos and DC motors connected to the board. Each servo connection is numbered, so that you can control multiple servos through attributes on this single object. After saving the values for the minimum and maximum pulse widths in constants, we then apply these settings to the first servo motor by calling `set_pulse_width_range`.

We then set the value of the angle attribute on the first servo, which will move the servo into angle 0. We pause for 3 seconds by calling the `sleep` method before changing the angle to 90, using the same angle attribute.

There's more...

Servo motors from different manufacturers will expect different settings for the minimum and maximum pulse widths. You can usually find the correct settings for a particular servo by checking the product's data sheet. The settings used in this recipe are specific to the servo models described at the start of the chapter. You can change these settings as required if you decide to use a different set of servos. The Python library for controlling the servos also lets you configure these settings for each servo. This lets you attach different servos with different settings at the same time by configuring each one separately.

The pulse widths are sometimes provided in milliseconds, and sometimes in microseconds. Just convert them to microseconds, as they are the units expected in this Python module. The servo used in this recipe was described as using 0.75 ms to 2.25 ms for its pulse width, which, when converted to microseconds, becomes 750 to 2,250.

See also

Here are a few references:

- An overview of the components found in servos can be found at `http://developer.wildernesslabs.co/Hardware/Reference/Peripherals/Servos/`.
- An explanation of the inner workings of servos can be found at `https://www.pc-control.co.uk/servo_control.htm`.

Setting the actuation range of a servo

Servos vary in the range of motion their arms have. For the angles, you make a request in your software to map correctly to the angles the servo actually moves in; you need to configure the servo with its actuation range. Once configured, you will be able to accurately move the arms connected to servos into their correct positions. This is an important step in configuring any project you plan to use servos in. If you don't do this, you will face a number of strange surprises where the servo arms keep moving to the wrong positions.

Getting ready

You will need access to the REPL on the Circuit Playground Express to run the code presented in this recipe.

How to do it...

Let's go over the steps required for this recipe:

1. Execute the next block of code in the REPL:

    ```
    >>> from adafruit_circuitplayground.express import cpx
    >>> from adafruit_crickit import crickit
    >>>
    >>> MIN_PULSE = 750
    >>> MAX_PULSE = 2250
    >>>
    >>> crickit.servo_1.set_pulse_width_range(MIN_PULSE, MAX_PULSE)
    ```

2. The pulse widths are now configured for the servo. Execute the following block of code to move the servo to its lowest position:

    ```
    >>> crickit.servo_1.angle = 0
    ```

3. Make note of the current position of the arm before running the next block of code. Run the next block of code to move the servo to the highest angle:

    ```
    >>> crickit.servo_1.angle = 180
    ```

4. Measure the angle between these two positions. You should find the angle to be 160 degrees. Run the next block of code to return the servo to angle 0 and configure the actuation range:

```
>>> crickit.servo_1.angle = 0
>>> crickit.servo_1.actuation_range = 160
```

5. Run the next block of code, and the software angle and the real-world angle should both be 160 degrees:

```
>>> crickit.servo_1.angle = 160
```

6. The following code should be inserted into the main.py file:

```
import time
from adafruit_circuitplayground.express import cpx
from adafruit_crickit import crickit

MIN_PULSE = 750
MAX_PULSE = 2250

crickit.servo_1.set_pulse_width_range(MIN_PULSE, MAX_PULSE)
crickit.servo_1.angle = 0
time.sleep(3)
crickit.servo_1.actuation_range = 160
crickit.servo_1.angle = 160
time.sleep(60)
```

When this script is executed, it will move servo 1 to the lowest angle for 3 seconds, and then move it to an angle of 160 degrees for 60 seconds.

How it works...

The first few lines of code will configure the pulse width settings for the servo. The angle will be set to 0 for 3 seconds before the actuation range is configured to the correct value for this specific servo as a value of 160 degrees. After this configuration, when the angle in the software is set as 160 degrees, the real-world movement should also be 160 degrees.

There's more...

Just as pulse widths vary between servos, so does the range of motion. Most servos won't give you a full 180 degrees of motion. One way to discover these settings is to not configure the actuation range, and then move the servo to 0 degrees and 180 degrees in your software.

You can then use a protractor to physically measure the angle moved by the servo. Once you have measured this value, you can then use this angle as the value for the actuation range. The following image shows the servo in this chapter being measured with a protractor at the lowest angle:

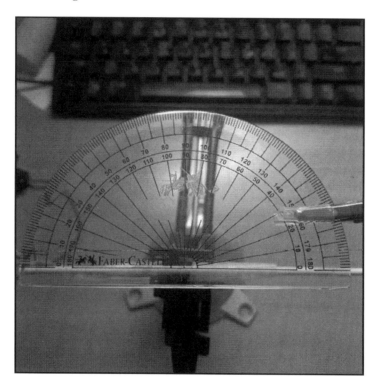

After the protractor has been put in place, the servo is moved to the highest angle. The following image shows the protractor measuring the angle as 160 degrees:

Protractors are the weapon of choice when you want to make accurate angle measurements in the real world.

See also

Here are a few references:

- Some details on setting the actuation range can be found at `https://learn.adafruit.com/using-servos-with-circuitpython/circuitpython`.
- A discussion of the range of motion of servos can be found at `https://learn.sparkfun.com/tutorials/hobby-servo-tutorial`.

Setting the angle of a servo

Once you have a correctly configured servo, you will be able to move the servo arm to exact angle positions. This recipe will move a servo to a number of angles and show what happens when you try to move servos to angles beyond their allowed range of motion.

Once we have the power to move servos to specific angles, we can start incorporating them into our projects to control robotic arms or to move other servo attachments to specific positions.

Getting ready

You will need access to the REPL on the Circuit Playground Express to run the code presented in this recipe.

How to do it...

Let's go over the steps required for this recipe:

1. Use the REPL to run the following lines of code:

```
>>> from adafruit_circuitplayground.express import cpx
>>> from adafruit_crickit import crickit
>>>
>>> MIN_PULSE = 750
>>> MAX_PULSE = 2250
>>>
>>> crickit.servo_1.set_pulse_width_range(MIN_PULSE, MAX_PULSE)
>>> crickit.servo_1.angle = 0
```

2. The servo should now be at the lowest angle. Execute the following block of code to move the servo to its highest position:

```
>>> crickit.servo_1.angle = 180
```

3. Run the following code to see what happens when you go past the maximum angle range:

```
>>> crickit.servo_1.angle = 190
Traceback (most recent call last):
  File "<stdin>", line 1, in <module>
  File "adafruit_motor/servo.py", line 111, in angle
ValueError: Angle out of range
```

4. Run the following block of code to return the servo to angle 0 and configure the actuation range to 160 degrees:

```
>>> crickit.servo_1.angle = 0
>>> crickit.servo_1.actuation_range = 160
```

5. Run the following block of code to see that 180 degrees is now considered an angle beyond the servo's range:

```
>>> crickit.servo_1.angle = 180
Traceback (most recent call last):
  File "<stdin>", line 1, in <module>
  File "adafruit_motor/servo.py", line 111, in angle
ValueError: Angle out of range
```

6. Run the following block of code, and the servo should move to its highest angle:

```
>>> crickit.servo_1.angle = 160
```

7. The following code should be put into the main.py file, and, when executed, it will move the servo to angles of 0, 45, 90, and 160, with a three-second delay between each movement:

```
import time
from adafruit_circuitplayground.express import cpx
from adafruit_crickit import crickit

MIN_PULSE = 750
MAX_PULSE = 2250

crickit.servo_1.set_pulse_width_range(MIN_PULSE, MAX_PULSE)
crickit.servo_1.angle = 0
crickit.servo_1.actuation_range = 160

crickit.servo_1.angle = 0
time.sleep(3)

crickit.servo_1.angle = 45
time.sleep(3)

crickit.servo_1.angle = 90
time.sleep(3)

crickit.servo_1.angle = 160
time.sleep(3)
```

How it works...

The first few lines of code will configure the pulse width settings and actuation range for the servo. Then, 4 different angles will be set on the servo. The angles are 0, 45, 90, and 160 degrees. After each angle is set, a delay of 3 seconds is applied by calling the `sleep` function on the time module.

There's more...

In this recipe, we experimented to see what would happen when we tried to set the angles on the servo both when the actuation range had not been configured, and once it had been configured. The default setting for the actuation range is 180 degrees. That is why, in all cases, a value of 190 degrees would be rejected. Once we configured the actuation range to 160, values such as 180 would, of course, be rejected, as they would be outside this range.

It's very helpful that the servo library has these checks, because if they weren't performed, bugs in your software application that set servo angles outside of the correct range could damage your servo. Also, throwing a `ValueError` exception with a clear exception message makes it easier to debug applications that have these bugs in them.

See also

Here are a few references:

- A project that controls the angles of servos using the CRICKIT can be found at `https://learn.adafruit.com/crickit-powered-owl-robot`.
- An example of creating motion with a servo and CircuitPython can be found at `https://learn.adafruit.com/hello-world-of-robotics-with-crickit`.

Sweeping a servo

In this recipe, you will learn how to create a script that continually moves a servo from the lowest to the highest angle and back again, in a sweeping motion. In some ways, the code is similar to the light animations that we have seen in previous chapters, as we will change the output of the board with time delays between each change to create an animated visual effect.

In the case of servos, though, it is the attached arm that will become animated with a sweeping motion. The approach used in this recipe can be adapted to any number of projects in which you want some servo attachments to continually sweep from one position to another.

Getting ready

You will need access to the REPL on the Circuit Playground Express to run the code presented in this recipe.

How to do it...

Let's go over the steps required for this recipe:

1. Run the following lines of code in the REPL:

```
>>> import time
>>> from adafruit_circuitplayground.express import cpx
>>> from adafruit_crickit import crickit
>>>
>>> MIN_PULSE = 750
>>> MAX_PULSE = 2250
>>> MAX_ANGLE = 160
>>> STEP = 10
>>> DELAY = 0.1
```

2. At this stage, the required Python libraries should be imported, and the different settings should be defined as constants for our script. Execute the following block of code to initialize the servo and move it to its lowest position:

```
>>> def init(servo):
...     servo.set_pulse_width_range(MIN_PULSE, MAX_PULSE)
...     servo.angle = 0
...     servo.actuation_range = MAX_ANGLE
...
...
...
>>> init(crickit.servo_1)
```

3. Run the following code to sweep the servo from angle 0 to 160:

```
>>> def sweep(servo, direction):
...     angle = int(servo.angle)
...     while 0 <= angle <= MAX_ANGLE:
```

```
...             print(angle)
...             servo.angle = angle
...             time.sleep(DELAY)
...             angle += STEP * direction
...
...
>>> sweep(crickit.servo_1, 1)
0
10
20
30
40
50
60
70
80
90
100
110
120
130
140
150
160
```

4. Run the following code to sweep the servo from angle 160 to 0:

```
>>> sweep(crickit.servo_1, -1)
160
150
140
130
120
110
100
90
80
70
60
50
40
30
20
10
0
```

5. The following code should be inserted into the `main.py` file, and, when executed, it will continually sweep the motor from angle 0 to 160, and then back to 0:

```
import time
from adafruit_circuitplayground.express import cpx
from adafruit_crickit import crickit

MIN_PULSE = 750
MAX_PULSE = 2250
MAX_ANGLE = 160
STEP = 10
DELAY = 0.1

def init(servo):
    servo.set_pulse_width_range(MIN_PULSE, MAX_PULSE)
    servo.angle = 0
    servo.actuation_range = MAX_ANGLE

def sweep(servo, direction):
    angle = int(servo.angle)
    while 0 <= angle <= MAX_ANGLE:
        print(angle)
        servo.angle = angle
        time.sleep(DELAY)
        angle += STEP * direction

def main():
    init(crickit.servo_1)
    while True:
        sweep(crickit.servo_1, 1)
        sweep(crickit.servo_1, -1)

main()
```

How it works...

First, a function called `init` is defined, which expects the name of the servo to initialize as its first argument. When this function is called, it will set the minimum and maximum pulse widths, set the angle to 0, and set the actuation range. Next, a function called `sweep` is defined. This function expects the first argument to be the servo to control, and the second argument to be an integer with the value 1 or –1, indicating the direction of the sweep.

A value of 1 will make the the angle increase, while a value of −1 will make the angle decrease. The first part of the sweep function will retrieve the current value of the servo's angle and type cast it to an integer and store it in a variable called `angle`. A loop is started, which will continue until the value of the angle has exceeded the allowed range of 0 to 160. In each iteration of the loop, the current angle is printed, and then the angle is applied to the servo before a sleep is applied; then, the angle is changed by the defined step value.

The `main` function is then defined, which, when called, will initialize the servo and move it to angle 0. Then, an infinite loop is started to perform two actions during each loop iteration. It will first call the sweep function to increase the angle from 0 to 160. Then, it will call the sweep function again, but this time, to reduce the angle from 160 to 0.

There's more...

As much as possible, no values are hardcoded in the `init` and `sweep` functions. Most of the values are provided as configurable constants set at the top of the script, or as arguments received as the function is called. This will make it much easier to tune the script for servos with other settings. You can also easily change the amount the angle changes during each `sweep` iteration and the speed at which the sweep is completed by increasing and lowering the values in these constants.

The program has also been broken into 3 different functions, in order to improve readability and encourage the reuse of different blocks of code into other projects. One of the interesting and relatively unique features of the Python programming language, which is fully supported in the MicroPython and CircuitPython editions, is the ability to chain comparison operations. This feature is used in the `sweep` function to check that the angle is between 0 and 160.

In other languages, you would usually have to express this using an `and` operator combined with two comparison operators. In Python, however, you can just chain the two comparison operators to achieve the same result in a more concise and readable way.

See also

Here are a few references:

- Documentation describing how comparisons can be chained can be found at `https://docs.python.org/3/reference/expressions.html#comparisons`.
- Documentation on the CRICKIT library can be found at `https://circuitpython.readthedocs.io/projects/crickit/en/latest/`.

Controlling servos with buttons

In this recipe, you will learn how to use the two push buttons on the Circuit Playground Express to control the angle of a servo. The script in this recipe will increase the servo angle each time push button A is pressed, and will decrease the angle each time push button B is pressed. These types of scripts are very useful whenever you want to create a project where people can directly control servos using different input controls, such as push buttons.

Getting ready

You will need access to the REPL on the Circuit Playground Express to run the code presented in this recipe.

How to do it...

Let's go over the steps required for this recipe:

1. Execute the following block of code in the REPL:

```
>>> import time
>>> from adafruit_circuitplayground.express import cpx
>>> from adafruit_crickit import crickit
>>>
>>> MIN_PULSE = 750
>>> MAX_PULSE = 2250
>>> MAX_ANGLE = 160
>>> STEP = 10
>>> DELAY = 0.1
```

2. The initial imports are done, and we are ready to define our functions. The following block of code will define and call a function to initialize the servo:

```
>>> def init(servo):
...     servo.set_pulse_width_range(MIN_PULSE, MAX_PULSE)
...     servo.angle = 0
...     servo.actuation_range = MAX_ANGLE
...
...
...
>>> init(crickit.servo_1)
```

3. Run the following code to move the servo by 10 degrees and inspect the value of angle:

```
>>> def move(servo, angle, direction):
...     new = angle + STEP * direction
...     if 0 <= new <= MAX_ANGLE:
...         angle = new
...         print(angle)
...         servo.angle = angle
...     return angle
...
...
>>> angle = 0
>>> angle = move(crickit.servo_1, angle, 1)
10
>>> angle
10
```

4. Run the following code to move the servo again, by another 10 degrees:

```
>>> angle = move(crickit.servo_1, angle, 1)
20
```

5. Run the following code to reduce the angle of the servo by 10 degrees:

```
>>> angle = move(crickit.servo_1, angle, -1)
10
```

6. The following code should be inserted into the main.py file:

```
import time
from adafruit_circuitplayground.express import cpx
from adafruit_crickit import crickit

MIN_PULSE = 750
MAX_PULSE = 2250
MAX_ANGLE = 160
STEP = 10
DELAY = 0.1


def init(servo):
    servo.set_pulse_width_range(MIN_PULSE, MAX_PULSE)
    servo.angle = 0
    servo.actuation_range = MAX_ANGLE


def move(servo, angle, direction):
```

```
        new = angle + STEP * direction
        if 0 <= new <= MAX_ANGLE:
            angle = new
            print(angle)
            servo.angle = angle
        return angle


def main():
    init(crickit.servo_1)
    angle = 0
    while True:
        if cpx.button_a:
            angle = move(crickit.servo_1, angle, 1)
        if cpx.button_b:
            angle = move(crickit.servo_1, angle, -1)
        time.sleep(DELAY)


main()
```

The script, once executed, will move the servo to a lower or higher angle each time push buttons A and B are pressed.

How it works...

After global constants and a servo initialization function are defined, we then continue to define two other functions. The move function accepts the servo, the current angle, and the movement direction as its three arguments. The expected new angle is then calculated based on the current angle step amount and the direction of movement. If this new angle is within the acceptable angle range, then its value is printed and applied to both the servo and the angle variable. Finally, the value of the angle variable is returned.

The main function that is defined and then called at the bottom of the script implements the main event loop. The servo variable is initialized and the angle variable is set to 0 before an infinite loop is started. During each iteration of the loop, if push button A is pressed, then the move function will be called to increase the servo angle. Then, push button B is checked, and, if it's pressed, the move function will be called to decrease the servo angle. Finally, a sleep function is applied at the end of each iteration of this loop.

There's more...

This basic event loop allows us to react to user input by moving the servo in different directions. We can extend the logic of this script in many directions. We could reduce the step angle from 10 to 1, for example, to get very fine control of the servo and change the angle by one degree at a time. We could also reduce the delay to speed up the movement in reaction to each button press. We could take the base script and add code that controls the pixels, in addition to the servo angles, as you press each push button.

See also

Here are a few references:

- A project that controls servos with push buttons can be found at `https://learn.adafruit.com/universal-marionette-with-crickit`.
- The source code for the `servo` objects can be found at `https://github.com/adafruit/Adafruit_Circuitpython_Motor`.

Controlling multiple servos

In this recipe, you will learn how to combine the use of the push buttons and slide switch to control multiple servos. Essentially, we will use the push buttons to control the angle of a specific servo. We will then use the slide switch to select which of the two connected servos we want to control.

This recipe builds on some of the past recipes and adds additional data structures and controls to manage the additional logic that is required to control multiple servos. This recipe will be very useful whenever you need to find ways to control more than one servo at a time.

Getting ready

You will need access to the REPL on the Circuit Playground Express to run the code presented in this recipe.

How to do it...

Let's go over the steps required for this recipe:

1. Use the REPL to run the following lines of code:

```
>>> import time
>>> from adafruit_circuitplayground.express import cpx
>>> from adafruit_crickit import crickit
>>>
>>> MIN_PULSE = 750
>>> MAX_PULSE = 2250
>>> MAX_ANGLE = 160
>>> STEP = 10
>>> DELAY = 0.1
>>>
>>> def init(servo):
...     servo.set_pulse_width_range(MIN_PULSE, MAX_PULSE)
...     servo.angle = 0
...     servo.actuation_range = MAX_ANGLE
...
...
...
>>>
```

2. The initial imports are done, and we have defined the `init` function to help initialize the servos. The following block of code will set up some data structures that will keep track of our angles and servos:

```
>>> servos = [crickit.servo_1, crickit.servo_4]
>>> angles = [0, 0]
```

3. The following block of code will initialize all the servos in our servos list:

```
>>> init(servos[0])
>>> init(servos[1])
```

4. Run the following code to set the switch variable, based on the slide switch position:

```
>>> switch = int(cpx.switch)
>>> switch
0
```

5. Run the following code to move the selected servo by 10 degrees:

```
>>> def move(servo, angle, direction):
...     new = angle + STEP * direction
...     if 0 <= new <= MAX_ANGLE:
...         angle = new
...         print(angle)
...         servo.angle = angle
...     return angle
...
...
...
>>> angles[switch] = move(servos[switch], angles[switch], 1)
10
```

6. Run the following code to inspect the angle's data structure before and after a call to the move function:

```
>>> angle = move(crickit.servo_1, angle, 1)
>>> angles
[10, 0]
>>> angles[switch] = move(servos[switch], angles[switch], 1)
20
>>> angles
[20, 0]
```

7. Change the slide switch position and run the following block of code to update the selected servo:

```
>>> switch = int(cpx.switch)
>>> switch
1
```

8. Run the following block of code to see how calling the move function moves the other servo:

```
>>> angles[switch] = move(servos[switch], angles[switch], 1)
10
>>> angles
[20, 10]
```

9. The following code should be inserted into the main.py file:

```
import time
from adafruit_circuitplayground.express import cpx
from adafruit_crickit import crickit

MIN_PULSE = 750
```

```
MAX_PULSE = 2250
MAX_ANGLE = 160
STEP = 10
DELAY = 0.1

def init(servo):
    servo.set_pulse_width_range(MIN_PULSE, MAX_PULSE)
    servo.angle = 0
    servo.actuation_range = MAX_ANGLE

def move(servo, angle, direction):
    new = angle + STEP * direction
    if 0 <= new <= MAX_ANGLE:
        angle = new
        print(angle)
        servo.angle = angle
    return angle

def main():
    servos = [crickit.servo_1, crickit.servo_4]
    angles = [0, 0]
    init(servos[0])
    init(servos[1])
    while True:
        switch = int(cpx.switch)
        if cpx.button_a:
            angles[switch] = move(servos[switch], angles[switch],
1)
        if cpx.button_b:
            angles[switch] = move(servos[switch], angles[switch],
-1)
        time.sleep(DELAY)

main()
```

Executing this script will move different servos, depending on the position of the slide switch and the presses on the push buttons.

How it works...

After global constants and a servo initialization function are defined, we will then continue to define two other functions. The move function follows the same structure that you saw in the previous recipe. The main function, however, has been expanded to have additional data structures and logic to handle dealing with multiple servos and the slide switch.

In the `main` function, a list called `servos` is created to point to the two servos to be controlled. A list called `angles` will keep track of the angles for each servo. Each servo is then initialized before entering into an infinite loop.

During each loop iteration, the value of the switch is converted from a Boolean value to the integer value 0 or 1. This will allow us to switch control between the two servos. Then, depending on whether push button A or B is pressed, the `move` function is called, provided with the correct `servo` object and angle. Finally, `sleep` is applied at the end of each loop.

There's more...

In this recipe, we have combined three input controls and two output servos in a way that makes interacting with the board a natural process. Part of the reason for this is that different physical input controls lend themselves to be mapped to different logical controls.

A slide switch is ideal for switching between two options, so it makes sense to use a slide switch when selecting between two servos. Push buttons work well when you want to repeatedly increase or reduce a value through repeated button presses.

See also

Here are a few references:

- Examples of interacting with the slide switch can be found at `https://learn.adafruit.com/circuitpython-made-easy-on-circuit-playground-express/slide-switch`.
- A number of Adafruit CRICKIT-related components can be found at `https://www.adafruit.com/category/972`.

Turning on a DC motor

In this recipe, you will learn how to control a DC motor using the Circuit Playground Express and CRICKIT board. DC motors are simpler to interact with than servos, since they don't need any initial configuration. This recipe will give you the basic skills required to turn DC motors on and off for your projects.

Getting ready

You will need access to the REPL on the Circuit Playground Express to run the code presented in this recipe.

How to do it...

Let's go over the steps required for this recipe:

1. Run the following lines of code in the REPL:

```
>>> from adafruit_crickit import crickit
>>> import time
>>>
>>> crickit.dc_motor_1.throttle = 1
```

2. The DC motor connected to the board should now start rotating at full speed. Run the following block of code to stop the DC motor from rotating:

```
>>> crickit.dc_motor_1.throttle = 0
```

3. The following block of code will stop and start the motor with a one-second delay:

```
>>> while True:
...         crickit.dc_motor_1.throttle = 1
...         time.sleep(1)
...         crickit.dc_motor_1.throttle = 0
...         time.sleep(1)
...
...
...
```

4. The following code should be inserted into the main.py file:

```
from adafruit_crickit import crickit
import time

while True:
    crickit.dc_motor_1.throttle = 1
    time.sleep(1)
    crickit.dc_motor_1.throttle = 0
    time.sleep(1)
```

This script, when executed, will start an infinite loop that keeps starting and stopping the motor.

How it works...

DC motors differ from servos, and therefore, they require less code and interaction to get them moving. After the library imports, an infinite loop is started.

In the first line of the loop, the `dc_motor_1` attribute on the `crickit` object is accessed. This object will let us interact with any DC motors connected to the first motor connection on the board. The `dc_motor_1` exposes an attribute called `throttle` that we can use to turn the motor on and off. If we set the value to 1, the motor starts, and a value of 0 switches off the motor.

In this way, the throttle is first set to 1 to turn the motor on; a 1 second sleep is applied before the motor is turned off, and another sleep of 1 second is applied. The loop then starts again, repeating the process.

There's more...

DC motors are different than the servos in a number of ways, as demonstrated in this recipe. It is true that they are easier to get started with than servos, since they don't need any initial configuration. On the flip side, however, they don't provide any precise control of the exact position you'd like to put the motor in.

There are, of course, things that DC motors are capable of doing that servos can't, such as a complete 360-degree rotational motion.

See also

Here are a few references:

- Documentation on using DC motors with the CRICKIT board can be found at `https://learn.adafruit.com/adafruit-crickit-creative-robotic-interactive-construction-kit/circuitpython-dc-motors`.
- A number of chassis that can be used to house the DC motors can be found at `https://learn.adafruit.com/adafruit-crickit-creative-robotic-interactive-construction-kit/recommended-chassis`.

Setting the speed and direction of a DC motor

In this recipe, you will learn how to control both the speed and the rotational direction of a specific DC motor. You will see that providing a positive or negative value to the throttle will let us control whether the motor will turn clockwise or counterclockwise. We can also provide fractional values to the throttle to control the power the motor is run at.

When you use DC motors to control wheels on a MicroPython-powered, computer-controlled vehicle, the techniques in this recipe will be very useful. They will let you speed the car up or slow it down. You can also use them to make the car go in reverse or come to a full stop.

Getting ready

You will need access to the REPL on the Circuit Playground Express to run the code presented in this recipe.

How to do it....

Let's go over the steps required for this recipe:

1. Execute the following block of code in the REPL:

    ```
    >>> from adafruit_crickit import crickit
    >>> import time
    >>> DELAY = 0.1
    >>>
    >>> crickit.dc_motor_1.throttle = 0.5
    ```

2. The DC motor will now run at 50% of its full speed. The following line of code will run the motor at a quarter of its full speed:

    ```
    >>> crickit.dc_motor_1.throttle = 0.25
    ```

3. The following block of code will move the motors in the opposite direction, at full speed:

    ```
    >>> crickit.dc_motor_1.throttle = -1
    ```

4. Run the following block of code to stop the motor:

```
>>> crickit.dc_motor_1.throttle = 0
```

5. When executed, the following block of code will define and call a function that will change the speed and direction of the motor from one direction to the opposite direction:

```
>>> from adafruit_crickit import crickit
>>> def change_throttle(motor, start, increment):
...         throttle = start
...         for i in range(21):
...             print(throttle)
...             motor.throttle = throttle
...             throttle += increment
...             throttle = round(throttle, 1)
...             time.sleep(DELAY)
...
...
>>> change_throttle(crickit.dc_motor_1, -1.0, 0.1)
-1.0
-0.9
-0.8
-0.7
-0.6
-0.5
-0.4
-0.3
-0.2
-0.1
0.0
0.1
0.2
0.3
0.4
0.5
0.6
0.7
0.8
0.9
1.0
>>>
```

6. The following code should be inserted into the main.py file:

```
from adafruit_crickit import crickit
import time
```

```
DELAY = 0.1


def change_throttle(motor, start, increment):
    throttle = start
    for i in range(21):
        print(throttle)
        motor.throttle = throttle
        throttle += increment
        throttle = round(throttle, 1)
        time.sleep(DELAY)


def main():
    while True:
        change_throttle(crickit.dc_motor_1, -1.0, 0.1)
        change_throttle(crickit.dc_motor_1, 1.0, -0.1)


main()
```

This script, when executed, will move the motor from one direction to the other, over and over again.

How it works...

The `change_throttle` function is defined, which will perform the bulk of the work in this recipe. It expects to receive the motor to control, the starting value for the throttle, and finally, the amount the throttle should be changed during each iteration. The function will initialize the `throttle` variable to the specified start value.

Then, a `for` loop will be started that will go from the lowest to the highest value of the throttle. It first prints the current throttle, and then applies the value of the `throttle` variable to the motor. The throttle is incremented and rounded to one decimal place. A delay is then applied before the next iteration.

The `main` function will enter into an infinite loop that calls the `change_throttle` function twice during each iteration. The first call will move the throttle value from −1.0 to 1.0, in increments of 0.1. The second call will move the throttle value from 1.0 to −1.0, in increments of −0.1.

There's more...

This recipe can be used to demonstrate running the motors at different speeds and different directions. It creates an almost visual animation, where you can see the motors slowing down and speeding up. You can see them moving at maximum speed in one direction, and then slowing down to move to the maximum speed in the other direction.

There are all sorts of creative experiments you can do to extend this recipe to new functionality. You could, for example, attach two wheels to the DC motor to make it move like a remote control car. You could configure the light sensor to react to a flashlight by speeding up the motor. Or, you could attach something else to the DC motor that turned based on a certain schedule. You could control the timing of when the motor is turned on, using the time module used in this recipe.

See also

Here are a few references:

- A project that uses both servos and DC motors with the CRICKIT board can be found at `https://learn.adafruit.com/adafruit-crickit-creative-robotic-interactive-construction-kit/bubble-bot`.
- Details on how to wire and control DC motors with the CRICKIT board can be found at `https://learn.adafruit.com/make-it-move-with-crickit/use-a-continuous-dc-motor-now`.

Controlling a DC motor with buttons

In this recipe, we will use push buttons to increase and decrease the speed of the DC motor. We can use the same script to change the direction of rotation with the push buttons. Essentially, one push button will make the motor increase speed in one direction, and the other push button will make the motor move more in the other direction. In this way, we can use the pair of push buttons to set a range of speeds in either direction and to bring the motor to a full stop.

As the script is run, the current speed and direction will be printed to the screen. This recipe can be useful in any project in which you want to have user input translated into motion. You could, for example, create a project in which you attach a pulley to a DC motor and use the push buttons to raise and lower the pulley.

Getting ready

You will need access to the REPL on the Circuit Playground Express to run the code presented in this recipe.

How to do it...

Let's go over the steps required for this recipe:

1. Use the REPL to run the following lines of code:

```
>>> from adafruit_crickit import crickit
>>> from adafruit_circuitplayground.express import cpx
>>> import time
>>>
>>> STEP = 0.1
>>> DELAY = 0.1
>>> MIN_THROTTLE = -1
>>> MAX_THROTTLE = 1
>>>
>>> throttle = 0
>>> crickit.dc_motor_1.throttle = throttle
```

2. The DC motor speed is set at 0 throttle. The following block of code will define a `move` function and call it three times, with parameters to increase the speed to 30% strength:

```
>>> def move(motor, throttle, direction):
...     new = throttle + STEP * direction
...     if MIN_THROTTLE <= new <= MAX_THROTTLE:
...         throttle = round(new, 1)
...         print(throttle)
...         motor.throttle = throttle
...     return throttle
...
...
...
>>> throttle = move(crickit.dc_motor_1, throttle, 1)
0.1
>>> throttle = move(crickit.dc_motor_1, throttle, 1)
0.2
>>> throttle = move(crickit.dc_motor_1, throttle, 1)
0.3
```

3. The following block of code will call the move function three times, to reduce the speed until the motor comes to a full stop:

```
>>> throttle = move(crickit.dc_motor_1, throttle, -1)
0.2
>>> throttle = move(crickit.dc_motor_1, throttle, -1)
0.1
>>> throttle = move(crickit.dc_motor_1, throttle, -1)
0.0
```

4. The following block of code will call the move function three more times, in the negative direction, to set the motor to 30% strength in the opposite direction:

```
>>> throttle = move(crickit.dc_motor_1, throttle, -1)
-0.1
>>> throttle = move(crickit.dc_motor_1, throttle, -1)
-0.2
>>> throttle = move(crickit.dc_motor_1, throttle, -1)
-0.3
```

5. The following block of code will call the move function three times in a direction that takes the motor from the opposite direction down to a full stop:

```
>>> throttle = move(crickit.dc_motor_1, throttle, 1)
-0.2
>>> throttle = move(crickit.dc_motor_1, throttle, 1)
-0.1
>>> throttle = move(crickit.dc_motor_1, throttle, 1)
0.0
```

6. The following code should be inserted into the main.py file, and, when executed, it will move the motor from one direction to the other, in response to presses on the push buttons:

```
from adafruit_crickit import crickit
from adafruit_circuitplayground.express import cpx
import time

STEP = 0.1
DELAY = 0.1
MIN_THROTTLE = -1
MAX_THROTTLE = 1

def move(motor, throttle, direction):
    new = throttle + STEP * direction
    if MIN_THROTTLE <= new <= MAX_THROTTLE:
        throttle = round(new, 1)
```

```
            print(throttle)
            motor.throttle = throttle
        return throttle

def main():
    throttle = 0
    while True:
        if cpx.button_a:
            throttle = move(crickit.dc_motor_1, throttle, 1)
        if cpx.button_b:
            throttle = move(crickit.dc_motor_1, throttle, -1)
        time.sleep(DELAY)

main()
```

How it works...

The `move` function is defined to control changes in the direction of movement on the motor. It can be called to either increase or decrease the movement in a specific rotational direction. The function takes the motor object, the current throttle, and the desired direction of movement. The new throttle value is calculated, and, if it is found to be within the acceptable range of the motor, the value will then be printed and applied to the motor.

The latest value of the throttle is then returned so that the main event loop can keep track of it. The `main` function contains an infinite loop, which acts as the main event loop. In this loop, presses on push button A will increase the motor's speed in one direction, and presses on push button B will increase the motor's speed in the opposite direction.

There's more...

This recipe provided the basic building blocks for taking user-generated input and generating output using DC motors. You can expand on this recipe in a similar way to others so that the slide switch will let you control more than one DC motor with the same script.

You can change the step value in the script to make the motors change speed and direction faster. Or, maybe you would like to reduce the step value, giving you more fine-grained control over the speed, at the cost of additional button presses.

See also

Here are a few references:

- A motor pulley that is compatible with the DC motors used in this chapter can be found at `https://www.adafruit.com/product/3789`.
- A project that uses DC motors with the CRICKIT board to control a pulley can be found at `https://learn.adafruit.com/adafruit-crickit-creative-robotic-interactive-construction-kit/marble-madness`.

9
Coding on the micro:bit

In this chapter, we will introduce the micro:bit microcontroller. We'll explore its features and its strengths compared to other microcontrollers. By the end of this chapter, you will have learned how to load your code on this microcontroller, control its LED grid display, as well as interact with the buttons that come on board. This chapter ends with a nice project so that you can create a countdown timer using this hardware. Each MicroPython board has its own strengths, and it's good to know what's out there so that you can choose the right hardware for your project.

In this chapter, we will cover the following topics:

- Using Mu to flash code onto the micro:bit
- Using Mu to get a REPL on the micro:bit
- Displaying a single character on the LED display
- Displaying a built-in image
- Displaying scrolling text
- Showing which button has been pressed
- Creating a countdown timer

Technical requirements

The code files for this chapter can be found in the `Chapter09` folder in this book's GitHub repository, available at `https://github.com/PacktPublishing/MicroPython-Cookbook`.

You will need the BBC micro:bit board and the Mu text editor for the recipes in this chapter.

The micro:bit

The Micro Bit was created by the **British Broadcasting Corporation (BBC)** as a board that could be used for educational purposes in the UK. It is about half the size of a credit card and is packed with a number of input and output sensors, which is surprising when you consider its size. It has both an accelerometer and a magnetometer. It has two push buttons and a reset button. There is a 5 x 5 array of LEDs that can act as a basic display to show different symbols and characters. The following photo shows what this board looks like:

The board supports a portable power supply by using an external battery pack with AAA batteries. A USB connection is used to connect the board to a computer to transfer scripts over and run the REPL.

Using Mu to flash code onto the micro:bit

This recipe will show you how to flash your Python scripts to the micro:bit. The Mu text editor has built-in support for flashing code to this type of board, and this recipe will take you through this process. Once we understand this, we can use it to develop and load whatever scripts we need onto the micro:bit board. This is an essential first step whenever you want to create projects and experiment with the micro:bit.

Getting ready

You will need to install the Mu text editor for this recipe. Follow the instructions in `Chapter 1`, *Getting Started with MicroPython*, regarding the installation of the Mu text editor.

How to do it...

Follow these steps to learn how to use mu to flash code onto the micro:bit:

1. Connect the micro:bit to your computer using a USB cable.
2. Start the Mu text editor application.
3. Click on the **Mode** button in the far-left corner of the application to bring up the following dialog:

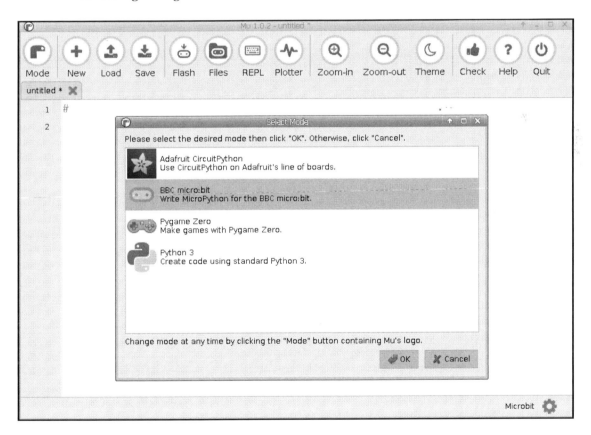

4. Select the **BBC micro:bit** option and press **OK**.

5. Put the following block of code in the main text editor window:

```
from microbit import display
display.show('x')
```

6. Press the **Flash** button on the toolbar to have the code flashed to the board. The following screenshot has the **Flash** button highlighted for reference:

7. If you look at the LED grid on the board, it should now display the x character.

How it works...

The micro:bit takes a different approach to loading your code on the board compared to Circuit Playground Express. The board requires that you use certain software that understands how to take your Python scripts and flash them onto these types of boards. The Mu text editor fully supports this MicroPython board. The initial steps were needed to configure Mu so that it is expected to interact with a connected micro:bit board. The script that was created is a simple script that imports the display object from the micro:bit Python library and uses it to display the x character on the LED display.

There's more...

The easiest program to get started with when flashing code onto the micro:bit is the Mu text editor. There are other options available, though, such as a command-line program called uFlash. The value of using the command-line approach is that it gives you the flexibility of using the text editor of your choice so that you can edit code and then flash it when you are ready to use the uFlash utility.

See also

Here are a few references regarding this recipe:

- Documentation on the uFlash command can be found at `https://uflash.readthedocs.io/en/latest/`.
- Details on the HEX file format that is used when flashing code onto the board can be found at `https://tech.microbit.org/software/hex-format/`.

Using Mu to get a REPL on the micro:bit

This recipe will build on the approach we covered in the previous recipe. Just as loading your scripts onto the board is essential, so is the REPL when it comes to debugging your scripts. The REPL will give you a much richer interface when you are trying to experiment with the board or trying to figure out what's wrong with your code. In the REPL, you can get tracebacks and see the output of print statements.

Getting ready

You will need to have the Mu text editor installed and configured, as well as your micro:bit board connected to your computer.

How to do it...

Follow these steps to learn how to use mu to get a REPL on the micro:bit:

1. Start the Mu text editor application.
2. Click on the REPL button in the toolbar, which is highlighted in the following screenshot:

3. The REPL interface should now appear in the lower half of the screen, as shown in the following screenshot:

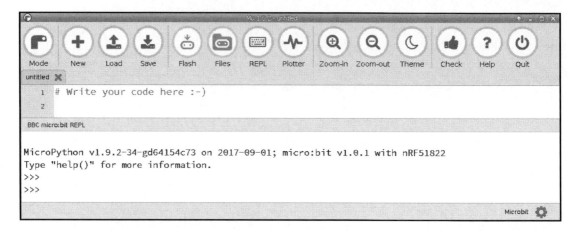

4. Run the following lines of code in the REPL:

```
>>> 1+1
2
```

5. Run the following block of code:

```
>>> import microbit
>>> microbit
<module 'microbit'>
```

The `microbit` library has now been imported.

How it works...

The Mu text editor has built-in REPL support for a number of boards, including the micro:bit. When you click the REPL button, the editor attempts to open a serial connection to the board. If successful, it starts a REPL session on the board.

The initial text that's printed out in the REPL shows the version of the MicroPython interpreter in use on the board. At this point, any commands you type in the REPL prompt will be sent to the board over the serial connection that's evaluated on the board. Then, their output will be returned to the computer to be displayed in the REPL screen.

There's more...

The MicroPython REPL comes with a number of useful functions to help you explore the different Python modules and objects that are available on the board. You can call the `help` function on different modules and objects to get details on what they do. When you're exploring a particular object and want to know the attributes and methods that are available on that object, you can use the `dir` function to list them in the REPL session.

See also

Here are a few references regarding this recipe:

- Documentation on the `help` function can be found at `https://docs.python.org/3/library/functions.html#help`.
- Documentation on the `dir` function can be found at `https://docs.python.org/3/library/functions.html#dir`.

Displaying a single character on the LED display

This recipe will show you how we can use the 5 x 5 array of LEDs that comes with the board to display characters and numbers. The display object has a `show` method that will do the mapping from characters and numbers to the bitmap image that needs to be displayed on the LEDs. These LEDs are one of the main forms of output on this board, so this recipe will provide you with a valuable means to interact with the scripts you put on the board.

Getting ready

You will need to have the Mu text editor installed and configured, as well as your Micro Bit board connected to your computer.

How to do it...

Follow these steps to learn how to display a single character on the LED display:

1. Run the following lines of code in the REPL:

```
>>> from microbit import display
>>> display.show('a')
```

2. The display should show the letter a now. Run the following block of code to display the number 1:

```
>>> display.show('1')
```

3. The following block of code will display the number 2 after it's run:

```
>>> display.show(2)
```

4. Run the following block of code to turn off the display:

```
>>> display.clear()
```

5. The following code should be put into the main text editor window and flashed to the board:

```
from microbit import display
import time

for i in range(3):
    display.show(i)
    time.sleep(1)
```

Once executed, this code will display the numbers 0, 1, and 2, with a 1-second delay between each change.

How it works...

The display object that is part of the micro:bit Python library has a show method on it that can be used to display numbers and characters on the display. The initial two examples called the method with an argument whose data type was string.

When the number 2 was shown, the value was given as an integer. This is possible as `show` accepts either strings or integers when it receives its input. The main script that is flashed in the recipe first imports the necessary libraries and then starts a `for` loop, which loops three times. In each loop, it displays the current number of the iteration starting from 0 and then sleeps for one second before looping again.

There's more...

It can be challenging dealing with such a limited display resolution of a 5 x 5 grid of LEDs. Thankfully, the Python module that comes with the micro:bit has done all the work of finding a way to display all the letters and characters on the display in a legible fashion. In this recipe, we have seen how we can provide strings and integers as data to display. In the next recipe, we will see that the same method can also receive other objects, such as image objects.

See also

Here are a few references regarding this recipe:

- Documentation on the `show` method can be found at `https://microbit-micropython.readthedocs.io/en/latest/display.html#microbit.display.show`.
- Documentation on the `clear` method can be found at `https://microbit-micropython.readthedocs.io/en/latest/display.html#microbit.display.clear`.

Displaying a built-in image

This recipe will show you how we can use the 5 x 5 array of LEDs to display one of the built-in images that's available with the micro:bit library. There are many images available, ranging from facial expressions to animal symbols. They are very much like emojis.

In this recipe, we will see how we can display the heart and the smiley icon on the display. When creating projects on the micro:bit, it can be useful to display symbols beyond text and numbers, as shown in this recipe. If you've made a game on the micro:bit, you might want to show a happy or sad face when the player loses or wins the game.

Getting ready

You will need to have the Mu text editor installed and configured, as well as your micro:bit board connected to your computer.

How to do it...

Follow these steps to learn how to display a built-in image:

1. Execute the following block of code in the REPL:

```
>>> from microbit import display, Image
>>> import time
>>>
>>> display.show(Image.HAPPY)
```

2. The display should show a happy face. Run the following block of code to show a heart icon:

```
>>> display.show(Image.HEART)
```

3. The following block of code will display a clock face pointing at 1 o'clock:

```
>>> display.show(Image.CLOCK1)
```

4. Run the following block of code to display a clock face animation that moves the clock face from 1 o'clock to 12 o'clock:

```
>>> CLOCK = [getattr(Image, 'CLOCK%s' % i) for i in range(1, 13)]
>>> for image in CLOCK:
...         display.show(image)
...         time.sleep(0.1)
...
...
...
>>>
```

5. The following code should be put into the main text editor window and flashed to the board:

```
from microbit import display, Image
import time

CLOCK = [getattr(Image, 'CLOCK%s' % i) for i in range(1, 13)]
while True:
    for image in CLOCK:
        display.show(image)
        time.sleep(0.1)
```

Once executed, this code will continually move the clock face from 1 o'clock to 12 o'clock, with a delay of 0.1 seconds between each change.

How it works...

The Image object that is a part of the microbit Python library has a collection of built-in images that can be accessed by referring to their attribute name. The show method accepts these image objects and will display them on the grid once they're called. The initial examples in the REPL show a happy face, heart, and a clock face, just by referring to the names of these images.

A list is then created that points to each of the 12 clock face images in the correct order from 1 to 12. This list can then be used to create a clock face animation. First, an infinite loop is started. During each iteration of the infinite loop, a for loop is started that will iterate through each of the 12 clock face images, displaying them and then pausing for 0.1 seconds before starting the next iteration. In this way, an animation is created of a clock face moving through the 12 positions on the clock.

There's more...

There are many more symbols and images than just the ones that were shown in this recipe. You can explore them in the REPL by either referring to the documentation or listing their names in the REPL using the built-in dir function.

The library also supports a mechanism that you can use to define your own custom images, which you can save in your code and reuse across projects. In this recipe, we showed you one way of creating image animations, but there is also built-in support for animations in the show method of the display object that can also be used.

See also

Here are a few references regarding this recipe:

- Documentation on creating your own images can be found at `https://microbit-micropython.readthedocs.io/en/latest/tutorials/images.html#diy-images`.
- Documentation on using the built-in support for creating animations can be found at `https://microbit-micropython.readthedocs.io/en/latest/tutorials/images.html#animation`.

Displaying scrolling text

This recipe will show you a technique that you can use to display text to the user using the scrolling text feature that is available with the `microbit` library. The LED grid is limited to showing one character at a time. By using the scrolling feature, you can show a message as a sequence of characters that scroll across the display.

In this way, you can create projects that display short messages to the user, even with the limited physical display that is available on the board. This recipe will also show you how to control the speed of this animation and how to have the text loop endlessly on the display.

Getting ready

You will need to have the Mu text editor installed and configured, as well as your micro:bit board connected to your computer.

How to do it...

Follow these steps to learn how to display scrolling text:

1. Use the REPL to run the following lines of code:

```
>>> from microbit import display
>>> display.scroll('hello')
```

2. The display should show the text `'hello'` scrolling across the display. The default delay is 150 milliseconds. The following block of code will scroll the text at double the normal speed:

```
>>> display.scroll('hello', delay=75)
```

3. The following block of code will display the same text at half the default speed:

```
>>> display.scroll('hello', delay=300)
```

4. Run the following block of code to display the text in an endless loop:

```
>>> display.scroll('hello', loop=True)
```

5. Terminate the endless loop by pressing *Ctrl + C*. You should see the following message:

```
Traceback (most recent call last):
  File "<stdin>", line 1, in <module>
KeyboardInterrupt:
>>>
```

6. The following code should be put into the main text editor window and flashed to the board:

```
from microbit import display

TEXT = [
    ('slow', 300),
    ('normal', 150),
    ('fast', 75),

]

for text, delay in TEXT:
    display.scroll(text, delay=delay)
```

Once executed, this code will scroll the text slow, normal, and fast, at three increasing speeds.

How it works...

The scroll method is a part of the display object and provides all the functionality we need to scroll text on the display. There is only one argument required, which is the text to display. Once you call this method, it will start the animation and display each character in the provided text and scroll the characters across the screen until the whole text is displayed.

The optional delay argument can be provided to control the speed at which the scroll animation is displayed. A lower value for the delay will create a faster animation, while a higher value will slow down the animation. The main script defines a list with three messages each, with a different setting for the the scroll delay. A for loop is then executed that will loop through each value and call the scroll method to display the specified text and apply a custom scroll delay for each message.

There's more...

There are other options provided by the scroll method that can come in handy. This method has the ability to run the scroll animation in the background. This can be useful when you want to let the message appear while your program performs some other action. You should be mindful of using the loop option that was presented in this recipe. Essentially, calling the show method in this way will have the call never return as it will start an infinite loop in the show method.

See also

Here are a few references regarding this recipe:

- Some simple examples of calling the scroll method can be found at https://microbit-micropython.readthedocs.io/en/latest/tutorials/hello.html.
- Documentation on the scroll method can be found at https://microbit-micropython.readthedocs.io/en/latest/display.html#microbit.display.scroll.

Showing which button has been pressed

This recipe will show you how to respond to either of the two push buttons on the board by displaying the button being pressed on the display each time the button is pressed. This will be the first recipe in this chapter where we will see how we can create an interactive project that responds to user input by displaying visual output through the onboard LED grid.

When you're creating your own projects, having access to two push buttons opens up a lot of possibilities in terms of creating interactive applications and games that respond to these inputs in different ways. This recipe will provide you with the basic building blocks so that you can start building these sorts of projects.

Getting ready

You will need to have the Mu text editor installed and configured, as well as your micro:bit board connected to your computer.

How to do it...

Follow these steps to learn how to show which button has been:

1. Run the following lines of code in the REPL:

```
>>> from microbit import display, button_a, button_b
>>>
>>> button_a.is_pressed()
False
```

2. Since button A is not being pressed, the value that's returned should be `False`. Hold down button A while you execute the following block of code:

```
>>> button_a.is_pressed()
True
```

3. Hold down button B while executing the following block of code:

```
>>> button_b.is_pressed()
True
```

4. The following code should be put into the main text editor window and flashed to the board:

```
from microbit import display, button_a, button_b

while True:
    if button_a.is_pressed():
        display.show('a')
    elif button_b.is_pressed():
        display.show('b')
    else:
        display.clear()
```

Once executed, this code will display the character a or b if either button A or B was pressed.

How it works...

After the initial imports, the main script enters an infinite loop. During each iteration, each of the two buttons will be polled to see whether it is currently being pressed. If either button A or B is pressed, then the character of the pressed button will be displayed on the screen. The final part of the loop is to check if neither button is pressed and then clear the contents of the screen.

There's more...

This recipe shows the basic structure of an event loop that continuously loops and check for events on the input sensors and takes actions in response to these events as they occur. You can take this basic recipe and expand it in many ways. For example, you could create a script that helps the user navigate and select between a list of menu options.

Each press of button A could display the next menu item. When button B is pressed, that menu item could then be selected. The overall structure of the program would remain the same in terms of an event loop and the checking of the state of each button during each loop iteration.

See also

Here are a few references regarding this recipe:

- An example of interacting with the push buttons can be found at `https://microbit-micropython.readthedocs.io/en/latest/tutorials/buttons.html`.
- Documentation on the `Button` class and its methods can be found at `https://microbit-micropython.readthedocs.io/en/latest/button.html`.

Creating a countdown timer

This recipe will show you how to create a countdown timer using the micro:bit board. The countdown timer is started each time someone presses the button A. It displays how many seconds are left before the countdown is complete. It will start at the number 9 and count down until the timer is complete, at which stage it will clear the screen. Consulting a recipe like this can be useful whenever you are thinking of creating a project that requires the incorporation of elapsed time into your script.

Getting ready

You will need to have the Mu text editor installed and configured, as well as your micro:bit board connected to your computer.

How to do it...

Follow these steps to learn how to create a countdown timer:

1. Execute the following block of code in the REPL:

```
>>> from microbit import display, button_a
>>> import time
>>>
>>> NUMBERS = list(range(9, 0, -1))
```

2. The list of numbers that are used for the countdown will is stored in the NUMBERS variable. The following block of code will show their values:

```
>>> NUMBERS
[9, 8, 7, 6, 5, 4, 3, 2, 1]
```

3. The following block of code will define and call the `countdown` function. You should see the display show a countdown from 9 to 1, with a one-second delay between each change:

```
>>> def countdown():
...     for i in NUMBERS:
...         display.show(i)
...         time.sleep(1)
...     display.clear()
...
...
...
>>>
>>> countdown()
```

4. The following code should be put into the main text editor window and flashed to the board:

```
from microbit import display, button_a
import time

NUMBERS = list(range(9, 0, -1))


def countdown():
    for i in NUMBERS:
        display.show(i)
        time.sleep(1)
    display.clear()


while True:
    if button_a.is_pressed():
        countdown()
```

Once executed, this code will display a 9-second countdown each time the push button A is pressed.

How it works...

After the initial imports, the main script enters into an infinite loop that keeps checking for a button press event on button A. If it detects button A being pressed, it will call the countdown function to start the countdown. The countdown function loops through the list of numbers from 9 to 1.

In each loop, it will display the number and pause for 1 second before continuing to the next iteration. Once all nine iterations have completed, it clears the screen to mark the end of the timer.

There's more...

This recipe could be extended so that when you press button B, a different timer is started. Maybe button B would start a timer to count up from 1 to 9. You could also make button A start a stopwatch, and button B could stop the stopwatch and display the elapsed time.

See also

Here are a few references regarding this recipe:

- Documentation on the running_time function can be found at https://microbit-micropython.readthedocs.io/en/latest/microbit.html#microbit.running_time.
- Documentation on the utime module, which can be used on the micro:bit, can be found at https://microbit-micropython.readthedocs.io/en/latest/utime.html.

Controlling the ESP8266 **10**

In this chapter, we will introduce the Adafruit Feather HUZZAH ESP8266 microcontroller. The ESP8266 is one of the most popular MicroPython hardware options when your embedded project needs to have support for internet connectivity. This connectivity is achieved using the board's built-in Wi-Fi capabilities.

This chapter will explore two main ways to get REPL access on the board: through a USB connection, and also wireless over Wi-Fi. We will also look at a number of recipes that cover different aspects of interacting with the Wi-Fi features on the board.

By the end of this chapter, you will have learned all the core skills necessary so that you can get productive with this board and start building your own embedded projects using this versatile and inexpensive piece of internet-connected hardware.

In this chapter, we will cover the following topics:

- Using the REPL over a serial connection
- Scanning for available Wi-Fi networks
- Configuring settings for AP mode
- Connecting to an existing Wi-Fi network
- Using the WebREPL over Wi-Fi
- Transferring files with the WebREPL CLI
- Controlling the blue and red LEDs

Technical requirements

The code files for this chapter can be found in the `Chapter10` folder of this book's GitHub repository, available at `https://github.com/PacktPublishing/MicroPython-Cookbook`.

CircuitPython 3.1.2 was used for all the recipes in this chapter.

The Adafruit Feather HUZZAH ESP8266

The ESP8266 is an inexpensive microcontroller that's manufactured by Espressif Systems. It can run MicroPython and supports a full TCP/IP stack. Its built-in Wi-Fi supports 802.11b/g/n. The Adafruit Feather HUZZAH ESP8266 is a development board that comes with USB support for power and data connectivity.

The processor on this board runs at 80 MHz and comes with 4 MB of flash storage. The board comes with nine GPIO pins that can be connected to a number of other components. The board comes in a number of different versions. The following photo shows what this board looks like with the headers option:

The board also comes in a stacking header configuration that makes it possible to plug in additional components on top of the board, such as OLED displays and buttons. These upgrades can be plugged right in, without the need for soldering or breadboards. The following photo shows this version of the board, which has a stacking header:

You can also make your projects portable by powering the board with a rechargeable lithium ion polymer battery. These batteries can be connected to the board using its JST connector. The following photo shows a board connected to a lithium ion polymer battery:

The board has a built-in LiPoly charger, which can show the charging status using the indicator LED. The battery can then be charged whenever the board is connected with the USB cable.

Where can you buy these?

This chapter uses the Adafruit Feather HUZZAH ESP8266 microcontroller. We recommend purchasing the version with a stacking header. The Adafruit Assembled Feather HUZZAH ESP8266 Wi-Fi microcontroller with stacking headers can be purchased directly from Adafruit (`https://www.adafruit.com/product/3213`).

Using the REPL over a serial connection

This recipe will show you how to get REPL access to the ESP8266 using a serial connection over USB. Even though the real power and excitement of this board comes from connecting to it wirelessly, the first thing we need to do is connect to it with a simple USB connection. Once this connection is set up, then you can proceed with the remaining recipes in this chapter, which set up your wireless settings so that you can unplug the board and interact with it completely wirelessly.

This recipe will help you get started with your own wireless embedded projects by setting up that initial connectivity to the board in order to establish wireless connectivity. It is also a valuable tool when you have a configured board that is facing connectivity issues and you want to get access to it to debug whatever Wi-Fi issues you might be facing.

Getting ready

Either macOS or a Linux computer can be used for this recipe, and you need the screen command to be available. On macOS, the screen application is built-in and thus requires no installation. On Ubuntu Linux, the screen command can be installed with the apt `install screen` command.

How to do it...

Follow these steps to learn how to use the REPL over a serial connection:

1. Connect the ESP8266 to your computer using a USB cable.
2. Open the Terminal application.

3. On most Linux systems, the name of the device should be /dev/ttyUSB0. Confirm that this device exists by running the following command in the Terminal:

```
$ ls /dev/ttyUSB0
/dev/ttyUSB0
```

4. The preceding command should run successfully if the ESP8266 was successfully detected by the operating system.

5. Run the following command to start a REPL session with the board:

```
$ sudo screen /dev/ttyUSB0 115200
```

6. The previous command will start the screen command and connect to a device called /dev/ttyUSB0 at a baud rate of 115,200 bits per second. If the connection was established successfully, you should see a message such as the following in the Terminal:

```
Adafruit CircuitPython 3.1.2 on 2019-01-07; ESP module with ESP8266
>>>
>>>
```

7. Execute the following code in the REPL:

```
>>> import math
>>> math.pow(8,2)
64.0
>>> 8**2
64
```

The preceding block of code will import the math library and calculate the value of 8 to the power of 2.

How it works...

The ESP8266 exposes a serial device over the USB connection. This serial device can then be interacted with using a Terminal emulator-like screen. Once the screen is connected, you can then gain access to the REPL and start executing Python code on the board. Whenever you execute Python code in the REPL, the commands are sent to the board to be executed, and then the results of the commands are transmitted back to the Terminal emulator over the serial connection.

There's more...

There are many excellent free Terminal emulators available on all major operating systems. `picocom` and `minicom` are popular alternatives to screen on Unix systems. On Windows, the Terminal emulator PuTTY can be used, while macOS has an application called CoolTerm that can be used for this purpose.

See also

Here are a few references regarding this recipe:

- Documentation on connecting to Adafruit Feather HUZZAH ESP8266 can be found at `https://learn.adafruit.com/adafruit-feather-huzzah-esp8266`.
- Details on the `picocom` command can be found at `https://github.com/npat-efault/picocom`.

Scanning for available Wi-Fi networks

This recipe will show you how to use the ESP8266 to list all Wi-Fi networks that are available and can be connected to. We will introduce the MicroPython network library and explore how to use its objects to initialize the onboard Wi-Fi hardware.

Once these components have been set up, we can use them to run a scan for wireless networks and store the results of that scan for further inspection. This recipe can provide you with useful techniques so that you can test the Wi-Fi capabilities of your board. Usually, listing wireless networks is the first step that's needed before you can proceed and connect to them later.

Getting ready

You will need access to the REPL on the ESP8266 to run the code presented in this recipe.

How to do it...

Follow these steps to learn how to scan for available Wi-Fi networks:

1. Run the following lines of code in the REPL:

```
>>> import network
>>> station = network.WLAN(network.STA_IF)
```

2. The network library has now been imported and a WLAN object has been created, which will provide a `station` interface. The following block of code will activate the `station` interface:

```
>>> station.active(True)
```

3. The following block of code will scan for all available wireless networks and store the results in the `networks` variable:

```
>>> networks = station.scan()
scandone
```

4. The following block of code will output the contents of the `networks` variable and show how many networks were found:

```
>>> networks
[(b'My WiFi', b'\x80*\xa8\x84\xa6\xfa', 1, -72, 3, 0), (b'Why Fi',
b'\xc8Q\x95\x92\xaa\xd0', 1, -92, 4, 0), (b'Wi Oh Wi',
b'd\xd1T\x9a\xb3\xcd', 1, -90, 3, 0)]
>>> len(networks)
3
```

5. Run the following lines of code:

```
>>> names = [i[0] for i in networks]
>>> names
[b'My WiFi', b'Why Fi', b'Wi Oh Wi']
```

Once executed, the code will extract the names of wireless networks and store them in a variable called `names`, which is then inspected.

How it works...

MicroPython provides a module called `network` that can be used to interact with the Wi-Fi hardware on the ESP8266. The WLAN object is instantiated and provided with `network.STA_IF` for its first argument. This will return an object that is created as a `station` interface.

The `station` interfaces are needed when you want to connect the board to existing Wi-Fi networks. Before a scan can be performed, the station must be activated by calling the `active` method with the `True` value. Then, the `scan` method can be called on the station, which will scan for available networks. This method returns a list of tuples that we store in the `networks` variable.

We can then count the number of networks using the `len` function and loop through this list of tuples to extract the name of each network. The name, or **Service Set Identifier (SSID)**, of each network will be stored in the first value of the tuple. This value is retrieved from each item in the `networks` variable using list comprehension, which we then save in the `names` variable.

There's more...

This recipe created a WLAN object as a `station` interface. In later recipes, we will learn how to create another type of WLAN object that can be used to configure the device as an AP. Besides using the `scan` method to get the names of the wireless networks, you can also inspect other details about each network, such as the channel it uses and the authentication mode it accepts.

It's very helpful that the `scan` method returns its results as a simple data structure that you can store and process in the rest of your program. This makes it possible to create projects that periodically scan the available networks and save the results to a log file.

See also

Here are a few references regarding this recipe:

- Documentation on the `scan` method can be found at `https://docs.micropython.org/en/latest/library/network.html#network.AbstractNIC.scan`.

- Documentation on the `active` method can be found at `https://docs.micropython.org/en/latest/library/network.html#network.AbstractNIC.active`.

Configuring settings for AP mode

This recipe will show you how to configure the **access point** (**AP**) mode on the ESP8266. Once configured, the board will become a Wi-Fi AP, and you can connect laptops and phones directly to the board using a standard Wi-Fi connection.

Wi-Fi is so ubiquitous that this feature becomes a very powerful way to offer connectivity. You can use the technique shown in this recipe to incorporate Wi-Fi AP functionality into your own projects. This lets you establish wireless connections between your board and a phone or laptop, even when there are no other access points available.

Getting ready

You will need access to the REPL on the ESP8266 to run the code presented in this recipe.

How to do it...

Follow these steps to learn how to configure the settings for AP mode:

1. Execute the following block of code in the REPL:

```
>>> import network
>>> ap = network.WLAN(network.AP_IF)
```

2. The `network` library has now been imported and a WLAN object has been created for AP mode. The following block of code will configure and activate the AP:

```
>>> ap.config(essid='PyWifi', password='12345678')
bcn 0
del if1
pm open,type:2 0
add if1
pm close 7
#7 ets_task(4020f4c0, 29, 3fff96f8, 10)
dhcp server
```

```
start:(ip:192.168.4.1,mask:255.255.255.0,gw:192.168.4.1)
bcn 100
>>> ap.active(True)
```

3. Search and join the AP called `PyWifi` using a phone or laptop. The following output should appear in the REPL:

```
>>> add 1
aid 1
station: b0:35:9f:2c:69:aa join, AID = 1

>>>
```

4. Connect another device to the same AP. You should see details of the joined device in the REPL output, as shown in the following block of code:

```
>>> add 2
aid 2
station: 34:2d:0d:8c:40:bb join, AID = 2

>>>
```

5. The board will also report devices that disconnect from the AP. Disconnect one of the connected devices from the AP—the following output should appear in the REPL:

```
>>> station: 34:2d:0d:8c:40:bb leave, AID = 2
rm 2

>>>
```

6. Run the following code in the REPL:

```
>>> ap.ifconfig()
('192.168.4.1', '255.255.255.0', '192.168.4.1', '8.8.8.8')
>>>
```

The preceding code will get details about the IP address and subnet mask of the AP.

How it works...

The MicroPython firmware provides functionality to create Wi-Fi access points using the ESP8266. To use this functionally, we must first create a WLAN object and pass it the `network.AP_IF` value for its first argument. This will return an object that can be used to enable AP mode. The `config` method is then called, passing the desired name of the Wi-Fi network and the password that will be used for devices to connect to the AP.

Finally, the AP must be activated by calling the `active` method with the `True` value. The board is then ready to receive connections. As devices join and leave the network, these details will be automatically printed as output to the REPL session.

There's more...

As we saw in this recipe, multiple devices can be connected to the board at the same time. You can use this recipe as a starting point to experiment with this feature. You can, for example, connect a laptop and mobile phone to the AP and attempt to ping different devices on the Wi-Fi network. You could even ping your mobile phone or the ESP8266 board from your laptop.

In later chapters, we'll learn how to run a web server on the board, and then you will be able to move beyond ping and interact with the board using your web browser over Wi-Fi.

See also

Here are a few references regarding this recipe:

- Documentation on the `config` method can be found at `https://docs.micropython.org/en/latest/library/network.html#network.AbstractNIC.config`.
- Documentation on the `ifconfig` method can be found at `https://docs.micropython.org/en/latest/library/network.html#network.AbstractNIC.ifconfig`.

Connecting to an existing Wi-Fi network

This recipe will show you how to connect the ESP8266 to an existing Wi-Fi network. There are many benefits to joining an existing Wi-Fi network. Doing so makes it possible to wirelessly access the board from different devices on your network. It also provides the board with internet connectivity through the Wi-Fi network's internet connection. You can use the approach shown in this recipe to connect your own embedded projects to different networks and help enable internet connectivity in these projects.

Getting ready

You will need access to the REPL on the ESP8266 to run the code presented in this recipe.

How to do it...

Follow these steps to learn how to connect to an existing Wi-Fi network:

1. Use the REPL to run the following lines of code:

```
>>> import network
>>> station = network.WLAN(network.STA_IF)
>>> station.active(True)
```

2. The WLAN object has now been created and activated. Use the following block of code to verify that the AP you want to connect to appears in the list of available networks:

```
>>> networks = station.scan()
scandone
>>> names = [i[0] for i in networks]
>>> names
[b'MyAmazingWiFi', b'Why Fi', b'Wi Oh Wi']
```

3. The following line of code will connect to the Wi-Fi AP:

```
>>> station.connect('MyAmazingWiFi', 'MyAmazingPassword')
ap_loss
scandone
state: 5 -> 0 (0)
rm 0
reconnect
>>> scandone
state: 0 -> 2 (b0)
```

```
state: 2 -> 3 (0)
state: 3 -> 5 (10)
add 0
aid 1
cnt

connected with MyAmazingWiFi, channel 6
dhcp client start...
ip:192.168.43.110,mask:255.255.255.0,gw:192.168.43.1

>>>
```

4. The following block of code will return a Boolean value that will indicate whether we are currently connected to the AP:

```
>>> station.isconnected()
True
```

5. The following lines of code will get details about our current network connection, including the board's IP address, subnet mask, gateway, and DNS server:

```
>>> station.ifconfig()
('192.168.43.110', '255.255.255.0', '192.168.43.1', '192.168.43.1')
>>>
```

6. Run the following block of code:

```
>>> station.active(False)
state: 5 -> 0 (0)
rm 0
del if0
mode : softAP(86:f3:eb:b2:9b:aa)
>>>
```

Once run, this code will make the board disconnect from the AP.

How it works...

The MicroPython firmware has the ability to connect to existing Wi-Fi access points using the ESP8266. To do this, you must create a WLAN object and pass it the network.STA_IF value for its first argument. This object is saved into a variable called station in this recipe. The station object is then activated by calling the active method with a True value. Once activated, the connect method can be called with the name of the AP to connect to and its associated password. Once called, the connect method will print out a lot of information as the connection proceeds.

We can then check whether or not we are connected at any time by calling the `isconnected` method on the station object. This will return the `True` value if we are connected, or the `False` value otherwise. Then, we can retrieve network details about our IP address and DNS server by calling the `ifconfig` method. Finally, the `active` method can be called with a `False` argument to make the board disconnect from the network.

There's more...

This recipe is packed with a number of different methods regarding the WLAN object that can be called and used. It showed you how to list networks, connect to them, poll the connection status, get network information about our current network, and how to disconnect from the network.

Using these methods, you can create a program that periodically scans nearby networks looking for a specific network. Whenever it is found, you can connect to it automatically. You could also write a different script that keeps polling the status of your network connectivity and updates a status LED that turns on to indicate that the Wi-Fi is connected, and off for disconnected.

See also

Here are a few references regarding this recipe:

- Documentation on the `connect` method can be found at `https://docs.micropython.org/en/latest/library/network.html#network.AbstractNIC.connect`.
- Documentation on the `isconnected` method can be found at `https://docs.micropython.org/en/latest/library/network.html#network.AbstractNIC.isconnected`.

Using the WebREPL over Wi-Fi

This recipe will show you how to use the WebREPL feature that is available on the ESP8266 board with MicroPython. The WebREPL is a service that can be started on the board and lets computers on your network wirelessly access the REPL through a web browser. We have seen how to access the REPL using the serial connection in the *Using the REPL over a serial connection* recipe in this chapter.

This recipe will equip you with the skills you need to get a REPL over Wi-Fi, making it possible to remotely debug and execute code on the board, even when you don't have a direct physical connection to it.

Getting ready

You will need access to the REPL on the ESP8266 to run the code presented in this recipe. You should follow the previous recipe, *Connecting to an existing Wi-Fi network*, before completing this recipe as you will use that recipe to connect the board to your network and get its IP address.

How to do it...

Follow these steps to learn how to use the WebREPL over Wi-Fi:

1. Run the following lines of code in the REPL:

   ```
   >>> import webrepl_setup
   ```

2. The WebREPL configuration wizard will now start, asking you a series of questions so that the service can be configured. Respond to the following question with the letter E to enable the service at boot-up:

   ```
   WebREPL daemon auto-start status: disabled

   Would you like to (E)nable or (D)isable it running on boot?
   (Empty line to quit)
   > E
   ```

3. The next set of questions will ask you to enter and confirm the WebREPL password:

   ```
   To enable WebREPL, you must set password for it
   New password (4-9 chars): secret123
   Confirm password: secret123
   ```

4. Answer y (yes) for the next question so that the board can be rebooted and have the changes applied:

```
Changes will be activated after reboot
Would you like to reboot now? (y/n) y
Rebooting. Please manually reset if it hangs.
state: 5 -> 0 (0)
rm 0
del if0
bcn 0
del if1
usl
load 0x40100000, len 31012, room 16
tail 4
chksum 0x61
load 0x3ffe8000, len 1100, room 4
tail 8
chksum 0x4e
load 0x3ffe8450, len 3264, room 0
tail 0
chksum 0x0f
csum 0x0f
boot.py output:
WebREPL daemon started on ws://192.168.4.1:8266
WebREPL daemon started on ws://0.0.0.0:8266
Started webrepl in normal mode
```

5. You can see from the preceding output that once the board is booted up, it will show that the WebREPL service has been started and the URL that can be used to access the service.

6. Download the WebREPL software from `https://github.com/micropython/webrepl` by clicking on the **Clone or download** button.

7. Extract the downloaded `.zip` file into any folder on your computer.

5. Open the `webrepl.html` file in any modern web browser. You should see the following interface appear in your web browser:

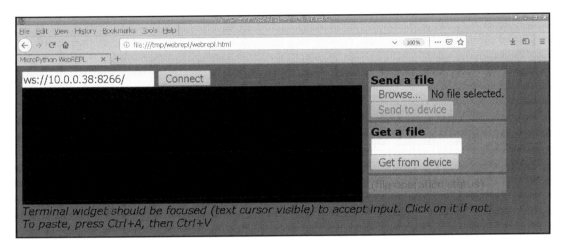

9. Enter the URL of your device's WebREPL service in the text box next to the **Connect** button. In the previous screenshot, the IP address of the board was `10.0.0.38`, so it's given the URL `ws://10.0.0.38:8266`.

10. Now, click on the **Connect** button and enter the WebREPL password when prompted. The following screenshot shows a WebREPL session where the `math` module is imported and the value of pi is displayed:

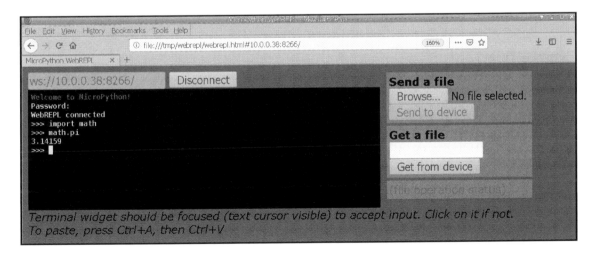

11. The WebREPL also has the ability to upload files to the board. You can take a Python script called `main.py` that you would like to be uploaded to the board and upload it using this feature.

12. Click on the **Browse...** button under **Send a file**.

13. Select your `main.py` file.

14. Click on the **Send to device** button.

15. The following screenshot shows an example of a successful upload message that will appear after you upload a file to the board:

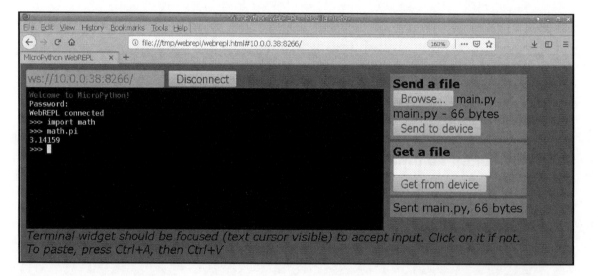

The message on the screen confirms that the file was sent and reports the number of bytes that were transmitted.

How it works...

The MicroPython firmware comes with a built-in WebREPL server. Once you import the `webrepl_setup` module, it will start an interactive wizard that will let you enable the service. Set its password and configure it to run each time you boot up the board. Once this service runs, it exposes a WebSocket service that can receive connections from the WebREPL client running in the browser.

The WebREPL client doesn't need any special installation—it is just an HTML file that can be extracted locally to you computer and then opened in your web browser. Through this client, you can now specify the address of the board you want to connect to, and establish a connection to the board. Once connected, you will have an interactive REPL session in the web browser, as well as the ability to upload files to the board.

There's more...

This recipe focused on one of the WebREPL clients. The client that was shown in this recipe is intended to run in your web browser and make the process of working with your board over Wi-Fi an easy process. There is also a WebREPL client that can be run from the Terminal using a **command-line interface** (**CLI**) instead of the web browser.

Unlike the web browser client, the CLI version is written completely in Python. This gives you a great opportunity to explore the internals of how WebREPL transfers files over web sockets. The CLI version will be explored in more depth in the next recipe.

See also

Here are a few references regarding this recipe:

- Documentation on accessing the WebREPL can be found at `https://docs.micropython.org/en/latest/esp8266/tutorial/repl.html#webrepl-a-prompt-over-wifi`.
- A guide on connecting to the WebREPL can be found at `https://learn.adafruit.com/micropython-basics-esp8266-webrepl/`.

Transferring files with the WebREPL CLI

This recipe will show you how we can use the WebREPL CLI to transfer files from a computer to the ESP8266 over Wi-Fi. This is a very powerful way of transferring files to the board. Each time you make changes to your Python code and want to try the latest change, you have to upload the file to the board. Doing this with your web browser over and over again can become tedious.

The beauty of using the CLI interface is that most Terminals remember their last executed commands, so you can rerun the last command with two simple keystrokes: you just press the *up* arrow key and the *Enter* key. This will make your cycle of code, upload, and run much faster and more productive.

Getting ready

You will need access to the REPL on the ESP8266 to run the code presented in this recipe. You should follow the previous recipe, *Using the WebREPL over Wi-Fi*, before tackling this recipe to ensure that the WebREPL is working correctly.

How to do it...

Follow these steps to learn how to transfer files with the WebREPL CLI:

1. Download the WebREPL software from `https://github.com/micropython/webrepl` by clicking on the **Clone or download** button.
2. Extract the downloaded `.zip` file into any folder on your computer.
3. The extracted files will contain a script called `webrepl_cli.py`.
4. Open a Terminal and change the working directory to the location of the `webrepl_cli.py` script.
5. Execute the following command in the Terminal to see the command's options:

```
$ python webrepl_cli.py --help
webrepl_cli.py - Perform remote file operations using MicroPython
WebREPL protocol
Arguments:
  [-p password] <host>:<remote_file> <local_file> - Copy remote
file to local file
  [-p password] <local_file> <host>:<remote_file> - Copy local file
to remote file
Examples:
  webrepl_cli.py script.py 192.168.4.1:/another_name.py
  webrepl_cli.py script.py 192.168.4.1:/app/
  webrepl_cli.py -p password 192.168.4.1:/app/script.py .
```

6. Run the following command to upload the `main.py` script to the board. You will need to enter the WebREPL password when prompted for it:

```
$ python webrepl_cli.py  main.py 10.0.0.38:/
Password:
op:put, host:10.0.0.38, port:8266, passwd:secret123.
main.py -> /main.py
Remote WebREPL version: (3, 1, 2)
Sent 73 of 73 bytes
```

7. The following command is very similar to the previous one:

```
$ python webrepl_cli.py -p secret123 main.py 10.0.0.38:/
op:put, host:10.0.0.38, port:8266, passwd:secret123.
main.py -> /main.py
Remote WebREPL version: (3, 1, 2)
Sent 73 of 73 bytes
```

The main difference is that the password is provided in the command line as a command-line option.

How it works...

This recipe starts with a simple command-line invocation of the `webrepl_cli.py` script to show details regarding the command-line options. It's a good idea to start with this command to at least verify that Python is executing the script successfully and producing the output you would expect.

The next time the command is called, it is used to upload the `main.py` script to the board. This is definitely a viable way of uploading scripts. However, its main downside is that you have to enter the password each time you upload the script. This can be addressed as it was in the previous example, where the password is provided on the command line. With the final example, the command can be run repeatedly with just a few key strokes.

There's more...

This command can be a real time-saver when you are repeatedly uploading scripts to your board. You can also take it and combine it with other command-line software that watches for changes in a specific folder. For example, you could have this command automatically upload any changes to `main.py` each time the file changes by combining these two pieces of software.

Please note that, as mentioned in this command's documentation, file transferring is still in alpha stage and has some known issues. If you find that the script is getting stuck after a few uploads, the most effective way to address this is to do a hard reset. This can be done by running the following block of code:

```
import machine
machine.reset()
```

This can also be done by pressing the reset button on the board.

See also

Here are a few references regarding this recipe:

- Documentation on performing hard resets can be found at `http://docs.micropython.org/en/v1.8.6/wipy/wipy/tutorial/reset.html`
- Documentation on using the `webrepl_cli.py` file to upload files can be found at `https://micropython-on-esp8266-workshop.readthedocs.io/en/latest/basics.html#uploading-files`.

Controlling the blue and red LEDs

The ESP8266 comes with two LEDs: one that's red, and another that's blue. Both of these LEDs can be controlled from the scripts you load on the board. This recipe will show you how you can control each one, and will end with an animation that blinks the lights between red and blue.

The techniques that are shown in this recipe can be used in your own projects whenever you want to signal some sort of status to your users. You might want to have a blinking blue light when you are scanning for a Wi-Fi network, or to light up the red light when your board has lost its network connectivity.

Getting ready

You will need access to the REPL on the ESP8266 to run the code presented in this recipe.

How to do it...

Follow these steps to learn how to control the blue and red LEDs:

1. Execute the following block of code in the REPL:

```
>>> from machine import Pin
>>> red = Pin(0, Pin.OUT)
>>> red.value(0)
```

2. The red LED should now be turned on. Run the following block of code to turn the red LED off:

```
>>> red.value(1)
```

3. The following block of code will turn on the blue LED:

```
>>> blue = Pin(2, Pin.OUT)
>>> blue.value(0)
```

4. The following code will switch the blue LED off:

```
>>> blue.value(1)
```

5. Run the following block of code:

```
>>> import time
>>>
>>> while True:
...        blue.value(0)
...        red.value(1)
...        time.sleep(1)
...        blue.value(1)
...        red.value(0)
...        time.sleep(1)
...
...
...
```

The preceding code will create a light animation that switches between the red and blue light with a one second delay between each change.

How it works...

First, the Pin object is imported from the machine module. This object will let us directly connect to the **general-purpose input/output (GPIO)** pins that come with the ESP8266 board. The red LED is connected on pin number 0. The Pin object that's assigned to the red variable is connected to the red LED. Once this object is created, setting its value to 0 turns the light on and setting its value to 1 turns the light off.

The blue variable is defined as the Pin object connected to GPIO pin 2, which maps to the blue LED. It can be turned on and off in the same way. The last part of this recipe is an infinite loop that first turns the blue LED on and the red LED off.

A sleep delay of 1 second is applied before the blue LED is switched off and the red LED is turned on. Another sleep delay of 1 second is applied before the loop starts again from the start, performing the same actions.

There's more...

This recipe shows you how to control the two LEDs that come with the board. Additional LEDs can be connected to the other available GPIO pins and can be controlled in a similar fashion. The board comes with 9 available GPIO pins. Beyond simple single color LEDs, the same GPIO pins can be used to connect NeoPixels, which offer a full range of colors, as they combine different levels of red, green, and blue LEDs.

See also

Here are a few references regarding this recipe:

- Documentation on interacting with pins and the GPIO can be found at `https://docs.micropython.org/en/latest/esp8266/quickref.html#pins-and-gpio`.
- A tutorial on interacting with the GPIO pins can be found at `https://docs.micropython.org/en/latest/esp8266/tutorial/pins.html`.

Interacting with the Filesystem

11

In this chapter, we will cover a number of recipes, all relating to interacting with the filesystem. The first recipe will touch on how to remount the filesystem on devices that require this before you can modify any files using your Python code.

Then, recipes on listing, removing, and creating files will be covered. Also, more advanced topics, such as calculating disk usage, will be covered. The recipes in this chapter will give you the tools you need to add filesystem interaction to your embedded projects. This can come in handy when you want to log sensor data to a file, or when you want your code to read and load a set of files into a data structure. It can also be helpful when you have to list a set of images to be displayed in your application.

In this chapter, we will be covering the following recipes:

- Remounting the filesystem
- Listing files
- Removing files
- Creating a directory
- Reading a file's contents
- Writing a file's contents
- Calculating disk usage

Technical requirements

The code files for this chapter can be found in the `Chapter11` folder in this book's GitHub repository, available at `https://github.com/PacktPublishing/MicroPython-Cookbook`.

CircuitPython 3.1.2 was used for all the recipes in this chapter.

Remounting the filesystem

This recipe will show you how to remount the filesystem so that it can have data written to it from your Python scripts. Some boards, such as Circuit Playground Express, will expose the connected device as a USB drive by default to make it easy to edit and save your code. The trade-off of this approach, however, is that your Python code cannot write or change any of the contents on the board's storage. On these boards, you must remount the filesystem to allow your script to write data to its filesystem.

By the end of this recipe, you'll know how to allow data to be written to the filesystem, and how to revert changes, which will become essential for certain projects. If, for example, you wanted to use Circuit Playground Express to record temperature readings to a log file, you would need to utilize this type of approach.

Getting ready

You will need access to the REPL on Circuit Playground Express to run the code presented in this recipe.

How to do it...

Follow these steps to learn how to remount the filesystem:

1. Run the following lines of code in the REPL:

```
>>> f = open('main.py')
```

2. The Python code was able to open a file for reading. However, if you try and open a file to write, as shown in the following code block, you will get an OSError instance because the filesystem is in read-only mode:

```
>>> f = open('hi.txt', 'w')
Traceback (most recent call last):
  File "<stdin>", line 1, in <module>
OSError: 30
>>>
```

3. We will now create a script that will remount the filesystem to allow the reading and writing of data.

4. The following code should be saved into the `boot.py` file. If the file doesn't exist, then you will have to create it:

```
import storage
storage.remount('/', False)
```

5. Eject the `CIRCUITPY` drive from your computer.

6. Unplug the board from your computer.

7. Reconnect the board to your computer.

8. Run the following lines of code in the REPL to confirm that your code can write data to a file on the board's storage:

```
>>> f = open('hi.txt', 'w')
>>> f.write('hi there')
8
>>> f.close()
```

9. The following block of code, when run in the REPL, will remove the `boot.py` file:

```
>>> import os
>>> os.remove('boot.py')
```

10. To apply these changes to the boot process, eject the `CIRCUITPY` drive from your computer again.

11. Unplug the board from your computer.

12. Reconnect the board to your computer.

13. You should be able to edit and save the contents of the `main.py` file, just like you did previously.

How it works...

Circuit Playground Express provides you with a way to enable reading and writing to the storage from your Python scripts. We put the code in the `boot.py` file as this script will be run early on in the boot process, before the `main.py` file (which will include our main code base).

In the `boot.py` script, we import the `storage` module and then calls its `remount` function with the second argument set as `False`, indicating that the filesystem should be mounted in read and write mode. Whenever we make changes to the `boot.py` file, whether it is creating or removing the file, we must do a hard reset on the board by unplugging and reconnecting the board for the changes to take effect. As shown in this recipe, the simplest way to revert this change is to delete the `boot.py` file from the REPL.

There's more...

Generally speaking, only boards that offer the USB-drive editing feature will require this extra step of remounting the filesystem. For example, the ESP8266 does not have the USB drive feature, and so it doesn't require this step. It's also important to note that once you enable writing to the filesystem from your code, you won't be able to edit your `main.py` file in your text editor. Whenever you want to go back to editing your code, you will have to remove the `boot.py` file. If your project only needs read-only access to the filesystem, to do things such as listing files and reading a file's contents, then you can run it safely in either mode.

See also

Here are a few references regarding this recipe:

- Documentation on the `mount` function can be found at `https://circuitpython.readthedocs.io/en/3.x/shared-bindings/storage/__init__.html#storage.mount`.
- Documentation on writing to the filesystem can be found at `https://learn.adafruit.com/cpu-temperature-logging-with-circuit-python/writing-to-the-filesystem`.

Listing files

This recipe will show you how you can list files and directories in MicroPython. We will also show the techniques that you can use to filter a listing so that it only includes files or only includes directories. Once you have the ability to interact with the filesystem in this way, you can use it in your own projects, where your code will accept a dynamic list of files on the board that doesn't need to be hardcoded in your program. In this way, the files might represent a set of configurable audio files that you want to play, or a collection of images that you will display on an attached screen.

Getting ready

You will need access to the REPL on Circuit Playground Express to run the code presented in this recipe.

How to do it...

Follow these steps to learn how to list files:

1. Execute the following block of code in the REPL:

```
>>> import os
>>> os.listdir()
['.fseventsd', '.metadata_never_index', '.Trashes', 'boot_out.txt',
'main.py', 'lib']
```

2. A listing of all the files and directories in the top-level folder will have been generated. The following block of code will generate the same listing, but a sorted one:

```
>>> sorted(os.listdir())
['.Trashes', '.fseventsd', '.metadata_never_index', 'boot_out.txt',
'lib', 'main.py']
```

3. We can also list files in a specific directory, as shown in the following block of code:

```
>>> os.listdir('.fseventsd')
['no_log']
```

4. The following block of code will check and show that the lib path is not a file:

```
>>> FILE_CODE  = 0x8000
>>>
>>> os.stat('lib')[0] == FILE_CODE
False
```

5. We will now confirm that main.py is detected as a file:

```
>>> os.stat('main.py')[0] == FILE_CODE
True
```

6. The following block of code defines and calls the `isfile` function on two paths to verify their type:

```
>>> def isfile(path):
...         return os.stat(path)[0] == FILE_CODE
...
...
...
>>> isfile('lib')
False
>>> isfile('main.py')
True
>>>
```

7. The following block of code will list all the files in the root path:

```
>>> files = [i for i in sorted(os.listdir()) if isfile(i)]
>>> files
['.Trashes', '.metadata_never_index', 'boot_out.txt', 'main.py']
```

8. Now, we will list all the directories in the root path:

```
>>> dirs = [i for i in sorted(os.listdir()) if not isfile(i)]
>>> dirs
['.fseventsd', 'lib']
```

9. The following code should be put into the `main.py` file:

```
import os

FILE_CODE = 0x8000


def isfile(path):
    return os.stat(path)[0] == FILE_CODE


def main():
    files = [i for i in sorted(os.listdir()) if isfile(i)]
    print('files:', files)
    dirs = [i for i in sorted(os.listdir()) if not isfile(i)]
    print('dirs:', dirs)


main()
```

When executed, this script will print out the sorted listing of files and directories in the root path.

How it works...

After importing the os module, a function called `isfile` is defined that will return `True` or `False`, depending on whether the provided path is a file or a directory. The `main` function is defined and called, after which it will generate a list of path names. The first list will retrieve the sorted list of paths and then filter the list so that only files are retained. This list is then printed. The same approach is then taken to get a list of directories and print them out.

There's more...

This recipe has introduced a number of techniques that can come in handy when dealing with files. It showed that file listings are not returned in alphabetical order by default, so if this is needed, the built-in `sorted` function can be used to sort the list of files. It also defines a function called `isfile` to inspect whether a specific path is a file. You could create an equivalent `isdir` function if so desired. This recipe also showed a simple approach of using list comprehensions to filter out the default listing to generate filtered lists of paths that contain only certain types of entries, such as files or directories.

See also

Here are a few references regarding this recipe:

- Documentation on the `listdir` function can be found at `https://circuitpython.readthedocs.io/en/3.x/shared-bindings/os/__init__.html#os.listdir`.
- Documentation on the `stat` function can be found at `https://circuitpython.readthedocs.io/en/3.x/shared-bindings/os/__init__.html#os.stat`.
- Documentation on the `isfile` function can be found at `https://docs.python.org/3/library/os.path.html#os.path.isfile`.

Removing files

This recipe will show you how you can remove files and directories in MicroPython. There are separate functions for deleting a file and deleting a directory. We will show you how to call these different functions for each type of path. Then, we will show you how you can create a generic function that can automatically remove either type of path.

There are many situations in the projects that you create where you need to resort to deleting files. You might create a project that logs data to a file. Log rotation is a mechanism that lets you create new log files periodically and remove old ones automatically. You will need functions that delete files in order to implement log rotation. The issue of removing files to conserve space becomes even more important in many MicroPython-embedded projects because you are often dealing with limited storage capacity on these boards.

Getting ready

You will need access to the REPL on Circuit Playground Express to run the code presented in this recipe. Make sure that you've completed the *Remounting the filesystem* recipe of this chapter, as you'll need write access to the storage system in order to remove files.

How to do it...

Follow these steps to learn how to remove files:

1. Create a file called hi.txt in the root path.
2. Use the REPL to run the following lines of code:

   ```
   >>> import os
   >>> os.remove('hi.txt')
   ```

3. The hi.txt file has now been deleted from the board's filesystem. Run the following block of code. It should go through an exception because the file does not exist anymore:

   ```
   >>> os.remove('hi.txt')
   Traceback (most recent call last):
     File "<stdin>", line 1, in <module>
   OSError: [Errno 2] No such file/directory
   >>>
   ```

4. Create a directory called mydir in the root path.
5. The following block of code will delete the mydir directory:

   ```
   >>> os.rmdir('mydir')
   ```

6. The following block of code defines the `isfile` function:

```
>>> FILE_CODE = 0x8000
>>>
>>> def isfile(path):
...     return os.stat(path)[0] == FILE_CODE
...
...
...
>>>
```

7. We can now define a function called `any_remove` that will remove any type of path:

```
>>> def any_remove(path):
...     func = os.remove if isfile(path) else os.rmdir
...     func(path)
...
...
...
>>>
```

8. Create a file called `hi.txt` and a directory called `mydir`.

9. Run the following block of code:

```
>>> any_remove('hi.txt')
>>> any_remove('mydir')
>>>
```

The preceding block of code has now deleted this file and directory using the same function call.

How it works...

The `any_remove` function that is defined first takes the path and sets a variable called `func`. This variable will store the callable that needs to be called to delete the provided path. The type of the path is checked and `func` is set as either `os.remove` or `os.rmdir`, depending on the type of path that's provided. This function is then called with the provided path to perform the actual deletion.

There's more...

This recipe has introduced a technique that you can use to create a convenience function that accepts any type of path and will call the correct underlying function to remove it. One thing to keep in mind is that you can only delete a directory that is empty. The functions and examples in this recipe support deleting directories that are empty, but will fail if called with a directory that has files inside it. You could extend the `delete` function to do recursive directory listings and then delete all the subfolders and directories.

See also

Here are a few references regarding this recipe:

- Documentation on the `remove` function can be found at `https://circuitpython.readthedocs.io/en/3.x/shared-bindings/os/__init__.html#os.remove`.
- Documentation on the `rmdir` function can be found at `https://circuitpython.readthedocs.io/en/3.x/shared-bindings/os/__init__.html#os.rmdir`.

Creating a directory

This recipe will show you how to create a directory in MicroPython. We will also show you how to create a function that can be called multiple times with the same path and will only create a directory if the directory doesn't exist yet. Then, we will define a function to behave just like the `makedirs` function, which is a part of the Python standard library but is not included in MicroPython.

These set of features can be useful whenever you need to create a project that might necessitate the creation a specific directory tree and then populate it with a certain set of files. It also helps to have access to these functions when you are working on a board such as the ESP8266, which will only let you create the directories you need through the REPL and your Python code.

Getting ready

You will need access to the REPL on Circuit Playground Express to run the code presented in this recipe. Make sure that you've completed the *Remounting the filesystem* recipe in this chapter since write access to the storage system is needed for this recipe.

How to do it...

Follow these steps to learn how to create a directory:

1. Run the following lines of code in the REPL:

    ```
    >>> import os
    >>> os.mkdir('mydir')
    ```

2. A directory called `mydir` has now been created. When you run the following block of code, an exception will be raised because the directory already exists:

    ```
    >>> os.mkdir('mydir')
    Traceback (most recent call last):
      File "<stdin>", line 1, in <module>
    OSError: [Errno 17] File exists
    >>>
    ```

3. The following block of code will define a function that returns `True` or `False`, depending on whether a path exists or not:

    ```
    >>> def exists(path):
    ...     try:
    ...         os.stat(path)
    ...     except OSError:
    ...         return False
    ...     return True
    ...
    ...
    ...
    >>>
    ```

4. The following block of code will call the `exists` function on two different paths to verify it is working correctly:

    ```
    >>> exists('main.py')
    True
    >>> exists('invalid_path')
    False
    ```

5. We can now define a function called `mkdir_safe`, which will only make directories when they don't exist:

```
>>> def mkdir_safe(path):
...     if not exists(path):
...         os.mkdir(path)
...
...
...
>>>
```

6. The following block of code will call the `mkdir_safe` function multiple times on the same path, with no exceptions being thrown:

```
>>> mkdir_safe('newdir')
>>> mkdir_safe('newdir')
```

7. We will now define a function that will recursively create directories:

```
>>> def makedirs(path):
...     items = path.strip('/').split('/')
...     count = len(items)
...     paths = ['/' + '/'.join(items[0:i + 1]) for i in
...     range(count)]
...     for path in paths:
...         os.mkdir(path)
...
...
...
>>>
```

8. Run the following block of code:

```
>>> makedirs('/top/middle/bottom')
```

The preceding block of code, when executed, will create three directories in the correct order, from top to bottom.

How it works...

In this recipe, three different functions were defined and used, each one performing a specific function. The `exists` function checks whether a path exists and returns `True` or `False`. This check attempted to call the `stat` function on a path and catches any `OSError` that might be raised. If the path exists, this exception won't be raised and a `True` value is returned; otherwise, a `False` value is returned.

The next function, `mkdir_safe`, simply checks if a path exists and only calls the `mkdir` function on paths that don't exist. Finally, the `makedirs` function is defined, which receives a path with multiple levels. The path is split into its separate pieces, and then the list of paths to be created is saved in a list in the correct order, from the highest path to the lowest path. Each path is looped through and created by calling the `mkdir` function.

There's more...

This recipe introduced three generic functions, each of which serve a specific purpose. By creating pieces of code in this fashion, it makes it easier to take pieces of one project and incorporate them into others. Two of the defined functions—`exists` and `makedirs`—are a part of the Python standard library, but are not found in MicroPython. This recipe demonstrates that, in many cases, even when there is some function in the Python standard library that you miss, you can frequently create your own implementation in MicroPython.

See also

Here are a few references regarding this recipe:

- Documentation on the `mkdir` function can be found at `https://circuitpython. readthedocs.io/en/3.x/shared-bindings/os/__init__.html#os.mkdir`.
- Documentation on the `makedirs` function can be found at `https://docs. python.org/3/library/os.html#os.makedirs`.
- Documentation on the `exists` function can be found at `https://docs.python. org/3/library/os.path.html#os.path.exists`.

Reading a file's contents

This recipe will show you how to read the contents of a file into variables in your scripts. This recipe will cover ways of reading in file contents as a string, as well as reading it in as a byte object. Many projects that you create will often need to open different data files, such as audio files, images, and text files. This recipe will provide you with the basic building blocks so that you can facilitate these interactions.

Getting ready

You will need access to the REPL on Circuit Playground Express to run the code presented in this recipe.

How to do it...

Follow these steps to learn how to read a file's contents:

1. Create a file called `hi.txt` in the root path with the following contents:

   ```
   hi there
   ```

2. Execute the following block of code in the REPL:

   ```
   >>> f = open('hi.txt')
   >>> data = f.read()
   >>> f.close()
   >>> data
   'hi there\n'
   ```

3. The contents of the file called `hi.txt` are read into a variable called `data`, which is then displayed as output. The following block of code also reads the file's contents into a variable, but uses the `with` statement:

   ```
   >>> with open('hi.txt') as f:
   ...       data = f.read()
   ...
   ...
   >>> data
   'hi there\n'
   ```

4. It is possible to read the file's contents into a variable with a single line of code, as shown in the following example:

   ```
   >>> data = open('hi.txt').read()
   >>> data
   'hi there\n'
   ```

5. Execute the following block of code:

   ```
   >>> data = open('hi.txt', 'rb').read()
   >>> data
   b'hi there\n'
   >>> type(data)
   <class 'bytes'>
   ```

The preceding block of code, when executed, will read the file's contents as a `bytes` object instead of a string.

How it works...

In this recipe, we have explored four different ways of reading data from a file. The first method uses the `open` function to get a file object. Then, data is read from this file object and closed. We can then improve upon this older style of file handling, as shown in the second example, by using the `with` statement, which will automatically close the file once we exit the `with` block. The third example opens and reads the contents all in one line. The `open` function accepts the file mode since it's the second argument. If we pass it the `rb` value, then it will open the file for reading in binary mode. This will then result in a bytes object being returned, instead of a string.

There's more...

You will need to choose the correct method of reading file data, depending on the data you expect to interact with. If your data files are plain text files, then the default text mode will suffice. However, if you're reading raw audio data in the `.wav` file format, which you will need to do to read in the data as binary data, exceptions may occur because the data might not be able to be decoded into strings.

See also

Here are a few references regarding this recipe:

- Documentation on the `open` function can be found at `https://docs.python.org/3/library/functions.html#open`.
- Documentation on the `with` statement can be found at `https://docs.python.org/3/reference/compound_stmts.html#with`.

Writing a file's contents

This recipe will show you how to write data to an output file. We will cover how to write strings, as well as bytes, to a file. We will then define a type of object to make it easier to perform these common operations of writing text and binary data to files. If you want to create a project that saves sensor data to a log file or records some user-generated data to the board's storage, then you will need to use many of the techniques we'll describe in this recipe.

Getting ready

You will need access to the REPL on Circuit Playground Express to run the code presented in this recipe. Make sure that you've completed the *Remounting the filesystem* recipe in this chapter as this recipe needs write access to the storage system.

How to do it...

Follow these steps to learn how to write a file's contents:

1. Use the REPL to run the following lines of code:

```
>>> with open('hi.txt', 'w') as f:
...     count = f.write('hi there')
...
...
...
>>> count
8
```

2. The text reading hi there has been written to a file called hi.txt using the file object's write method. The number of bytes written is then returned and displayed. The following block of code will take a bytes object and give it to the write method so that it can write the data to the provided file:

```
>>> with open('hi.txt', 'wb') as f:
...     count = f.write(b'hi there')
...
...
...
>>> count
8
>>>
```

---

[272]

3. The following block of code will define a `Path` class with two methods. One method will initialize new objects, while the other will generate a representation of the object:

```
>>> class Path:
...     def __init__(self, path):
...         self._path = path
...
...     def __repr__(self):
...         return "Path(%r)" % self._path
...
...
>>>
>>> path = Path('hi.txt')
>>> path
Path('hi.txt')
>>>
```

4. After executing the following block, we will have a `Path` class with two additional methods so that we can write text and binary data to a file:

```
>>> class Path:
...     def __init__(self, path):
...         self._path = path
...
...     def __repr__(self):
...         return "Path(%r)" % self._path
...
...     def write_bytes(self, data):
...         with open(self._path, 'wb') as f:
...             return f.write(data)
...
...     def write_text(self, data):
...         with open(self._path, 'w') as f:
...             return f.write(data)
...
...
>>>
>>> path = Path('hi.txt')
>>> path.write_text('hi there')
8
>>> path.write_bytes(b'hi there')
8
```

5. Save the following block of code into a file called `pathlib.py` so that it can be imported:

```
class Path:
    def __init__(self, path):
        self._path = path

    def __repr__(self):
        return "Path(%r)" % self._path

    def write_bytes(self, data):
        with open(self._path, 'wb') as f:
            return f.write(data)

    def write_text(self, data):
        with open(self._path, 'w') as f:
            return f.write(data)
```

6. The following code should be put into the `main.py` file:

```
from pathlib import Path

Path('hi.txt').write_text('hi there')
```

When this script gets executed, it will write the text `hi there` message into the `hi.txt` file.

How it works...

In this recipe, we started off by showing the two most straightforward ways of writing bytes and text data to files. Then, we created a class called `Path`, which we build in two stages. The first version lets us create `Path` objects that keep track of their path and return a human-readable representation when requested.

Then, we added helper methods to assist in writing text data or binary data. The name of the class and its methods follow the same naming and functionality as the `Path` object in the Python `pathlib` module, which comes with the standard library. The final code block shows a simple example of importing the `pathlib` module and calling its `write_text` method to save some text to a file.

There's more...

You might find yourself in a situation in some projects where you have to interact with files, their paths, and have to write and read data frequently. In these situations, it can be very helpful to be equipped with a class that simplifies your access to files. The `Path` object that was defined in this recipe is great for this purpose. We have also followed the same naming and functionality of a module that is part of Python's standard library. This will make our code more readable and portable when we want to run it on a computer that has a full Python installation.

See also

Here are a few references regarding this recipe:

- Documentation on the `write_bytes` method can be found at `https://docs.python.org/3/library/pathlib.html#pathlib.Path.write_bytes`.
- Documentation on the `write_text` method can be found at `https://docs.python.org/3/library/pathlib.html#pathlib.Path.write_text`.

Calculating disk usage

This recipe will show you how to check a number of figures related to the storage system. We will retrieve the filesystem's block size, the total number of blocks, and the number of free blocks. We can then use these figures to calculate a number of useful figures, such as the total disk capacity and how much space is used and free on the disk.

We'll then package all this code into a function to make it easier to call whenever we need access to this information. You can use the techniques shown in this recipe to achieve a number of things in your projects. For example, you could use it to find out how much total storage is available on the device since this varies between different boards. You can even use it to decide if the disk is getting too full and whether your script should delete some old log files.

Getting ready

You will need access to the REPL on Circuit Playground Express to run the code presented in this recipe.

How to do it...

Follow these steps to learn how to calculate disk usage:

1. Run the following lines of code in the REPL:

```
>>> import os
>>> stats = os.statvfs('/')
>>> stats
(1024, 1024, 2024, 1040, 1040, 0, 0, 0, 0, 255)
```

2. We have now retrieved all the key filesystem information, but it is presented as a tuple, which makes it difficult to know which figure relates to what. In the following block of code, we will assign the values we care about to more human-readable variable names:

```
>>> block_size = stats[0]
>>> total_blocks = stats[2]
>>> free_blocks = stats[3]
```

3. Now that we have this key information in human-readable variables, we can proceed with the following block of code to calculate the main values we are interested in:

```
>>> stats = dict()
>>> stats['free'] = block_size * free_blocks
>>> stats['total'] = block_size * total_blocks
>>> stats['used'] = stats['total'] - stats['free']
>>> stats
{'free': 1064960, 'used': 1007616, 'total': 2072576}
```

4. The following block of code will wrap all this logic into a single function:

```
>>> def get_disk_stats():
...     stats = os.statvfs('/')
...     block_size = stats[0]
...     total_blocks = stats[2]
...     free_blocks = stats[3]
...     stats = dict()
```

```
...         stats['free'] = block_size * free_blocks
...         stats['total'] = block_size * total_blocks
...         stats['used'] = stats['total'] - stats['free']
...         return stats
...
>>>
>>> get_disk_stats()
{'free': 1064960, 'used': 1007616, 'total': 2072576}
>>>
```

5. The following function will format the values, represented as bytes, in a more human-readable fashion:

```
>>> def format_size(val):
...         val = int(val / 1024)              # convert bytes to KiB
...         val = '{:,}'.format(val)           # add thousand
separator
...         val = '{0: >6} KiB'.format(val)    # right align amounts
...         return val
...
...
...
>>> print('total space:', format_size(stats['total']))
total space:  2,024 KiB
>>>
```

6. We can now create a function that prints a number of key figures related to total disk size and usage:

```
>>> def print_stats():
...         stats = get_disk_stats()
...         print('free space: ', format_size(stats['free']))
...         print('used space: ', format_size(stats['used']))
...         print('total space:', format_size(stats['total']))
...
...
...
>>> print_stats()
free space:   1,040 KiB
used space:     984 KiB
total space:  2,024 KiB
>>>
```

7. The following code should be put into the `main.py` file:

```python
import os

def get_disk_stats():
    stats = os.statvfs('/')
    block_size = stats[0]
    total_blocks = stats[2]
    free_blocks = stats[3]
    stats = dict()
    stats['free'] = block_size * free_blocks
    stats['total'] = block_size * total_blocks
    stats['used'] = stats['total'] - stats['free']
    return stats

def format_size(val):
    val = int(val / 1024)          # convert bytes to KiB
    val = '{:,}'.format(val)       # add thousand separator
    val = '{0: >6} KiB'.format(val) # right align amounts
    return val

def print_stats():
    stats = get_disk_stats()
    print('free space: ', format_size(stats['free']))
    print('used space: ', format_size(stats['used']))
    print('total space:', format_size(stats['total']))

print_stats()
```

When this script gets executed, it will print out details on the free, used, and total disk space.

How it works...

The `statvfs` function returns a number of key figures relating to the filesystem that is on the board. We care about three values in this tuple, which map to the `block_size`, `total_blocks`, and `free_blocks` variables. We can multiply these values together to calculate the amount of free, used, and total disk space in terms of bytes. Then, the `format_size` function is defined to convert bytes values into KiB, add a thousand separator, and right-align the values. The `print_stats` function simply combines all this code by getting the filesystem's `stats` and calling the `format_size` function on each value.

There's more...

Circuit Playground Express comes with 2 MB of flash storage, which can be seen in the output of this recipe. MicroPython uses the FAT format for its filesystem. One thing that you can experiment with is adding a number of files on the board and then rerunning the script to see the changes in filesystem usage. Keep in mind that for you to see these changes reflected on a number of boards, you will have to eject the USB device and plug it back in to get the latest filesystem usage figures.

See also

Here are a few references regarding this recipe:

- Documentation on the `statvfs` function can be found at `https://circuitpython.readthedocs.io/en/3.x/shared-bindings/os/__init__.html#os.statvfs`.
- Details on the information returned by `statvfs` can be found at `http://man7.org/linux/man-pages/man3/statvfs.3.html`.

12
Networking

This chapter will introduce a variety of topics related to performing network operations. Simple low-level examples, such as performing DNS lookups using the low-level socket libraries, will be presented. HTTP client and server implementations will also be presented. We will then show you how to create an application that lets you control the LEDs on board the microcontroller using a web browser.

This chapter will help you create a MicroPython project that needs to fetch information from the internet. This can help you whenever you want to provide a way for people to use their web browsers on their phones and computers to directly connect and interact with your MicroPython boards.

In this chapter, we will be covering the following topics:

- Performing a DNS lookup
- Creating a function to wait for internet connectivity
- Performing an HTTP request using raw sockets
- Performing an HTTP request using the urequests library
- Fetching JSON data from a RESTful web service
- Creating an HTTP server
- Creating a web handler module
- Controlling LEDs through the web server
- Developing a RESTful API to control the LEDs

Technical requirements

The code files for this chapter can be found in the Chapter12 folder in this book's GitHub repository, available at https://github.com/PacktPublishing/MicroPython-Cookbook.

This chapter uses the Adafruit Feather HUZZAH ESP8266. CircuitPython 3.1.2 was used for all the recipes in this chapter. You should apply the configuration we described in the *Connecting to an existing Wi-Fi network* recipe from Chapter 10, *Controlling the ESP8266*. This recipe will let you run all the recipes in this chapter that connect to the internet, as well as the recipes that involve you connecting to your board from your computer.

Performing a DNS lookup

This recipe will show you how to write code that will run on MicroPython to perform a DNS lookup. Whenever our applications try and connect to the host, one of the first steps is to look up the hostname using the DNS protocol and get the host's IP address so that you can open a connection to that IP address.

This recipe shows you how to perform that DNS lookup, and then takes those lines of code and packages them into a function that you can call whenever you want to get the IP address of a specific host. This recipe can be useful in your projects whenever you want to keep track of a hostname and its related IP address, or when you face networking issues on your devices or network and want some simple tests to troubleshoot what's going on.

Getting ready

You will need access to the REPL on the ESP8266 to run the code presented in this recipe.

How to do it...

Follow these steps to learn how to perform a DNS lookup:

1. Run the following lines of code in the REPL:

```
>>> import socket
>>>
>>> addr_info = socket.getaddrinfo('python.org', 80)
>>> addr_info
[(2, 1, 0, '', ('45.55.99.72', 80))]
```

2. We've used the `getaddrinfo` function to perform a DNS lookup on
   `python.org` and get its IP address. The following block of code will access the
   specified string in the returned data structure that contains the IP address:

   ```
   >>> ip = addr_info[0][-1][0]
   >>> ip
   '45.55.99.72'
   ```

3. We can now wrap this code up in a function that returns the IP address for a
   given hostname:

   ```
   >>> def get_ip(host, port=80):
   ...     addr_info = socket.getaddrinfo(host, port)
   ...     return addr_info[0][-1][0]
   ...
   ...
   ...
   >>>
   ```

4. We will call this function with a number of different hostnames to verify that it is
   working correctly:

   ```
   >>> get_ip('python.org')
   '45.55.99.72'
   >>> get_ip('micropython.org')
   '176.58.119.26'
   >>> get_ip('pypi.org')
   '151.101.0.223'
   ```

5. The following code should be put into the `main.py` file:

   ```
   import socket
   import time

   BOOTUP_WIFI_DELAY = 5

   def get_ip(host, port=80):
       addr_info = socket.getaddrinfo(host, port)
       return addr_info[0][-1][0]

   def main():
       print('applying wifi delay...')
       time.sleep(BOOTUP_WIFI_DELAY)
       print('performing DNS lookup...')
       hosts = ['python.org', 'micropython.org', 'pypi.org']
   ```

```
for host in hosts:
    print(host, get_ip(host))

main()
```

When this script is executed, it will perform DNS lookups on three hostnames and print out the results of each lookup.

How it works...

The `get_ip` function that is defined will receive the hostname as its the first argument and will perform a DNS lookup on the hostname, before returning the IP address at the end of each function call. There is one optional argument that specifies the TCP port to use when connecting to the host. The TCP port default value is set to port `80`. This is the port number for the HTTP protocol. This means that this function will work for hosts that are hosting a web server.

The `main` function sleeps for five seconds to allow the board to establish a connection to the Wi-Fi network on boot-up before performing the DNS lookups. Then, the `main` function loops through three hostnames and performs a DNS lookup on each one, printing out the hostname and returned IP of each entry through the `for` loop.

There's more...

This script performs its task well enough, but there is room for improvement. The five-second delay is sufficient on most Wi-Fi networks. There are, however, networks that will take longer, so this value should be increased. But if we set this value very high and the network is fast to connect, then we are unnecessarily waiting too long. In the next recipe, we will introduce a way to wait for internet connectivity that will address both limitations in a much more effective fashion. Any time you use hardcoded sleep values in your code, you should dig deep and try to find better solutions.

See also

Here are a few references regarding this recipe:

- Documentation on the `getaddrinfo` function can be found at `https://docs.python.org/3/library/socket.html#socket.getaddrinfo`.

- An example of using `getaddrinfo` on MicroPython can be found at `https://docs.micropython.org/en/latest/esp8266/tutorial/network_tcp.html#star-wars-asciimation`.

Creating a function to wait for internet connectivity

This recipe will show you how to write a function that polls the status of your Wi-Fi connection on boot-up. We will name this function `wait_for_networking`. Once it has detected that a connection has been successfully established and that an IP address has been assigned over DHCP, then the `wait_for_networking` function will return.

Whenever you have a project that requires internet connectivity, you will face this issue at boot-up. If your script starts immediately, connecting to the internet before the network connection has come up, it will raise exceptions and fail to continue. Using the method in this recipe will let you start the rest of your program's execution once the network connection is properly established.

Getting ready

You will need access to the REPL on the ESP8266 to run the code presented in this recipe.

How to do it...

Follow these steps to learn how to create a function that waits for internet connectivity:

1. Execute the following block of code in the REPL:

```
>>> import network
>>> import time
>>>
>>> station = network.WLAN(network.STA_IF)
>>> station.isconnected()
False
```

2. When the code is run early enough, it will return a `False` value. Calling `isconnected` again, but at a later stage, will result in the following output:

```
>>> station.isconnected()
True
```

3. The following block of code can be used to retrieve the assigned IP address once the network is connected:

```
>>> ip = station.ifconfig()[0]
>>> ip
'10.0.0.38'
```

4. The following function brings all this code together into one function that will wait until a network connection is established and an IP address is allocated to the device. It then returns the IP address:

```
>>> def wait_for_networking():
...     station = network.WLAN(network.STA_IF)
...     while not station.isconnected():
...         print('waiting for network...')
...         time.sleep(1)
...     ip = station.ifconfig()[0]
...     print('address on network:', ip)
...     return ip
...
...
...
>>>
>>> ip = wait_for_networking()
address on network: 10.0.0.38
>>> ip
'10.0.0.38'
>>>
```

5. The following code should be put into the `netcheck.py` file:

```
import network
import time

def wait_for_networking():
    station = network.WLAN(network.STA_IF)
    while not station.isconnected():
        print('waiting for network...')
        time.sleep(1)
    ip = station.ifconfig()[0]
```

```
print('address on network:', ip)
return ip
```

6. The following block of code should be put into the `main.py` file:

```
from netcheck import wait_for_networking

def main():
    ip = wait_for_networking()
    print('main started')
    print('device ip:', ip)

main()
```

When this script is executed, it will wait for a network connection to be established and then print out the IP address assigned to the device.

How it works...

In this recipe, we created a Python module called `netcheck`. The `wait_for_networking` function in that module will create a WLAN object called `station`. The `station` object will be used to poll the network at 1-second intervals until a network connection is established. Then, it will get the assigned IP from the `station` object using the `ifconfig` method. This IP address is then returned to the calling function. The main script in this recipe simply imports the `wait_for_networking` function from the `netcheck` module and calls it at the start of its execution, before printing out the returned IP address.

There's more...

So many network connected projects should only start their main block of code once the network is connected. When you run Python on a typical computer, the operating system takes care of the process of ensuring all network connections are up before starting other services for you. In the case of MicroPython, there is no operating system—it's just your script running on bare metal. You have to take these things into account so that your code can run correctly.

See also

Here are a few references regarding this recipe:

- Documentation on the **Dynamic Host Configuration Protocol (DHCP)** can be found at `https://tools.ietf.org/html/rfc2131`.
- Documentation on how `systemd` on Linux handles detecting network connectivity can be found at `https://www.freedesktop.org/wiki/Software/systemd/NetworkTarget/`.

Performing an HTTP request using raw sockets

This recipe will use the `socket` library that comes with both MicroPython and Python to perform an HTTP request. We will create a function that receives a URL as its input and returns the response from the requested web server after performing the HTTP request. We will also create a function that can parse a URL and return the hostname and path components of the URL. These pieces will be needed to perform the HTTP request.

There's a whole class of MicroPython projects that will want to connect to web servers on the internet and fetch different results. You will see one way to do this using the `socket` library, which gives you direct access to TCP sockets to read and write bytes of data from them.

Getting ready

You will need access to the REPL on the ESP8266 to run the code presented in this recipe.

How to do it...

Follow these steps to learn how to perform an HTTP request using raw sockets:

1. Use the REPL to run the following lines of code:

```
>>> import socket
>>> import time
>>>
>>> def parse_url(url):
```

```
...        return url.replace('http://', '').split('/', 1)
...
...
...
>>>
```

2. We have successfully created the `parse_url` function, which takes a URL and returns the `host` and `path` components:

```
>>> url = 'http://micropython.org/ks/test.html'
>>> host, path = parse_url(url)
>>> host
'micropython.org'
>>> path
'ks/test.html'
>>>
```

3. `parse_url` is then called with an example URL to demonstrate its functionality. In the following block of code, we define and call a function to look up the IP address for a specific hostname:

```
>>> HTTP_PORT = 80
>>> def get_ip(host, port=HTTP_PORT):
...        addr_info = socket.getaddrinfo(host, port)
...        return addr_info[0][-1][0]
...
...
...
>>> ip = get_ip(host)
>>> ip
'176.58.119.26'
>>>
```

4. We can now define the `fetch` function, which receives a URL as its input and retrieves its content from a web server:

```
>>> HTTP_REQUEST = 'GET /{path} HTTP/1.0\r\nHost: {host}\r\n\r\n'
>>> BUFFER_SIZE = 1024
>>>
>>> def fetch(url):
...        host, path = parse_url(url)
...        ip = get_ip(host)
...        sock = socket.socket()
...        sock.connect((ip, 80))
...        request = HTTP_REQUEST.format(host=host, path=path)
...        sock.send(bytes(request, 'utf8'))
...        response = b''
```

```
...          while True:
...              chunk = sock.recv(BUFFER_SIZE)
...              if not chunk:
...                  break
...              response += chunk
...          sock.close()
...          body = response.split(b'\r\n\r\n', 1)[1]
...          return str(body, 'utf8')
...
...
...
>>>
```

5. We can now call this function and inspect the results that it returns:

```
>>> html = fetch('http://micropython.org/ks/test.html')
>>> html
'<!DOCTYPE html>\n<html lang="en">\n    <head>\n
<title>Test</title>\n    </head>\n    <body>\n
<h1>Test</h1>\n          It\'s working if you can read this!\n
</body>\n</html>\n'
>>> print(html)
<!DOCTYPE html>
<html lang="en">
    <head>
        <title>Test</title>
    </head>
    <body>
        <h1>Test</h1>
        It's working if you can read this!
    </body>
</html>

>>>
```

6. The following code should be put into the `main.py` file:

```
from netcheck import wait_for_networking
import socket

HTTP_REQUEST = 'GET /{path} HTTP/1.0\r\nHost: {host}\r\n\r\n'
HTTP_PORT = 80
BUFFER_SIZE = 1024

def parse_url(url):
    return url.replace('http://', '').split('/', 1)

def get_ip(host, port=HTTP_PORT):
```

```
        addr_info = socket.getaddrinfo(host, port)
        return addr_info[0][-1][0]

def fetch(url):
    host, path = parse_url(url)
    ip = get_ip(host)
    sock = socket.socket()
    sock.connect((ip, 80))
    request = HTTP_REQUEST.format(host=host, path=path)
    sock.send(bytes(request, 'utf8'))
    response = b''
    while True:
        chunk = sock.recv(BUFFER_SIZE)
        if not chunk:
            break
        response += chunk
    sock.close()
    body = response.split(b'\r\n\r\n', 1)[1]
    return str(body, 'utf8')

def main():
    wait_for_networking()
    html = fetch('http://micropython.org/ks/test.html')
    print(html)

main()
```

When this script gets executed, it will fetch the content of a specific URL and output the returned results.

How it works...

The parse_url function will return the two main parts of the URL that we are interested in. This is done by removing the initial part of the URL and performing a single string split using the / character. Once these operations are performed, we will be left with the hostname and path part of the URL, which we can then return. The fetch function first calls parse_url and get_ip to get the hostname, path, and IP address information for a given URL. Once this is done, a socket connection is created to the web server.

The HTTP request is created by filling in the template called HTTP_REQUEST. This request is then transmitted over the network to the web server. The results are continually read as a series of chunks until the end of the response is reached. These chunks of data are concatenated together into a variable called response.

The response has both the HTTP headers and body in the response. We are only interested in the body portion, so we use the `split` method to extract it. Once extracted, it is converted from a `bytes` object into a string and returned. The `main` function, when called, will wait for network connectivity and then call the `fetch` function to get the HTML content of the URL. This content is then printed out.

There's more...

A lot is going on in this recipe. In a way, this is a great way to learn about TCP sockets, HTTP, HTML, and URLs, because all the low-level details are exposed to you. MicroPython doesn't ship with the higher-level HTTP request libraries that come with the Python standard library.

So, when you want to write code from scratch that fetches content from a web server, you have to use the `socket` library in the same way that was presented in this recipe. In the next recipe, we will see that there is a Python module that works with MicroPython that we can add to our projects to make performing these HTTP requests much simpler.

See also

Here are a few references regarding this recipe:

- Documentation on the `send` method on MicroPython socket objects can be found at `https://docs.micropython.org/en/latest/library/usocket.html#usocket.socket.send`.
- Documentation on the `recv` method on MicroPython socket objects can be found at `https://docs.micropython.org/en/latest/library/usocket.html#usocket.socket.recv`.

Performing an HTTP request using the urequests library

This recipe will use the `urequests` library, which was specially written to work with MicroPython. It provides a convenient way to connect to web servers and perform HTTP requests. This library provides an object that you can use to perform all your HTTP interactions. After the request is completed, you can access different attributes of this object to get a variety of information on the completed request.

This recipe will explore using this library and the different attributes that you might want to access on its objects. When you start creating MicroPython projects that need to make HTTP requests, this library will take care of a lot of the low-level details of making these requests. This will keep your code simpler and more readable, and lets you focus on the task at hand instead of getting bogged down with low-level TCP socket details.

Getting ready

You will need access to the REPL on the ESP8266 to run the code presented in this recipe.

How to do it...

Follow these steps to learn how to perform an HTTP request using `urequests`:

1. Download `urequests.py` from `https://github.com/micropython/ micropython-lib/blob/master/urequests/urequests.py`.
2. Save this Python module on your board's top-level directory.
3. Run the following lines of code in the REPL:

```
>>> import urequests
>>>
>>> url = 'http://micropython.org/ks/test.html'
>>> req = urequests.get(url)
```

4. We now have a completed HTTP request, and its results are stored in the `req` variable. The following block of code will output the HTML response we received from the web server:

```
>>> req.text
'<!DOCTYPE html>\n<html lang="en">\n    <head>\n
<title>Test</title>\n    </head>\n    <body>\n
<h1>Test</h1>\n         It\'s working if you can read this!\n
</body>\n</html>\n'
>>> print(req.text)
<!DOCTYPE html>
<html lang="en">
    <head>
        <title>Test</title>
    </head>
    <body>
        <h1>Test</h1>
        It's working if you can read this!
    </body>
```

```
</html>

>>>
```

5. We can also access the raw content in its binary form, as shown in the following block of code:

```
>>> req.content
b'<!DOCTYPE html>\n<html lang="en">\n     <head>\n
<title>Test</title>\n     </head>\n     <body>\n
<h1>Test</h1>\n          It\'s working if you can read this!\n
</body>\n</html>\n'
>>>
```

6. The `status_code` attribute provides us with the HTTP status code of the response:

```
>>> req.status_code
200
```

7. The following block of code will attempt to access a page that doesn't exist:

```
>>> url = 'http://micropython.org/no_such_page_exists'
>>> req = urequests.get(url)
```

8. We can now inspect the values of the status code and the explanatory text:

```
>>> req.status_code
404
>>> req.reason
b'Not Found'
>>>
```

9. The following code should be put into the `main.py` file:

```
from netcheck import wait_for_networking
import urequests

def main():
    wait_for_networking()
    url = 'http://micropython.org/ks/test.html'
    html = urequests.get(url).text
    print(html)

main()
```

When this script is executed, it will use the `urequests` library to fetch the content of a specific URL and output the page's HTML content.

How it works...

The urequests library provides a function called get that lets you perform HTTP GET requests on web servers. Once you call this function, it will return an object that has a number of useful properties that you can then access to retrieve the results of this request.

You can get the raw response as a bytes object by accessing the content attribute, or you can get the value as a string by accessing the text attribute. Finally, you can use the status_code and reason attributes to check whether a request was successful or failed, and what the reason for its failure was. This code is then wrapped up and put into the main function. When the main function is called, it will connect to the web server and output the contents of the returned HTML document.

There's more...

This recipe shows a nice way of getting productive in MicroPython HTTP requests without having to go to a very low level of detail. It's a great example of how a well-designed library can make your code more readable and maintainable.

This library provides a number of HTTP methods, beyond a basic HTTP GET request. The HEAD, POST, PUT, PATCH, and DELETE methods are all made available too. They can all be accessed using function names that match the request method. This can be very useful at times when you're interacting with web services that need the correct HTTP method to be specified for them to work correctly. If you are getting warning messages each time you make HTTP calls using the urequests library, you can try and use the fix_urequests_warnings.py file to fix this issue. You can find this script in the Chapter12 folder of this book's GitHub repository.

See also

Here are a few references regarding this recipe:

- Documentation on the list of HTTP response status codes can be found at https://developer.mozilla.org/en-US/docs/Web/HTTP/Status.
- The popular requests library is what the design of urequests is based on, and can be found at http://docs.python-requests.org/en/master/.

Fetching JSON data from a RESTful web service

This recipe will show you an example of connecting to a server on the internet in order to consume its RESTful web service. The web service will provide data in JSON format, which will then be parsed so that we can access different parts of the returned dataset.

We will consume a web service that provides the current location of the **International Space Station (ISS)**. Since the ISS moves at an incredible speed of 28,000 km/h, we can watch its position, which is expressed in terms of longitude and latitude, change as we repeatedly call this web service. Whenever you want to create a MicroPython project that connects to the rich world of internet-based web services, you can use the techniques covered in this recipe as a starting point to build these connections.

Getting ready

You will need access to the REPL on the ESP8266 to run the code presented in this recipe.

How to do it...

Follow these steps to learn how to fetch JSON data from a RESTful web service:

1. Execute the following block of code in the REPL:

```
>>> import urequests
>>> import time
>>>
>>> ISS_API_URL = 'http://api.open-notify.org/iss-now.json'
>>> req = urequests.get(ISS_API_URL)
```

2. We have successfully connected to the web service and retrieved the space station's position. The following block of code will inspect the data that has been returned to us:

```
>>> req.text
'{"timestamp": 1555012195, "iss_position": {"latitude": "-33.1779",
"longitude": "45.0667"}, "message": "success"}'
>>>
```

3. The data is provided in JSON format. We can use the following block of code to parse the text data and generate a set of nested dictionaries:

```
>>> data = req.json()
>>> data
{'message': 'success', 'iss_position': {'longitude': '45.0667',
'latitude': '-33.1779'}, 'timestamp': 1555012195}
```

4. The following block of code shows how we can access the latitude and longitude data from the returned data structure:

```
>>> data['iss_position']['latitude']
'-33.1779'
>>> data['iss_position']['longitude']
'45.0667'
```

5. Now, we will create and call the `track_space_station` function, which will track the space station's position every second over a period of 10 seconds:

```
>>> req.status_code
>>> def track_space_station():
...     for i in range(10):
...         data = urequests.get(ISS_API_URL).json()
...         position = data['iss_position']
...         print(i, 'lat: {latitude} long:
{longitude}'.format(**position))
...         time.sleep(1)
...
...
...
>>> track_space_station()
0 lat: -38.5192 long: 52.4146
1 lat: -38.5783 long: 52.5069
2 lat: -38.6570 long: 52.6302
3 lat: -38.7355 long: 52.7538
4 lat: -38.7943 long: 52.8467
5 lat: -38.8726 long: 52.9708
6 lat: -38.9507 long: 53.0952
7 lat: -39.0092 long: 53.1887
8 lat: -39.0871 long: 53.3136
9 lat: -39.1454 long: 53.4075
>>>
```

6. The following code should be put into the `main.py` file:

```
from netcheck import wait_for_networking
import urequests
import time

ISS_API_URL = 'http://api.open-notify.org/iss-now.json'

def track_space_station():
    for i in range(10):
        data = urequests.get(ISS_API_URL).json()
        position = data['iss_position']
        print(i, 'lat: {latitude} long:
{longitude}'.format(**position))
        time.sleep(1)

def main():
    wait_for_networking()
    track_space_station()

main()
```

When this script is executed, it will track the position of the ISS and display the changes in the latitude and longitude each second for a fixed period of time.

How it works...

We defined a constant called `ISS_API_URL` that has the URL that we can use to retrieve information on where the ISS is currently located. When we call this API by performing an HTTP GET request, the server returns its output in JSON format. We can then use the `json` method on the returned request object to parse this response into Python data structures. We can access the `iss_position` key and the latitude and longitude information within that dictionary. The rest of the `track_space_station` function just loops for 10 iterations, with a 1-second sleep between each loop, before calling the API and printing its parsed results.

There's more...

This recipe is a great example of how rich and varied the world of web services can be. You can connect these tiny low-powered microcontrollers to all sorts of rich information sources. JSON is the most popular serialization format for these web services, so it's a very powerful feature to have built-in support for parsing this format with MicroPython.

MicroPython also fully supports creating JSON output so that you can equally submit data to web services from your MicroPython project. You could connect some sensors to your boards and continually upload sensor data in JSON format to a remote server using web services.

See also

Here are a few references regarding this recipe:

- Documentation on the ISS Current Location API can be found at `http://open-notify.org/Open-Notify-API/ISS-Location-Now/`.
- Documentation on the JSON format can be found at `https://www.json.org/`.

Creating an HTTP server

This recipe will show you how we can create a web server in MicroPython that will serve web pages with dynamic content on the ESP8266. Each time a browser visits the web server, it will display the current uptime of the board in seconds.

We'll ensure that the web page that's generated will render well on computer web browsers, as well as phone browsers. It can be a very powerful tool for the projects you create, as that you have the ability to interact with them from any phone or computer on your network using a web browser.

This recipe shows you how to create projects like this, where you can submit any live sensor data or information straight to people's browsers, regardless of whether they connect from their phone or desktop computer.

Getting ready

You will need access to the REPL on the ESP8266 to run the code presented in this recipe.

How to do it...

Follow these steps to learn how to create an HTTP server:

1. Use the REPL to run the following lines of code:

```
>>> from netcheck import wait_for_networking
>>> import socket
>>> import time
>>>
>>> HTTP_PORT = 80
>>> TCP_BACKLOG = 0
```

2. At this stage, we have all the necessary Python modules imported and constants defined. The following block of code will define an HTML template that we will use to generate pages before submitting them to the connecting browsers:

```
>>> TEMPLATE = """\
... <!DOCTYPE HTML>
... <html lang="en">
... <head>
...     <title>ESP8266</title>
...     <meta charset="UTF-8">
...     <link rel="icon" href="data:,">
...     <meta name="viewport" content="width=device-width">
... </head>
... <body>
...     <h1>ESP8266</h1>
...     uptime: {uptime}s
...     </body>
...     </html>
... """
>>>
```

3. The following function is defined and called, and will bind and listen to the default HTTP port:

```
>>> def socket_listen():
...     sock = socket.socket()
...     sock.bind(('0.0.0.0', HTTP_PORT))
...     sock.listen(TCP_BACKLOG)
...     return sock
```

```
...
...
...
>>> ip = wait_for_networking()
address on network: 10.0.0.38
>>> sock = socket_listen()
```

4. The following block of code defines and calls the `serve_requests` function, which will be in charge of serving any requests that are made to the web server. The function is called, and then the web server is visited by a browser three separate times. Each time a request is served, its details are printed out:

```
>>> def serve_requests(sock, ip):
...     print('webserver started on http://%s/' % ip)
...     start = time.monotonic()
...     while True:
...         conn, address = sock.accept()
...         print('request:', address)
...         request = conn.makefile('rwb')
...         while True:
...             line = request.readline()
...             if not line or line == b'\r\n':
...                 break
...         uptime = time.monotonic() - start
...         html = TEMPLATE.format(uptime=uptime)
...         conn.send(html)
...         conn.close()
...
...
...
>>>
>>> serve_requests(sock, ip)
webserver started on http://10.0.0.38/
request: ('10.0.0.151', 47290)
request: ('10.0.0.151', 47292)
request: ('10.0.0.151', 47294)
```

5. The following code should be put into the `main.py` file:

```
from netcheck import wait_for_networking
import socket
import time

HTTP_PORT = 80
TCP_BACKLOG = 0
TEMPLATE = """\
<!DOCTYPE HTML>
<html lang="en">
```

```
<head>
    <title>ESP8266</title>
    <meta charset="UTF-8">
    <link rel="icon" href="data:,">
    <meta name="viewport" content="width=device-width">
</head>
<body>
    <h1>ESP8266</h1>
    uptime: {uptime}s
</body>
</html>
"""

def socket_listen():
    sock = socket.socket()
    sock.bind(('0.0.0.0', HTTP_PORT))
    sock.listen(TCP_BACKLOG)
    return sock

def serve_requests(sock, ip):
    print('webserver started on http://%s/' % ip)
    start = time.monotonic()
    while True:
        conn, address = sock.accept()
        print('request:', address)
        request = conn.makefile('rwb')
        while True:
            line = request.readline()
            if not line or line == b'\r\n':
                break
        uptime = time.monotonic() - start
        html = TEMPLATE.format(uptime=uptime)
        conn.send(html)
        conn.close()

def main():
    ip = wait_for_networking()
    sock = socket_listen()
    serve_requests(sock, ip)

main()
```

When this script is executed, it will kick off a web server each time the board boots up, which will display a message with the server's uptime each time it is visited by a browser.

How it works...

One of the first things that are defined in the script is the HTML template. This template will generate valid HTML5 web pages, which will render correctly on both mobiles and desktops.

The `icon` link tag is present to prevent web browsers from unnecessarily asking for `favicon.ico` files. The `socket_listen` function is called to bind and listen to the default HTTP port. The `serve_requests` function is then called and will endlessly serve all incoming HTTP requests. The start time of the web server is recorded in a variable called `start`. We will use this to calculate the server uptime for each request.

We call the `accept` method, which will block the code until a new request comes to the web server. Once we receive this new request, we consume all the HTTP request headers by repeatedly calling the `readline` method until we have detected the end of the request headers. We can now generate our HTML response and send it to the HTTP client using the `send` method. After transmitting the response, we close the connection with the client.

There's more...

You can take this recipe and extend it in many ways. You could read data from different sensors and buttons connected to the board and send this data back to the browser. You can also easily change and add more content to the template.

Currently, it only has HTML content, but there is nothing preventing you from adding CSS, JavaScript, and image content to your responses. The board comes with 4 MB of flash memory, so there is a good amount of room on the board to add all of this content. The following screenshot shows the page that was generated from this recipe shown on a desktop browser:

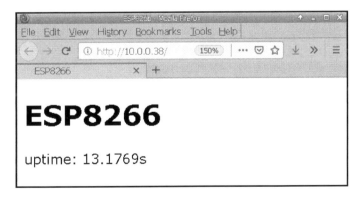

The following screenshot is taken from the browser on an Android smartphone:

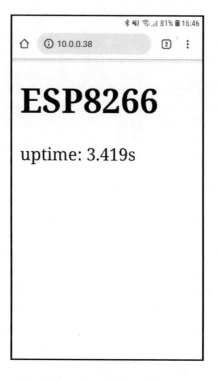

The way the HTML is designed in this recipe is to make it easy to have one code base serve both categories of devices.

See also

Here are a few references regarding this recipe:

- Documentation on the `bind` method can be found at `https://docs.micropython.org/en/latest/library/usocket.html#usocket.socket.bind`.
- Documentation on the `listen` method can be found at `https://docs.micropython.org/en/latest/library/usocket.html#usocket.socket.listen`.

Creating a web handler module

This recipe will show you how we can take a lot of the code and logic involved in handling sockets, parsing HTTP request headers, and generating HTML, and bundle it all into a single Python module. Once we have it in one module, we can import this module and pass it our web handler, which will do all the heavy lifting for us.

You will find this recipe useful when you are creating projects that create a web-based application on your microcontroller and you want to get productive fast, without getting bogged down in all the low-level details of sockets and parsing HTTP headers.

Getting ready

You will need access to the REPL on the ESP8266 to run the code presented in this recipe.

How to do it...

Follow these steps to learn how to create a web handler module:

1. Run the following lines of code in the REPL:

```
>>> from netcheck import wait_for_networking
>>> import socket
>>>
>>> HTTP_PORT = 80
>>> TCP_BACKLOG = 0
>>> BASE_TEMPLATE = """\
... <!DOCTYPE HTML>
... <html lang="en">
... <head>
...     <title>MicroPython</title>
...     <meta charset="UTF-8">
...     <link rel="icon" href="data:,">
...     <meta name="viewport" content="width=device-width">
... </head>
... <body>
... %s
... </body>
... </html>
... """
>>>
```

2. We have created a variable called BASE_TEMPLATE that will act as a generic template. Now, we can fill its body tag with any content we desire. The following block of code defines socket_listen, which does the initial socket configuration for the server:

```
>>> def socket_listen():
...         sock = socket.socket()
...         sock.bind(('0.0.0.0', HTTP_PORT))
...         sock.listen(TCP_BACKLOG)
...         return sock
...
...
...
```

3. The following block of code has a function that receives the web handler as an argument. When called, it will handle incoming requests so that it can collect their request headers, and then parse the HTTP method and requested path. This information is then passed to the handler, which will return the HTML content to be sent to the HTTP client:

```
>>> def serve_requests(sock, ip, handler):
...         print('webserver started on http://%s/' % ip)
...         while True:
...             conn, address = sock.accept()
...             stream = conn.makefile('rwb')
...             request = b''
...             while True:
...                 line = stream.readline()
...                 request += line
...                 if not line or line == b'\r\n':
...                     break
...             request = str(request, 'utf8')
...             method, path, _ = request.split(' ', 2)
...             client_ip = address[0]
...             print('request:', client_ip, method, path)
...             html = handler(request, method, path)
...             conn.send(html)
...             conn.close()
...
...
...
>>>
```

4. The `run_server` function is then defined in the following block of code. It is provided with a handler, and will create the sockets and call `serve_requests` to start serving all incoming requests:

```
>>> def run_server(handler):
...     ip = wait_for_networking()
...     sock = socket_listen()
...     serve_requests(sock, ip, handler)
...
...
...
>>>
```

5. The following block of code shows an example handler that creates a web application that generates random numbers each time anyone visits it:

```
>>> import random
>>>
>>> def handler(request, method, path):
...     body = 'random: %s' % random.random()
...     return BASE_TEMPLATE % body
...
...
...
>>> run_server(handler)
address on network: 10.0.0.38
webserver started on http://10.0.0.38/
request: 10.0.0.151 GET /hotneumm
request: 10.0.0.151 GET /
request: 10.0.0.151 GET /
request: 10.0.0.151 GET /
```

6. The following code should be put into the `web.py` file:

```
from netcheck import wait_for_networking
import socket

HTTP_PORT = 80
TCP_BACKLOG = 0
BASE_TEMPLATE = """\
<!DOCTYPE HTML>
<html lang="en">
<head>
    <title>MicroPython</title>
    <meta charset="UTF-8">
    <link rel="icon" href="data:,">
    <meta name="viewport" content="width=device-width">
</head>
```

```
<body>
%s
</body>
</html>
"""
def socket_listen():
    sock = socket.socket()
    sock.bind(('0.0.0.0', HTTP_PORT))
    sock.listen(TCP_BACKLOG)
    return sock

def serve_requests(sock, ip, handler):
    print('webserver started on http://%s/' % ip)
    while True:
        conn, address = sock.accept()
        stream = conn.makefile('rwb')
        request = b''
        while True:
            line = stream.readline()
            request += line
            if not line or line == b'\r\n':
                break
        request = str(request, 'utf8')
        method, path, _ = request.split(' ', 2)
        client_ip = address[0]
        print('request:', client_ip, method, path)
        html = handler(request, method, path)
        conn.send(html)
        conn.close()

def run_server(handler):
    ip = wait_for_networking()
    sock = socket_listen()
    serve_requests(sock, ip, handler)
```

7. Then, put the following code in the `main.py` file:

```
from web import BASE_TEMPLATE, run_server
import random

def handler(request, method, path):
    body = 'random: %s' % random.random()
    return BASE_TEMPLATE % body

def main():
    run_server(handler)

main()
```

When this script is executed, it will start a web server at boot-up that generates random numbers whenever people visit it.

How it works...

The bulk of this recipe is the code in the `web` Python module. This code provides the `BASE_TEMPLATE` variable, which can be filled with any content in its `body` tag. Then, three functions are defined in the module.

The `socket_listen` function has logic that we are familiar with; that is, setting up the socket, binding it, and making it listen to port `80`. The `serve_requests` function now receives a handler and will collect the HTTP request headers in a variable called `request`. This `request` is then parsed to extract the HTTP method in use and the requested path. These three variables are then passed to the provided handler, which returns an HTML response to be transmitted to the HTTP client. The `run_server` function is the main point of entry into this module. You can call it and provide it with your handler, and it will set up the server and start processing requests.

The code in the `main.py` file imports the `web` module and passes the handler it has defined. Its handler simply generates a random number for each HTTP request and sends this number back to the web browser.

There's more...

This recipe lends itself to being extended. The bulk of the code related to socket handling and dealing with byte conversion is all done by the `web` module. You can import this module and start creating web applications on your MicroPython board in a relatively short amount of time.

You can also extend the `web` module to add more features. You could create more built-in templates or parse the HTTP headers further to get access to more request information automatically.

See also

Here are a few references regarding this recipe:

- Documentation on the `accept` method can be found at `https://docs.micropython.org/en/latest/library/usocket.html#usocket.socket.accept`.
- Documentation on the `close` method can be found at `https://docs.micropython.org/en/latest/library/usocket.html#usocket.socket.close`.

Controlling LEDs through the web server

This recipe will show you how to create a web-based application that will let people see the status of the red and blue LED lights, as well as turn each of them on and off. This recipe will help you whenever you want to create projects that control the output of different hardware components, such as LEDs, screens, or speakers through a web-based application that can be accessed from computers and phones alike.

Getting ready

You will need access to the REPL on the ESP8266 to run the code presented in this recipe.

How to do it...

Follow these steps to learn how to control LEDs through the web server:

1. Execute the following block of code in the REPL:

```
>>> from web import BASE_TEMPLATE, run_server
>>> from machine import Pin
>>>
>>> pins = dict(red=Pin(0, Pin.OUT), blue=Pin(2, Pin.OUT))
>>> state = dict(red=True, blue=True)
>>>
>>>
```

2. The `pins` and `state` variables have been created so that we can keep track of the status of the red and blue LEDs, as well as access their `Pin` objects. The following block of code will define the HTML `BODY` template and will show the current state of the LEDs, as well as provide buttons to toggle them on and off:

```
>>> BODY = """
... Red: {red}<br/>
... Blue: {blue}<br/><br/>
... Toggle Colors:<br/><br/>
... <form action="/red" method=post><input type=submit
value=Red></form><br/>
... <form action="/blue" method=post><input type=submit
value=Blue></form><br/>
... """
>>>
```

3. The following block of code has a function that will format Boolean values into the `On` and `Off` labels for the HTML content we will generate:

```
>>> def format(value):
...         return 'On' if value else 'Off'
...
...
...
>>>
>>> format(True)
'On'
>>> format(False)
'Off'
>>>
```

4. The `gen_body` function generates the body portion of the HTML content:

```
>>> def gen_body():
...         data = {k: format(v) for k, v in state.items()}
...         return BODY.format(**data)
...
...
...
>>> gen_body()
'\nRed: On<br/>\nBlue: On<br/><br/>\nToggle
Colors:<br/><br/>\n<form action="/red" method=post><input
type=submit value=Red></form><br/>\n<form action="/blue"
method=post><input type=submit value=Blue></form><br/>\n'
>>>
```

5. The `toggle_color` function will switch the LED on and off. The first call will switch the red LED off, while then the second call will switch it back on:

```
>>> def toggle_color(color):
...     state[color] = not state[color]
...     pin_value = 0 if state[color] else 1
...     pins[color].value(pin_value)
...
...
...
>>> toggle_color('red')
>>> toggle_color('red')
```

6. The `handler` function will toggle colors for POST requests, and for all requests, it will return the generated HTML body, which shows the LEDs' statuses and provides toggle buttons:

```
>>> def handler(request, method, path):
...     if method == 'POST':
...         color = path.replace('/', '')
...         toggle_color(color)
...     return BASE_TEMPLATE % gen_body()
...
...
...
>>>
```

7. The following code should be put into the `main.py` file:

```
from web import BASE_TEMPLATE, run_server
from machine import Pin

pins = dict(red=Pin(0, Pin.OUT), blue=Pin(2, Pin.OUT))
state = dict(red=True, blue=True)

BODY = """
Red: {red}<br/>
Blue: {blue}<br/><br/>
Toggle Colors:<br/><br/>
<form action="/red" method=post><input type=submit
value=Red></form><br/>
<form action="/blue" method=post><input type=submit
value=Blue></form><br/>
"""

def format(value):
    return 'On' if value else 'Off'
```

```
def gen_body():
    data = {k: format(v) for k, v in state.items()}
    return BODY.format(**data)

def toggle_color(color):
    state[color] = not state[color]
    pin_value = 0 if state[color] else 1
    pins[color].value(pin_value)

def handler(request, method, path):
    if method == 'POST':
        color = path.replace('/', '')
        toggle_color(color)
    return BASE_TEMPLATE % gen_body()

def main():
    pins['red'].value(0)
    pins['blue'].value(0)
    run_server(handler)

main()
```

When this script is executed, it will start a web application that shows the current status of the LEDs and provides buttons that can be used to toggle the LEDs on and off.

How it works...

The `format` function takes Boolean values and returns values to indicate the light status of On or Off. The `gen_body` function will then loop through all the LED state values and format them so that they can fill the HTML template. This template is then filled and returned. The `toggle_color` function receives the name of the LED to toggle and then updates the state data structure before accessing the `Pin` object in order to apply the change to the LEDs. The `handler` function will take incoming requests and toggle the LEDs if the request is a POST request. Then, it will always return the generated body to show the latest values of the LEDs and provide the buttons to toggle them on and off. The `main` function initializes the LED `Pin` objects, and then calls the `run_server` function with the defined handler so that it can start processing incoming requests.

There's more...

This recipe provides all the controls we need to inspect the current settings of the LEDs and switch them on and off. We can, however, extend and improve it in many ways. We could add some CSS to improve the look and feel of the application. We could also use some rich JavaScript controls that can create animations when someone interacts with the UI controls so that they act more like toggle buttons.

See also

Here are a few references regarding this recipe:

- Documentation on a toggle control for web browsers can be found at `http://www.bootstraptoggle.com/`.
- Documentation on the HTTP `POST` method can be found at `https://developer.mozilla.org/en-US/docs/Web/HTTP/Methods/POST`.

Developing a RESTful API to control the LEDs

This recipe will show you how to create a RESTful API hosted on the ESP8266 that will let API clients inquire about the status of the LEDs, as well as toggle them on and off. In previous recipes, we've seen how you can use MicroPython as a client to access RESTful web services.

Now, we will flip this around, and provide RESTful web services so that other devices and computers on the network can connect to the board and control its hardware. You will find this recipe very useful whenever you need to have other computers and devices on the network remotely connect to your projects and control components on them.

Getting ready

You will need access to the REPL on the ESP8266 to run the code presented in this recipe. You will also need the `curl` command-line tool, which can be downloaded from `https://curl.haxx.se/download.html`.

How to do it...

Follow these steps to learn how to develop a RESTful API to control the LEDs:

1. Use the REPL to run the following lines of code:

```
>>> from web import BASE_TEMPLATE, run_server
>>> from machine import Pin
>>> import json
>>>
>>> pins = dict(red=Pin(0, Pin.OUT), blue=Pin(2, Pin.OUT))
>>> state = dict(red=True, blue=True)
```

2. We have imported the `json` library and set up the `pins` and `state` variables. The following block of code will define the `JSON_HEADERS` template, which we will use to provide the HTTP response headers for our JSON responses:

```
>>> JSON_HEADERS = '''\
... HTTP/1.1 200 OK
... Content-Type: application/json
...
... '''
>>>
```

3. The following block of code will perform the LED toggling for the RESTful API calls:

```
>>> def toggle_color(color):
...     state[color] = not state[color]
...     pin_value = 0 if state[color] else 1
...     pins[color].value(pin_value)
...
...
...
>>>
```

4. The `handler` function in the following code will toggle LEDs when a request uses the `POST` method. In all cases, it will return the values of the state variable in JSON serialized form:

```
>>> def handler(request, method, path):
...     if method == 'POST':
...         color = path.replace('/', '')
...         toggle_color(color)
...     return JSON_HEADERS + json.dumps(state) + '\n'
...
...
```

```
   ...
   >>>
```

5. The following code should be put into the `main.py` file:

```python
from web import BASE_TEMPLATE, run_server
from machine import Pin
import json

pins = dict(red=Pin(0, Pin.OUT), blue=Pin(2, Pin.OUT))
state = dict(red=True, blue=True)
JSON_HEADERS = '''\
HTTP/1.1 200 OK
Content-Type: application/json

'''

def toggle_color(color):
    state[color] = not state[color]
    pin_value = 0 if state[color] else 1
    pins[color].value(pin_value)

def handler(request, method, path):
    if method == 'POST':
        color = path.replace('/', '')
        toggle_color(color)
    return JSON_HEADERS + json.dumps(state) + '\n'

def main():
    pins['red'].value(0)
    pins['blue'].value(0)
    run_server(handler)

main()
```

6. Execute the `main.py` script so that we can start accessing the RESTful APIs.
7. Download and install the `curl` command line on your computer (`https://curl.haxx.se/download.html`).
8. Run the following command in the Terminal:

```
$ curl http://10.0.0.38/
{"red": true, "blue": true}
```

9. This will retrieve the status of the LEDs. Execute the following command to switch the red LED off:

```
$ curl -X POST http://10.0.0.38/red
{"red": false, "blue": true}
```

10. When we run the following command, the red LED will be switched back on:

```
$ curl -X POST http://10.0.0.38/red
{"red": true, "blue": true}
```

The `curl` command line is an excellent way to test and interact with most RESTful APIs.

How it works...

The structure of the code is very similar to the previous recipe. Some of the main differences are that the `JSON_HEADERS` template provides the necessary HTTP response headers to indicate that the content type of the response will be JSON. The `dumps` function in the `json` module is also used to generate the JSON data from the state data structure. The server needs to be started before we can test and interact with the APIs through `curl`. The first `curl` command simply performs a GET request, which returns the status of the LEDs. We then use the `-X` option in `curl` to specify that we want to use the POST method so that we can toggle the LEDs on and off.

There's more...

This recipe offers a basic set of APIs so that we can control the lights on the board. We could extend it to respond to requests on how long the server has been running or its disk usage. You could create an API that lets you remotely list and delete files. RESTful APIs are very powerful tools that you can use to glue many different scripts and computers together across the network. The approach that we used in this recipe can be extended to provide more services and features with relative ease.

See also

Here are a few references regarding this recipe:

- Documentation on using the `curl` command for HTTP POST requests can be found at `https://ec.haxx.se/http-post.html`.
- A tutorial on RESTful APIs can be found at `https://www.restapitutorial.com/`.

13
Interacting with the Adafruit FeatherWing OLED

This chapter will introduce you to the Adafruit FeatherWing **organic light-emitting diode (OLED)** display. The Adafruit Feather is a standard board arrangement, which allows upgrades to those boards to be plugged into each other. These can run either stacked on top of each other or as standalone boards. FeatherWings are accessories that can be plugged into these Feather boards.

In this chapter, we will plug the Adafruit FeatherWing OLED display into the Adafruit Feather HUZZAH ESP8266 MicroPython board. This will create the powerful combination of a microcontroller with internet connectivity, which has a display that can output text graphics and interact with the user using three hardware push buttons that are a part of the display.

The recipes in this chapter will help you build a whole array of projects. You can make little MicroPython boards that display a menu, which you can navigate through, and each selected action could post sensor data to other servers on your network or to the internet. You could also use it to fetch data from servers on command and display it on the screen. This chapter will focus on all the main features of the display, such as displaying texts, lines, and rectangle graphics, as well as interacting with the built-in buttons that come with the display.

In this chapter, we will be covering the following recipes:

- Detecting button presses with GPIO pins
- Connecting to the SSD1306 display
- Filling and clearing the display
- Setting pixels on the display
- Drawing lines and rectangles on the display
- Writing text on the display
- Inverting colors on the display

The Adafruit FeatherWing OLED

The FeatherWing OLED display uses an OLED that has a number of benefits compared to other display technologies. For example, it has a much lower power consumption than other display technologies. This makes it very useful for embedded projects, where the power requirements need to be kept as low as possible.

OLEDs also have a much higher contrast ratio than other display technologies, making the text and graphics being displayed much clearer. The screen comes with three user buttons and has a number of different options in terms of headers and screen resolution. The following photograph shows one of these displays attached to an Adafruit Feather HUZZAH ESP8266 board:

The board comes in a configuration with loose headers that require soldering and another version with assembled headers that require no soldering. The board that is shown in the preceding photograph uses assembled headers and plugs right into the ESP8266 mainboard with no need for soldering.

Where to buy it

This chapter uses the Assembled Adafruit FeatherWing OLED – 128 x 32 OLED Add-on for Feather. This FeatherWing can be purchased directly from Adafruit (`https://www.adafruit.com/product/3045`).

Technical requirements

The code files of this chapter can be found in the `Chapter13` folder of the following GitHub repository: `https://github.com/PacktPublishing/MicroPython-Cookbook`.

This chapter uses the Adafruit Feather HUZZAH ESP8266 board and the Assembled Adafruit FeatherWing OLED – 128 x 32 OLED Add-on for Feather board. CircuitPython 3.1.2 was used for all the recipes in this chapter.

This chapter requires some specific modules from the CircuitPython library, and they will be mentioned at the beginning of each recipe. For details on downloading and extracting these libraries, you can refer to the *Updating the CircuitPython library* recipe from `Chapter 1`, *Getting Started with MicroPython*. Version 20190212 of the CircuitPython library is used for all the recipes in this chapter.

Detecting button presses with GPIO pins

This recipe will demonstrate how to check the state of the three push buttons that come with the Adafruit FeatherWing OLED. We will poll each of these three buttons and continually print out their state so that we can detect the moment a button is pressed and when it is realized.

Each of these push buttons is attached to a different GPIO pin, so we will use a dictionary to map the button names to their associated GPIO pins. The physical buttons on the board are labeled *A*, *B*, and *C*. We will use the same naming to map the button events to print statements in the script.

This recipe is useful because it will enable your project to take different actions, depending on which buttons are being pressed. Because there are three buttons on this board, you have a lot of options in terms of how you can design your application. For example, you could make two of the buttons up and down menu options, while the third button could allow users to choose a menu option. Alternatively, you could have one button that increases a setting value and another button that decreases a setting value.

Getting ready

You will need access to the REPL on the ESP8266 to run the code presented in this recipe.

How to do it...

Let's perform the following steps:

1. Run the following lines of code in the REPL:

```
>>> from machine import Pin
>>> import time
>>>
>>> PINS = dict(a=0, b=16, c=2)
```

2. We have now imported the necessary Python libraries and have set up a PINS dictionary, which will map the button names to their associated GPIO pins as follows:

```
>>> def get_buttons():
...     return dict(
...         a=Pin(PINS['a'], Pin.IN, Pin.PULL_UP),
...         b=Pin(PINS['b']),
...         c=Pin(PINS['c'], Pin.IN, Pin.PULL_UP),
...     )
...
...
...
>>> buttons = get_buttons()
```

3. The get_buttons function will return a dictionary that maps each button to its associated Pin object. On this board, buttons A and C require PULL_UP to be configured while button B does not. Run the following block of code and it will return a value of 1, which indicates that button A is not pressed:

```
>>> buttons['a'].value()
1
```

4. Hold down button A while running the next block of code, and the Pin value will show that the button is being pressed:

```
>>> buttons['a'].value()
0
```

5. The next block of code creates the `names` list, which has a sorted list of the button names. We define a function called `get_status`, which will return the status of each of the three buttons:

```
>>> names = sorted(PINS.keys())
>>>
>>> def get_status(names, buttons):
...         items = [format(i, buttons) for i in names]
...         return ' '.join(items)
...
...
...
>>>
```

6. When run, the following block of code calls the `get_status` function and returns the current state of the push buttons:

```
>>> get_status(names, buttons)
'a: False b: False c: False'
```

7. Hold down button B while running the next block of code and the status of push button B will show that it is being pressed:

```
>>> get_status(names, buttons)
'a: False b: True c: False'
```

8. The following code should be added to the `main.py` file:

```
from machine import Pin
import time

PINS = dict(a=0, b=16, c=2)

def format(name, buttons):
    pressed = not buttons[name].value()
    return '{name}: {pressed}'.format(name=name, pressed=pressed)

def get_status(names, buttons):
    items = [format(i, buttons) for i in names]
    return ' '.join(items)

def get_buttons():
    return dict(
        a=Pin(PINS['a'], Pin.IN, Pin.PULL_UP),
        b=Pin(PINS['b']),
        c=Pin(PINS['c'], Pin.IN, Pin.PULL_UP),
    )
```

```
def main():
    names = sorted(PINS.keys())
    buttons = get_buttons()
    while True:
        status = get_status(names, buttons)
        print(status)
        time.sleep(0.1)

main()
```

When this script is executed, it will continually print out the status of each of the buttons with a delay of 0.1 seconds between each loop.

How it works...

This recipe defines a data structure called PINS, which will map each of the three buttons to their correct GPIO pin on the ESP8266. The get_buttons function creates Pin objects for each of these buttons with their correct PULL_UP settings. This get_buttons function is called in the main function and the returned dictionary is saved in the buttons variable.

The names variable is simply the sorted list of button names. It is created to ensure that the status update is always presented in alphabetical order. The get_status function loops through each button and calls the format function to generate the status line, which gets printed out each time the status is checked. The main loop enters into an infinite loop, printing the button status in each iteration, and then pausing for 0.1 seconds before continuing to the next loop.

There's more...

When using GPIO pins to interact with push buttons, they need to be properly configured. The correct pins need to be used and the PULL_UP settings need to be applied correctly to each pin configuration. These settings can usually be found with the board's documentation.

In the case of this board, the reason why push button B doesn't require a PULL_UP setting is that the button and hardware level have a 100k pull-up value included, and so that addresses the issue that the ESP8266 doesn't have an internal pull-up on pin 16. However, the other two buttons do require PULL_UP to be set up.

See also

For more information, you can refer to the following documentation:

- More documentation on the FeatherWing OLED pinouts can be found at `https:/` `/learn.adafruit.com/adafruit-oled-featherwing/pinouts`.
- Further documentation on the `Pin` object in the `machine` module can be found at `https://docs.micropython.org/en/latest/library/machine.Pin.` `html#machine.Pin`.

Connecting to the SSD1306 display

This recipe will show you how to use the `adafruit_ssd1306` library to connect to the FeatherWing OLED display. The recipe will show you how to initialize the **Inter-Integrated Circuit (I2C)** bus that the OLED display is connected to. Then, we can create an `SSD1306_I2C` object that connects to the display using the I2C bus.

This recipe will help you in a number of ways; there are a whole array of components that connect using I2C, so this recipe will give you exposure to this technology so that you are familiar with it whenever you need to use it in your own projects.

You will gain an understanding of how to use a display library that can work with MicroPython, which can then be included in any projects that you might want to add a display to.

Getting ready

You will need access to the REPL on the ESP8266 to run the code presented in this recipe. Version 20190212 of the CircuitPython library is used for this recipe.

How to do it...

Let's perform the following steps:

1. Download the CircuitPython library bundle. You will need both the `.mpy` and `.py` versions of the bundle.
2. Extract both of the `.zip` files to your computer.
3. It is not necessary to install all the libraries in the bundle on the ESP8266.

4. Three specific libraries are required to connect to the display.
5. The `adafruit_bus_device` and `adafruit_framebuf` libraries should have their `.mpy` files installed on the ESP8266. The files for these libraries should be transferred to the ESP8266 and into the `.lib` folder.
6. Execute the following code in the REPL to verify that these two libraries were installed correctly on the board:

```
>>> import adafruit_bus_device
>>> import adafruit_framebuf
```

8. The `adafruit_ssd1306` library should have the `.py` version of the `adafruit_ssd1306.py` file in the library.
9. The library will try to use the built-in `framebuf` MicroPython library instead of `adafruit_framebuf`. The library will fail to connect to the display if it uses the `framebuf` library for its frame buffer manipulation. To fix this issue, download and run the `fix_framebuf_import.py` file in the same directory as `adafruit_ssd1306.py`. You can find this script in the `Chapter13` folder of the book's GitHub repository.
10. Upload the fixed version of the `adafruit_ssd1306.py` file to the board's root directory.
11. Run the following block of code to verify that the `adafruit_ssd1306` library was installed correctly on the board:

```
>>> import adafruit_ssd1306
>>>
```

12. At this stage, all additional libraries have been installed and imported successfully. Run the following block of code to import the libraries that are required to initialize the I2C bus:

```
>>> import board
>>> import busio
```

13. Run the following block of code to initialize the I2C bus:

```
>>> i2c = busio.I2C(board.SCL, board.SDA)
>>>
```

14. Run the following code to create an `SSD1306_I2C` display object:

```
>>> buttons['a'].value()
>>> oled = adafruit_ssd1306.SSD1306_I2C(128, 32, i2c)
>>>
```

15. Add the following code to the `main.py` file:

```python
import adafruit_ssd1306
import board
import busio

def main():
    print('initialize I2C bus')
    i2c = busio.I2C(board.SCL, board.SDA)
    print('create SSD1306_I2C object')
    oled = adafruit_ssd1306.SSD1306_I2C(128, 32, i2c)
    print('ALL DONE')

main()
```

When this script gets executed, it will initialize the I2C bus and create an `SSD1306_I2C` object.

How it works...

The libraries that are required to interact with the FeatherWing OLED are not a part of the CircuitPython firmware, so they require further installation before they can be used. Three libraries need to be installed, and they are called `adafruit_ssd1306`, `adafruit_bus_device`, and `adafruit_framebuf`.

The `adafruit_ssd1306` library is the main library that we will interact with and it relies on the other libraries we have installed to work correctly. Once these libraries are installed, we can then start importing them and using their code to connect to the display. The first step is to initialize the I2C bus. This is done by creating an I2C object and passing it references to the SCL and SDA pins. The object is then saved in the `i2c` variable. An `SSD1306_I2C` object is created by passing it the values of `128` and `32`, which refer to the display resolution since we are using the 128 x 32 OLED. The other parameter that is passed is the `i2c` object.

There's more...

I2C is a very popular protocol for a whole range of devices. I2C is relatively simple to connect to and use, which is one of the reasons why it is widely used with many microcontrollers. It only requires two wires to connect to it and can use the general-purpose I/O pins that come with many microcontroller boards.

A single connection can control multiple devices, which adds to its flexibility. One of the downsides of this protocol, however, is its low speeds compared to other protocols. This means that we can use it for a small monochrome display, but if we wanted to control a display with a higher resolution and more colors, then it wouldn't be fast enough.

See also

For more information, you can refer to the following:

- More details on the I2C protocol can be found at `https://i2c.info/`.
- Further documentation on installing the CircuitPython SSD1306 library can be found at `https://learn.adafruit.com/adafruit-oled-featherwing/circuitpython-and-python-setup`.

Filling and clearing the display

This recipe will show you how to use the `adafruit_ssd1306` library to connect to the FeatherWing OLED display. It will demonstrate how to initialize the I2C bus that the OLED display is connected to. Then, we can create an `SSD1306_I2C` object that connects to the display using the I2C bus. This recipe will help you in a number of ways.

There are a whole array of components that can connect using I2C; this recipe will give you exposure to this technology so that you are familiar with it whenever you need to use it in your own projects. The recipe will also help you with the first steps for using a display library that can work with MicroPython, which can then be included in any projects that you might want to add a display to.

Getting ready

You will need access to the REPL on the ESP8266 to run the code presented in this recipe.

How to do it...

Let's perform the following steps:

1. Use the REPL to run the following lines of code:

```
>>> import adafruit_ssd1306
>>> import board
>>> import busio
```

2. The required libraries have now all been imported. Run the next block of code to create the `i2c` object and the `SSD1306_I2C` object called `oled`:

```
>>> i2c = busio.I2C(board.SCL, board.SDA)
>>> oled = adafruit_ssd1306.SSD1306_I2C(128, 32, i2c)
```

3. Using the following block of code, set all the pixels on the screen to the color white and apply the changes to the display by calling the `show` method:

```
>>> oled.fill(1)
>>> oled.show()
```

4. Now, we will turn off all the pixels on the screen with the following block of code:

```
>>> oled.fill(0)
>>> oled.show()
```

5. The following code block will loop 10 times and repeatedly turn all the pixels on the screen on and off, creating a blinking-screen effect:

```
>>> for i in range(10):
...         oled.fill(1)
...         oled.show()
...         oled.fill(0)
...         oled.show()
...
...
...
>>>
```

6. Add the following code to the `main.py` file:

```python
import adafruit_ssd1306
import board
import busio

def main():
    i2c = busio.I2C(board.SCL, board.SDA)
    oled = adafruit_ssd1306.SSD1306_I2C(128, 32, i2c)
    for i in range(10):
        oled.fill(1)
        oled.show()
        oled.fill(0)
        oled.show()

main()
```

When this script gets executed, it will make the screen flash black and white 10 times.

How it works...

The `main` function first sets up the `i2c` object and saves the `SSD1306_I2C` object as a variable called `oled`. The `oled` object has two methods that we will use in this recipe. The `fill` method receives one argument and fills all the pixels on the display to either white or black. If `1` is provided, then the pixels will become white, otherwise, they will become black (or turned off).

The `show` method must be called after each change for the changes to take effect on the display. A `for` loop is started that will loop 10 times and turn the display all white and then all black during each iteration.

There's more...

The two `fill` and `show` methods are great starting points for when you are interacting with the display, as they are relatively easy to use. Even though they seem simple, they are needed for a lot of operations.

In later recipes, we will explore how to draw lines, rectangles, and text. In all of these cases, we will need to call `show` for the changes to be rendered to the screen. We will also frequently call `fill` to clear the contents of the screen before we write or draw something new on the display.

See also

For more information, you can refer to the following:

- Examples of using `fill` and `show` can be found at `https://circuitpython.readthedocs.io/projects/ssd1306/en/latest/examples.html`.
- Further documentation on the `SSD1306_I2C` object can be found at `https://circuitpython.readthedocs.io/projects/ssd1306/en/latest/api.html`.

Setting pixels on the display

This recipe will demonstrate how to turn individual pixels on the screen on and off. The recipe starts by setting pixels with specific *x* and *y* coordinates to indicate on or off. Then, we'll create a simple animation that repeatedly draws pixels in a certain direction, and so creating a line that grows in length. We will place this simple line animation into its own function so that we can call it multiple times and create a type of zigzag line animation.

You will find this recipe useful for when you start controlling the display from your projects and want control over individual pixels. The operation of controlling individual pixels becomes the building block to produce ever more complex drawings.

Getting ready

You will need access to the REPL on the ESP8266 to run the code presented in this recipe.

How to do it...

Let's perform the following steps:

1. Run the following lines of code in the REPL:

```
>>> import adafruit_ssd1306
>>> import board
>>> import busio
>>>
>>> BLACK = 0
>>> WHITE = 1
>>>
>>> i2c = busio.I2C(board.SCL, board.SDA)
>>> oled = adafruit_ssd1306.SSD1306_I2C(128, 32, i2c)
```

2. Define the BLACK and WHITE constants, which represent the values for the two possible pixel colors. Then, set up the i2c and oled objects. The following block of code will clear the contents of the screen:

```
>>> oled.fill(BLACK)
>>> oled.show()
```

3. The following block of code will draw the pixel at (*x*, *y*), that is, position (0, 0) for the color white:

```
>>> oled.pixel(0, 0, WHITE)
>>> oled.show()
```

4. The following block of code will turn the pixel off at position (0, 0) by setting its color to black:

```
>>> oled.pixel(0, 0, BLACK)
>>> oled.show()
```

5. The following code will set the color of the pixel at position (10, 30) to white:

```
>>> oled.pixel(10, 30, WHITE)
>>> oled.show()
```

6. The following code block will clear the screen, and then loop 10 times, setting a diagonal line of pixels on, one after the other, as an animation that will appear like a growing line:

```
>>> oled.fill(BLACK)
>>> oled.show()
>>>
>>> for i in range(10):
...         oled.pixel(i, i, WHITE)
...         oled.show()
...
...
...
>>>
```

7. Using the following code block, define a function that will perform a line animation from a starting position of (*x*, *y*) and will then move steps in the *x* and *y* direction for a certain count of iterations:

```
>>> def animate_pixel(oled, x, y, step_x, step_y, count):
...         for i in range(count):
...             x += step_x
...             y += step_y
```

```
...             oled.pixel(x, y, WHITE)
...             oled.show()
...
...
...
>>>
```

8. The following code block will clear the screen and call `animate_pixel` to draw a line from position (0, 0) to (30, 30), composed of 30 pixels:

```
>>> oled.fill(BLACK)
>>> oled.show()
>>> animate_pixel(oled, x=0, y=0, step_x=1, step_y=1, count=30)
```

9. The following block of code will then draw a line from position (30, 30) to (60, 0). The line will continue where the last animation completed but move in a different direction:

```
>>> animate_pixel(oled, x=30, y=30, step_x=1, step_y=-1, count=30)
```

10. Now define a function called `zig_zag`, which will draw four line animations. Each one will continue from the point the last one finished at, as follows:

```
>>> def zig_zag(oled):
...         animate_pixel(oled, x=0, y=0, step_x=1, step_y=1, count=30)
...         animate_pixel(oled, x=30, y=30, step_x=1, step_y=-1,
...         count=30)
...         animate_pixel(oled, x=60, y=0, step_x=1, step_y=1,
count=30)
...         animate_pixel(oled, x=90, y=30, step_x=1, step_y=-1,
...         count=30)
...
...
...
>>>
```

11. Run the following block of code to clear the display and run the `zig_zag` line animation:

```
>>> oled.fill(BLACK)
>>> oled.show()
>>> zig_zag(oled)
```

12. Add the following code to the `main.py` file:

```python
import adafruit_ssd1306
import board
import busio

BLACK = 0
WHITE = 1

def animate_pixel(oled, x, y, step_x, step_y, count):
    for i in range(count):
        x += step_x
        y += step_y
        oled.pixel(x, y, WHITE)
        oled.show()

def zig_zag(oled):
    animate_pixel(oled, x=0, y=0, step_x=1, step_y=1, count=30)
    animate_pixel(oled, x=30, y=30, step_x=1, step_y=-1, count=30)
    animate_pixel(oled, x=60, y=0, step_x=1, step_y=1, count=30)
    animate_pixel(oled, x=90, y=30, step_x=1, step_y=-1, count=30)

def main():
    i2c = busio.I2C(board.SCL, board.SDA)
    oled = adafruit_ssd1306.SSD1306_I2C(128, 32, i2c)
    zig_zag(oled)

main()
```

When this script gets executed, it will draw four line animations in a zigzag pattern.

How it works...

After the `main` function has set up the `oled` object, it calls the `zig_zag` function. The `zig_zag` function makes four calls to the `animate_pixel` function. Each call moves the line in a different diagonal direction.

Each new line animation starts off where the last one finished so that it appears as one long animation from start to finish. The `animate_pixel` function takes a starting x and y position and loops for the number of iterations specified by the `count` variable.

In each loop iteration, the values of x and y are changed by the specified x and y step values. Once the new values are calculated, a pixel is drawn at that position and the `show` method is called to show it immediately.

There's more...

This recipe started off with a few simple examples of setting pixels on and off and the different positions on the display. Then, it expanded to do a simple animation and an even more involved zigzag animation. The following photograph shows what this animation looks like on the display once it is complete:

Many more different types of shapes and animations can be created by using the math module that comes with MicroPython. The sine and cosine functions can be used to draw wave animations. We can also use these trigonometric functions to draw circles and ellipses.

See also

For more information, you can refer to the following:

- More documentation on drawing pixels on the FeatherWing OLED can be found at https://learn.adafruit.com/adafruit-oled-featherwing/circuitpython-and-python-usage.
- More documentation on the sin function in the math module can be found at https://docs.micropython.org/en/latest/library/math.html#math.sin.

Drawing lines and rectangles on the display

This recipe will demonstrate how to use the methods that come with the `SSD1306_I2C` object, which will let us draw horizontal lines, vertical lines, squares, and rectangles. We can now move beyond setting individual pixels and explore drawing a wider range of shapes using the methods that come out of the box with the `adafruit_ssd1306` display library.

You will find this recipe useful for when you want to draw some different shapes; for example, to build a simple user interface on the display. There is enough resolution on the display to draw a number of boxes and borders that represent different parts of your user interface.

Getting ready

You will need access to the REPL on the ESP8266 to run the code presented in this recipe.

How to do it...

Let's perform the following steps:

1. Execute the following block of code in the REPL:

```
>>> import adafruit_ssd1306
>>> import board
>>> import busio
>>>
>>> BLACK = 0
>>> WHITE = 1
>>>
>>> i2c = busio.I2C(board.SCL, board.SDA)
>>> oled = adafruit_ssd1306.SSD1306_I2C(128, 32, i2c)
>>> oled.fill(BLACK)
>>> oled.show()
```

2. The necessary modules are imported, `oled` is created, and then the display is cleared. Using the following block of code, draw a vertical line starting at coordinates (0, 0) with a height of 20 pixels:

```
>>> oled.vline(x=0, y=0, height=20, color=WHITE)
>>> oled.show()
```

3. In a similar fashion, draw a horizontal line starting at coordinates (0, 0) with a width of 80 pixels:

```
>>> oled.hline(x=0, y=0, width=80, color=WHITE)
>>> oled.show()
```

4. A rectangle at position (0, 0) having a width of 10 pixels and height of 20 pixels can be drawn using the next block of code:

```
>>> oled.rect(x=0, y=0, width=10, height=20, color=WHITE)
>>> oled.show()
```

5. The following function will draw the HI text. The H character will be drawn using vertical lines and one horizontal line. The I character will then be drawn using a single vertical line:

```
>>> def draw_hi(oled):
...     print('drawing H')
...     oled.vline(x=50, y=0, height=30, color=WHITE)
...     oled.hline(x=50, y=15, width=30, color=WHITE)
...     oled.vline(x=80, y=0, height=30, color=WHITE)
...     oled.show()
...     print('drawing I')
...     oled.vline(x=100, y=0, height=30, color=WHITE)
...     oled.show()
...
...
...
>>>
```

6. The following code block will clear the screen and call the draw_hi function to render the message, HI, on the display:

```
>>> oled.fill(BLACK)
>>> oled.show()
>>> draw_hi(oled)
drawing H
drawing I
>>>
```

7. Using the following code block, define a function that will perform an animation involving boxes, which are of a certain size and are shifted in position by step *x* and *y* in each iteration:

```
>>> def animate_boxes(oled, x, y, step_x, step_y, size, count):
...     for i in range(count):
...         oled.rect(x, y, width=size, height=size, color=WHITE)
```

```
...             oled.show()
...             x += step_x
...             y += step_y
...
...
...
>>>
```

8. Next, use the following code block to call `animate_boxes` and draw six boxes in a diagonal formation:

```
>>> animate_boxes(oled, x=0, y=0, step_x=5, step_y=5, size=5,
count=6)
```

9. Define and call the `draw_x_boxes` function, which draws a set of boxes in two diagonal lines to create a large letter X made of small boxes:

```
>>> def draw_x_boxes(oled):
...         animate_boxes(oled, x=0, y=0, step_x=5, step_y=5, size=5,
count=6)
...         animate_boxes(oled, x=0, y=25, step_x=5, step_y=-5, size=5,
count=6)
...
...
...
>>>
>>> draw_x_boxes(oled)
```

10. Add the following code to the `main.py` file:

```
import adafruit_ssd1306
import board
import busio

BLACK = 0
WHITE = 1

def draw_hi(oled):
    print('drawing H')
    oled.vline(x=50, y=0, height=30, color=WHITE)
    oled.hline(x=50, y=15, width=30, color=WHITE)
    oled.vline(x=80, y=0, height=30, color=WHITE)
    oled.show()
    print('drawing I')
    oled.vline(x=100, y=0, height=30, color=WHITE)
    oled.show()

def animate_boxes(oled, x, y, step_x, step_y, size, count):
```

```
            for i in range(count):
                oled.rect(x, y, width=size, height=size, color=WHITE)
                oled.show()
                x += step_x
                y += step_y

        def draw_x_boxes(oled):
            animate_boxes(oled, x=0, y=0, step_x=5, step_y=5, size=5,
        count=6)
            animate_boxes(oled, x=0, y=25, step_x=5, step_y=-5, size=5,
        count=6)

        def main():
            i2c = busio.I2C(board.SCL, board.SDA)
            oled = adafruit_ssd1306.SSD1306_I2C(128, 32, i2c)
            draw_x_boxes(oled)
            draw_hi(oled)

        main()
```

When this script gets executed, it will draw a letter X made up of small boxes and draw the
HI text, which is made of vertical and horizontal lines.

How it works...

The draw_hi function uses the vline and hline methods on the oled object to draw the
three lines that will make up H. After the letter H is drawn, a vertical line is drawn using
vline to represent the letter I.

Calling the draw_x_boxes function will, in turn, call the animate_boxes function. The
first call to the animate_boxes function draws six boxes in a diagonal direction to make
the first part of the X character. The second call to animate_boxes also makes six boxes,
but from a different starting position and going in a different direction. The second call will
cut through the first line to form the X character.

There's more...

The line drawing and rectangle drawing methods can be combined in many different ways to create all sorts of shapes and drawings. The following photograph shows what the display will look like once you run the `main.py` script in this recipe:

In the next recipe, we will learn how to draw text on the display. It is very useful to combine box and line drawings and then render text on different parts of the display.

See also

For more information, you can refer to the following:

- Further documentation on the main features of the FeatherWing OLED can be found at `https://learn.adafruit.com/adafruit-oled-featherwing/overview`.
- More documentation on the `busio` module can be found at `https://circuitpython.readthedocs.io/en/3.x/shared-bindings/busio/__init__.html`.

Writing text on the display

This recipe will demonstrate how to write text output to the FeatherWing OLED. The recipe will show you how to control the position and content of the text to be displayed. A text animation will be created to perform a countdown on the display, and then a function will be created to show all lowercase, uppercase, and digit characters on the screen at the same time.

This recipe will help you whenever you have some information that you want to communicate with people using your devices. Because the display can show three rows of text, it gives a lot of room for presenting all sorts of information.

Getting ready

You will need access to the REPL on the ESP8266 to run the code presented in this recipe.

How to do it...

Let's perform the followings steps:

1. Download the CircuitPython library bundle.
2. Extract the bundle of `.zip` files to your computer.
3. Copy the `font5x8.bin` font file, which is located in the bundle of the ESP8266 root folder.
4. Use the REPL to run the following lines of code:

```
>>> import adafruit_ssd1306
>>> import board
>>> import busio
>>>
>>> BLACK = 0
>>> WHITE = 1
>>>
>>> i2c = busio.I2C(board.SCL, board.SDA)
>>> oled = adafruit_ssd1306.SSD1306_I2C(128, 32, i2c)
>>> oled.fill(BLACK)
>>> oled.show()
```

5. We now have the display cleared and are ready to show some text on the screen. Using the following block of code, display the `'hello'` text on the screen drawn at position (0, 0) in the color white:

```
>>> oled.text('hello', 0, 0, WHITE)
>>> oled.show()
```

6. Use the following block of code to clear the screen and show three lines of text:

```
>>> oled.fill(BLACK)
>>> oled.show()
>>>
>>> oled.text('line 1', 0, 0, WHITE)
>>> oled.text('line 2', 0, 10, WHITE)
>>> oled.text('line 3', 0, 20, WHITE)
>>> oled.show()
```

7. Define a function and then call it; this will count down from the number 10 to 0 on the display:

```
>>> def countdown(oled, start):
...     for i in range(start, -1, -1):
...         oled.fill(BLACK)
...         oled.text(str(i), 0, 0, WHITE)
...         oled.show()
...
...
...
>>>
>>> countdown(oled, 10)
```

8. Using the following block of code, define a constant called ALPHA_NUMERIC. It contains all the lowercase, uppercase, and digit characters, which are organized in a structure that will fit on the display:

```
>>> ALPHA_NUMERIC = [
...     'abcdefghijklmnopqrstu',
...     'vwxyzABCDEFGHIJKLMNOP',
...     'QRSTUVWXYZ0123456789',
... ]
```

9. Using the following block of code, define and call the show_alpha_numeric function, which loops through the ALPHA_NUMERIC list and shows each string on a separate line:

```
>>> def show_alpha_numeric(oled):
...     for i, text in enumerate(ALPHA_NUMERIC):
```

```
...             oled.text(text, 0, 10 * i, WHITE)
...             oled.show()
...
...
...
>>> oled.fill(BLACK)
>>> show_alpha_numeric(oled)
```

10. Add the following code to the `main.py` file:

```python
import adafruit_ssd1306
import board
import busio

BLACK = 0
WHITE = 1
ALPHA_NUMERIC = [
    'abcdefghijklmnopqrstu',
    'vwxyzABCDEFGHIJKLMNOP',
    'QRSTUVWXYZ0123456789',
]

def countdown(oled, start):
    for i in range(start, -1, -1):
        oled.fill(BLACK)
        oled.text(str(i), 0, 0, WHITE)
        oled.show()

def show_alpha_numeric(oled):
    for i, text in enumerate(ALPHA_NUMERIC):
        oled.text(text, 0, 10 * i, WHITE)
        oled.show()

def main():
    i2c = busio.I2C(board.SCL, board.SDA)
    oled = adafruit_ssd1306.SSD1306_I2C(128, 32, i2c)
    oled.fill(BLACK)
    countdown(oled, 10)
    oled.fill(BLACK)
    show_alpha_numeric(oled)

main()
```

When this script gets executed, it will perform a count down animation and then display some alphanumeric text.

How it works...

The countdown function starts a for loop that will count from 10 to 0. During each iteration, the screen is cleared and then the current number is displayed on the screen. The ALPHA_NUMERIC variable combines lowercase, uppercase, and digit characters in a format that is structured over three lines. The display can show 3 rows and 21 columns of text. This data fits within these limits so that all the characters can be displayed clearly without any cropping of text. The countdown function loops through each line of text and displays it at the correct position so that the 3 rows of text on the screen get filed correctly.

There's more...

The sky is the limit when it comes to what you can represent using textual output. The output you displayed could be as varied as sensor readings to the latest news headlines fetched live from the internet. The following photograph shows the display after the show_alpha_numeric function is called:

Even though the screen is physically quite small, it has a good resolution, and the font that comes with the CircuitPython library bundle has done a good job of using the limited screen space efficiently. This has made it possible to show three lines of text on a very small display.

See also

For more information, you can refer to the following:

- More documentation on a MicroPython project that creates an OLED watch can be found at `https://learn.adafruit.com/micropython-oled-watch`.
- Further documentation on the I2C communication protocol can be found at `https://learn.sparkfun.com/tutorials/i2c/all`.

Inverting colors on the display

This recipe will demonstrate how to use the `invert` feature to flip the color of all the pixels. This can be used for when you are displaying white text on a black background, and then want the colors to be flipped so that the screen shows black text on a white background. A number of key operations on the display, such as clearing the screen, can be quite slow compared to features such as invert. We can take advantage of these performance differences to use invert when we want fast, visual feedback to appear to people using the screen.

This recipe will help you whenever you are creating a project using a slow microcontroller and you need to find creative ways to make the device more responsive so that you can improve its usability.

Getting ready

You will need access to the REPL on the ESP8266 to run the code presented in this recipe.

How to do it...

Let's perform the following steps:

1. Run the following lines of code in the REPL:

```
>>> import adafruit_ssd1306
>>> import board
>>> import busio
>>>
>>> BLACK = 0
>>> WHITE = 1
>>>
```

```
>>> i2c = busio.I2C(board.SCL, board.SDA)
>>> oled = adafruit_ssd1306.SSD1306_I2C(128, 32, i2c)
>>> oled.fill(BLACK)
>>> oled.show()
```

2. After the initial setup, the `oled` object is available for us to start inverting the screen. Use the following block of code to display some white text on a black background:

```
>>> oled.invert(True)
```

3. The screen will now have black text on a white background. To flip the colors back, run the following code:

```
>>> oled.invert(False)
```

4. The `invert` feature is much faster than some of the other methods that are used to update the screen. Use the following function to time this speed difference:

```
>>> def measure_time(label, func, args=(), count=3):
...     for i in range(count):
...         start = time.monotonic()
...         func(*args)
...         total = (time.monotonic() - start) * 1000
...         print(label + ':', '%s ms' % total)
...
...
...
>>>
```

5. Use the next block of code to call the `measure_time` function, and time how long the `fill` operation takes in milliseconds:

```
>>> measure_time('fill', oled.fill, [BLACK])
fill: 1047.85 ms
fill: 1049.07 ms
fill: 1046.14 ms
>>>
```

6. Now time the `show` method, and you will see that it is faster than `fill`:

```
>>> measure_time('show', oled.show, [])
show: 62.0117 ms
show: 62.0117 ms
show: 61.0352 ms
>>>
```

7. Use the following code to check the speed of the `text` method:

```
>>> measure_time('text', oled.text, ['hello', 0, 0, WHITE])
text: 74.9512 ms
text: 75.1953 ms
text: 80.0781 ms
>>>
```

8. Finally, the `invert` method has its speed checked, as follows:

```
>>> measure_time('invert', oled.invert, [True])
invert: 0.976563 ms
invert: 1.95313 ms
invert: 0.976563 ms
>>>
```

9. Add the following code to the `main.py` file:

```
import adafruit_ssd1306
import board
import busio
import time

BLACK = 0
WHITE = 1

def measure_time(label, func, args=(), count=3):
    for i in range(count):
        start = time.monotonic()
        func(*args)
        total = (time.monotonic() - start) * 1000
        print(label + ':', '%s ms' % total)

def main():
    i2c = busio.I2C(board.SCL, board.SDA)
    oled = adafruit_ssd1306.SSD1306_I2C(128, 32, i2c)
    oled.fill(BLACK)
    oled.show()

    measure_time('fill', oled.fill, [BLACK])
    measure_time('show', oled.show, [])
    measure_time('text', oled.text, ['hello', 0, 0, WHITE])
    measure_time('invert', oled.invert, [True])

main()
```

When this script gets executed, it prints out the performance results for a number of screen-related operations.

How it works...

The `measure_time` function, by default, loops for three rounds. It saves the current time in the `start` variable, calls the function being tested, and then calculates the total execution time of the function call. This value is converted into milliseconds and the result is then printed out. The `main` function calls `measure_time` four times. It calls it to measure the execution time of `fill`, `show`, `text`, and the `invert` method.

There's more...

Looking at the performance results, a number of things are quite evident. The good thing is that the results are pretty consistent. In this recipe, we have taken three readings for each measurement. It's always a good idea to take more than one sample when measuring execution speed. From the samples, it seems that a call to `fill` is approximately 500 times slower than a call to `invert`. For an application to feel responsive, operations shouldn't take more than 100 milliseconds, or it will appear to be sluggish or unresponsive. Operations such as `invert`, `text`, and `show` perform at a good speed. But since `fill` takes so long, we might want to call `invert` before performing `fill` so that users get a sign that our application is responding to their inputs.

See also

For more information, you can refer to the following:

- More documentation on a CircuitPython project that uses the OLED display and the ESP8266 can be found at `https://learn.adafruit.com/circuitpython-totp-otp-2fa-authy-authenticator-friend`.
- Further details on OLEDs can be found at `https://www.oled-info.com/oled-introduction`.

14
Building an Internet of Things (IoT) Weather Machine

In this chapter, we will create an internet-connected weather machine that will tell us the weather in random cities at the press of a button. In order to produce this working device, we will combine a number of concepts and technologies that we have covered in the book .

We'll use some of the networking techniques shown in Chapter 12, *Networking*, as well as the display logic shown in Chapter 13, *Interacting with the Adafruit FeatherWing OLED*, covering how to interact with the FeatherWing OLED. These different technologies will be combined to create a device that responds to touch button events by fetching live weather data using RESTful APIs and presenting them on an **organic light-emitting diode (OLED)** display.

This chapter can be a useful source of information to help you create internet-connected devices with MicroPython that are easy to interact with and will give a rich set of visual outputs.

In this chapter, we will be covering the following topics:

- Retrieving weather data from the internet
- Creating a function to get a city's weather
- Randomly selecting cities
- Creating a Screen object for text handling
- Creating a function to show a city's weather
- Providing visual feedback when fetching weather data
- Creating a function to display the weather for a random city
- Creating an IoT button to show the weather around the world

Technical requirements

The code files of this chapter can be found in the `Chapter14` folder of the following GitHub repository: `https://github.com/PacktPublishing/MicroPython-Cookbook`.

This chapter uses the Adafruit Feather HUZZAH ESP8266 and the Assembled Adafruit FeatherWing OLED 128x32 OLED add-on for Feather. CircuitPython 3.1.2 was used for all the recipes in this chapter. You will need to apply the configuration described in the *Connecting to an existing Wi-Fi network* recipe from `Chapter 10`, *Controlling the ESP8266*. The `wait_for_networking` function described in the *Creating a function to wait for internet connectivity* recipe from `Chapter 12`, *Networking*, will also be used in this chapter. You will also need to perform the steps described in `Chapter 13`, *Interacting with the Adafruit FeatherWing OLED*.

The recipes in this chapter use the weather API service provided by Openweather. This service is free to use, but you must register and obtain an **API key (APPID)** to use the service. The API key will be needed to run the code in this chapter. You can visit `https://openweathermap.org/appid` to get an API key.

Retrieving weather data from the internet

This recipe will show you how to connect to the internet using the ESP8266 and fetch live weather data using RESTful web services. The service that we will be using has up-to-date weather information for over 100,000 cities around the world. A very large amount of weather information for each location is provided, so this recipe will show how we can drill down to the items that are of most interest to us.

This recipe can be useful in your projects whenever you need to pass different parameters to a RESTful call or when the returned results are very large and you need to find ways to navigate through these large datasets.

Getting ready

You will need access to the REPL on the ESP8266 to run the code presented in this recipe.

How to do it...

Let's follow the steps required in this recipe:

1. Run the following lines of code in the REPL:

```
>>> import urequests >>> >>> API_URL =
'http://api.openweathermap.org/data/2.5/weather' >>>
```

2. The API_URL variable has now been defined, which we will use to access the weather API. In the next block of code, we define APPID and city to get weather data for. Make sure to replace the APPID value with your actual APPID value. We will now build the URL by combining these variables, which we we can then access:

```
>>> APPID = 'put-your-API-key(APPID)-here'
>>> city = 'Berlin'
>>> url = API_URL + '?units=metric&APPID=' + APPID + '&q=' + city
```

3. The following block of code will connect to the weather API and retrieve the weather data:

```
>>> response = urequests.get(url)
>>> response
<Response object at 3fff1b00>
```

4. We know that the response uses JSON format, so we can parse it and inspect how many top-level keys are in the data:

```
>>> data = response.json()
>>> len(data)
13
```

5. The next block of code inspects the parsed weather data. There is a lot of nested data, so it is difficult to digest in its current form:

```
>>> data
{'cod': 200, 'rain': {'1h': 0.34}, 'dt': 1555227314, 'base':
'stations', 'weather': [{'id': 500, 'icon': '10d', 'main': 'Rain',
'description': 'light rain'}, {'id': 310, 'icon': '09d', 'main':
'Drizzle', 'description': 'light intensity drizzle rain'}], 'sys':
{'message': 0.0052, 'country': 'DE', 'sunrise': 1555215098,
'sunset': 1555264894, 'id': 1275, 'type': 1}, 'name': 'Berlin',
'clouds': {'all': 75}, 'coord': {'lon': 13.39, 'lat': 52.52},
'visibility': 7000, 'wind': {'speed': 3.6, 'deg': 40}, 'id':
2950159, 'main': {'pressure': 1025, 'humidity': 93, 'temp_min':
2.22, 'temp_max': 3.89, 'temp': 3.05}}
```

6. MicroPython doesn't have the `pprint` module. We will copy and paste the output of the data and run the following on a Python REPL on a computer:

```
>>> data = {'cod': 200, 'rain': {'1h': 0.34}, 'dt': 1555227314,
'base': 'stations', 'weather': [{'id': 500, 'icon': '10d', 'main':
'Rain', 'description': 'light rain'}, {'id': 310, 'icon': '09d',
'main': 'Drizzle', 'description': 'light intensity drizzle rain'}],
'sys': {'message': 0.0052, 'country': 'DE', 'sunrise': 1555215098,
'sunset': 1555264894, 'id': 1275, 'type': 1}, 'name': 'Berlin',
'clouds': {'all': 75}, 'coord': {'lon': 13.39, 'lat': 52.52},
'visibility': 7000, 'wind': {'speed': 3.6, 'deg': 40}, 'id':
2950159, 'main': {'pressure': 1025, 'humidity': 93, 'temp_min':
2.22, 'temp_max': 3.89, 'temp': 3.05}}
```

7. Run the next block of code on the computer's REPL, and we will get a more structured representation of the data:

```
>>> import pprint
>>> pprint.pprint(data)
{'base': 'stations',
 'clouds': {'all': 75},
 'cod': 200,
 'coord': {'lat': 52.52, 'lon': 13.39},
 'dt': 1555227314,
 'id': 2950159,
 'main': {'humidity': 93,
          'pressure': 1025,
          'temp': 3.05,
          'temp_max': 3.89,
          'temp_min': 2.22},
 'name': 'Berlin',
 'rain': {'1h': 0.34},
 'sys': {'country': 'DE',
         'id': 1275,
         'message': 0.0052,
         'sunrise': 1555215098,
         'sunset': 1555264894,
         'type': 1},
 'visibility': 7000,
 'weather': [{'description': 'light rain',
              'icon': '10d',
              'id': 500,
              'main': 'Rain'},
             {'description': 'light intensity drizzle rain',
              'icon': '09d',
              'id': 310,
              'main': 'Drizzle'}],
 'wind': {'deg': 40, 'speed': 3.6}}
```

```
>>>
```

8. We can return to the MicroPython REPL now and run the following lines of code to inspect the `main` key:

```
>>> data['main']
{'pressure': 1025, 'humidity': 93, 'temp_min': 2.22, 'temp_max':
3.89, 'temp': 3.05}
```

9. The next lines of code will give us access to the temperature and humidity values of Berlin:

```
>>> data['main']['temp']
3.05
>>> data['main']['humidity']
93
>>>
```

10. You can access the wind section of the data with the following lines of code:

```
>>> data['wind']
{'speed': 3.6, 'deg': 40}
>>> data['wind']['speed']
3.6
```

In this way, we can drill down further and get the wind speed value for the requested city.

How it works...

After importing the `urequests` library, we define a number of variables so that we can proceed and prepare the URL to perform the API call. The `API_URL` is a fixed constant that will not change between calls to the web service. Then, we define a variable to store the API key and city values. These values are combined to make the final URL, which we then call using the `urequests` library's `get` function.

The `return` response is parsed and the output is displayed. Because the data structure is so large, we use a trick to move this data to the REPL on a computer where we can use the `pprint` function and get a much clearer output format of the returned data. This makes it much easier to identify the different parts of the data structure and start accessing different data elements in the nested data structure. We then use the keys in the dictionary to access the humidity, temperature, and wind speed of the city of Berlin.

There's more...

The use of API keys is widespread in the world of web services. This recipe is a great example of how we can take these keys and include them in our API calls so that they can be processed successfully. We also showed the trick of copying data structures from our MicroPython REPL to a Python REPL on a computer. This lets us bounce between these two worlds and access some modules, such as `pprint`, that are available on computers but not on MicroPython.

See also

Here are a few references for further information:

- Documentation on the `pprint` module can be found at `https://docs.python.org/3/library/pprint.html`.
- Documentation on accessing weather data by city name can be found at `https://openweathermap.org/current#name`.

Creating a function to get a city's weather

In this recipe, we will create a function to connect to the weather API and fetch the weather data for a particular city. We don't want to hardcode values such as our API keys directly in our source code. So, this recipe will also show you how to create a JSON formatted configuration file that can store different settings, such as the API key. The application will then read in the values from this configuration file at boot up and use them for the calls to the weather web services.

This recipe will be particularly useful to you whenever you want to keep configuration values separate from your code base, whether it be for security reasons or to just tweak these settings more easily without changing your application's source code. This can also help you in your own projects to organize the API calls into reusable functions.

Getting ready

You will need access to the REPL on the ESP8266 to run the code presented in this recipe.

How to do it...

Let's follow the steps required in this recipe:

1. Execute the next block of code in the REPL:

```
>>> from netcheck import wait_for_networking
>>> import urequests
>>> import json
>>>
>>> CONF_PATH = 'conf.json'
>>> API_URL = 'http://api.openweathermap.org/data/2.5/weather'
```

2. The CONF_PATH variable defines the location of our JSON configuration file.

3. The following content should be put into the conf.json file on the board's root folder. Replace the value of APPID with your actual APPID value:

```
{"APPID": "put-your-API-key(APPID)-here"}
```

4. The next block of code defines a function that will read and parse the settings provided in your configuration file. The values of these settings are then returned to the calling function:

```
>>> def get_conf():
...     content = open(CONF_PATH).read()
...     return json.loads(content)
...
...
...
>>>
```

5. We will now call the get_conf function and store its results into a variable called conf. The value of APPID is retrieved and saved into a variable for future use:

```
>>> conf = get_conf()
>>> APPID = conf['APPID']
```

6. The following block of code defines a function that receives a city name and performs the weather API call for that city and returns the parsed weather data:

```
>>> def get_weather(APPID, city):
...     url = API_URL + '?units=metric&APPID=' + APPID + '&q='
...     + city
...     return urequests.get(url).json()
...
```

```
...
...
>>>
```

7. The next block of code calls the `get_weather` function for the city of London and stores the result in a variable called `data`. A number of different data fields are then accessed and printed out:

```
>>> data = get_weather(APPID, 'London')
>>>
>>> print('temp:', data['main']['temp'])
temp: 7.87
>>> print('wind:', data['wind']['speed'])
wind: 3.1
>>> print('name:', data['name'])
name: London
>>> print('country:', data['sys']['country'])
country: GB
>>>
```

8. The next block of code should be put into the `main.py` file.

```
from netcheck import wait_for_networking
import urequests
import json

CONF_PATH = 'conf.json'
API_URL = 'http://api.openweathermap.org/data/2.5/weather'

def get_conf():
    content = open(CONF_PATH).read()
    return json.loads(content)

def get_weather(APPID, city):
    url = API_URL + '?units=metric&APPID=' + APPID + '&q=' + city
    return urequests.get(url).json()

def main():
    wait_for_networking()
    conf = get_conf()
    APPID = conf['APPID']
    data = get_weather(APPID, 'London')
    print('temp:', data['main']['temp'])
    print('wind:', data['wind']['speed'])
    print('name:', data['name'])
    print('country:', data['sys']['country'])

main()
```

When this script is executed, it will connect to the weather API and print out a number of retrieved data elements for the city of London.

How it works...

The main script first calls `wait_for_networking` to ensure that networking is up and running before making any API calls. It then retrieves the applications configuration data by calling `get_conf`, which parses the JSON data stored in the configuration file.

The value of `APPID` is then accessed from the configuration settings. An API call is then made using the `get_weather` function. This function receives the `APPID` value and name of the city to fetch information on. With these two values, it can prepare the URL and make the API call.

The results are then parsed and returned to the `main` function. The data structure is then accessed to get a number of values from the returned API call and print them out with their associated labels.

There's more...

This recipe shows a generic technique to store values such as your API keys outside your source code. JSON is a useful file format for storing configuration values, particularly when working with MicroPython, since it has built-in support for parsing this file format. Some applications also use the popular `.ini` file format for configuration files, which has support in the Python standard library. This Python module is not available as part of the main libraries in MicroPython, so it's best to avoid it in your MicroPython projects when you can.

See also

Here are a few references for further information:

- Documentation on the `json` module can be found at `https://docs.python.org/3/library/json.html`.
- Documentation on the `configparser` module used to parse INI files can be found at `https://docs.python.org/3/library/configparser.html`.

Randomly selecting cities

In this recipe, we will use the `random` module to randomly select cities from a fixed list of cities. We first create a global variable called `CITIES` to store these values. We can then use a specific function in the `random` module that is for the specific purpose of selecting random items from a list of values.

The recipe will then loop 10 times and make a random selection from the list of cities and output details of the selected city. This recipe will be particularly useful to you whenever you have a project that needs to select a certain option randomly from a fixed list of values. You might, for example, create a dice-rolling MicroPython project that should choose from the values one to six on each roll.

Getting ready

You will need access to the REPL on the ESP8266 to run the code presented in this recipe.

How to do it...

Let's follow the steps required in this recipe:

1. Use the REPL to run the following lines of code:

```
>>> import random
>>>
>>> CITIES = ['Berlin', 'London', 'Paris', 'Tokyo', 'Rome', 'Oslo',
'Bangkok']
```

2. We have now defined a list of cities that we can make a random selection from. The next code shows one of the simplest ways of getting random data from the `random` Python module:

```
>>> random.random()
0.0235046
>>> random.random()
0.830886
>>> random.random()
0.0738319
```

3. For our purposes, we can use the `choice` function, as it will randomly select an item from a list. The following block of code uses this method to randomly select three cities:

```
>>> random.choice(CITIES)
'Rome'
>>> random.choice(CITIES)
'Berlin'
>>>
>>> random.choice(CITIES)
'Oslo'
```

4. The following block of code will loop 10 times and print out a randomly selected city in each iteration:

```
>>> for i in range(10):
...     city = random.choice(CITIES)
...     print('random selection', i, city)
...
...
...
random selection 0 London
random selection 1 Tokyo
random selection 2 Oslo
random selection 3 Berlin
random selection 4 Bangkok
random selection 5 Tokyo
random selection 6 London
random selection 7 Oslo
random selection 8 Oslo
random selection 9 London
>>>
```

5. The next block of code should be put into the `main.py` file:

```
import random

CITIES = ['Berlin', 'London', 'Paris', 'Tokyo', 'Rome', 'Oslo',
'Bangkok']

def main():
    for i in range(10):
        city = random.choice(CITIES)
        print('random selection', i, city)

main()
```

When this script is executed, it will print out 10 randomly selected cities.

How it works...

We first import the `random` module that will be used to perform the random selection of cities. The `random` function is called repeatedly to verify that we can get random numbers from the module. We have created a variable called `CITIES`, which is our list of cities that we want to make random selections from. The `choice` function in the `random` module is then used to pick a random choice from this list. The `main` function provides a demonstration of this logic by calling the `choice` function 10 times and printing out the results of each call.

There's more...

This chapter only needs random numbers to be chosen to create a level of unpredictability in the operation of the weather machine. Because of this, we don't need to worry about the quality of the random numbers being generated. If, however, we need random numbers for the purpose of some cryptographic operation, then we would need to be more careful of how these numbers are generated. We would also need to go into detail in terms of how the random number generator is initialized with a call to the `seed` function.

See also

Here are a few references for further information:

- Documentation on the `choice` function can be found at `https://docs.python.org/3/library/random.html#random.choice`.
- Documentation on the `seed` function can be found at `https://docs.python.org/3/library/random.html#random.seed`.

Creating a Screen object for text handling

In this recipe, we will create a `Screen` object that will make it easier to write a multi-line output to the FeatherWing OLED display. The weather machine that we are building will want to take advantage of the multi-line output capabilities of the OLED display.

To facilitate this output, this recipe will create an object that receives multi-line text and will properly position the text in its associated *x* and *y* coordinates. You will find this recipe useful for any projects where you are writing text content to the display frequently and want an automatic way to handle the multi-line output.

Getting ready

You will need access to the REPL on the ESP8266 to run the code presented in this recipe.

How to do it...

Let's follow the steps required in this recipe:

1. Run the following lines of code in the REPL:

```
>>> import adafruit_ssd1306
>>> import board
>>> import busio
>>>
>>> BLACK = 0
>>> WHITE = 1
>>>
>>> MESSAGE = """\
... top line %s
... middle line
... last line
... """
>>>
```

2. We have imported the necessary modules and created a variable called MESSAGE that we will use to generate multi-line output messages. The next block of code will create the basic structure of the Screen object with a constructor that receives the oled display object:

```
>>> class Screen:
...     def __init__(self, oled):
...         self.oled = oled
...         self.oled.fill(BLACK)
...         self.oled.show()
...
...
...
>>>
```

3. In the following lines of code, we create an object to interact with the display and an instance of the Screen class:

```
>>> i2c = busio.I2C(board.SCL, board.SDA)
>>> oled = adafruit_ssd1306.SSD1306_I2C(128, 32, i2c)
>>> screen = Screen(oled)
```

4. We will now add a method to the `Screen` object that will be responsible for writing the multi-line text to the display:

```
>>> class Screen:
...     def __init__(self, oled):
...         self.oled = oled
...         self.oled.fill(BLACK)
...         self.oled.show()
...
...     def write(self, text):
...         self.oled.fill(BLACK)
...         lines = text.strip().split('\n')
...         for row, line in enumerate(lines):
...             self.oled.text(line, 0, 10 * row, WHITE)
...         self.oled.show()
...
...
...
>>>
```

5. We now create a `Screen` object and call its `write` method. You should see the `'hello'` text appear on the display now:

```
>>> screen = Screen(oled)
>>> screen.write('hello')
```

6. The next block of code will print a multi-line message to the display that takes up three lines:

```
>>> screen.write('multi \n line \n output')
>>>
```

7. Run the following code to display 10 different multi-line messages on the display:

```
>>> for i in range(10):
...     print(i)
...     screen.write(MESSAGE % i)
...
...
...
0
1
2
3
4
5
```

```
6
7
8
9
>>>
```

8. The following code should be put into the `screen.py` file:

```python
import adafruit_ssd1306
import board
import busio

BLACK = 0
WHITE = 1

class Screen:
    def __init__(self, oled):
        self.oled = oled
        self.oled.fill(BLACK)
        self.oled.show()

    def write(self, text):
        self.oled.fill(BLACK)
        lines = text.strip().split('\n')
        for row, line in enumerate(lines):
            self.oled.text(line, 0, 10 * row, WHITE)
        self.oled.show()

def get_oled():
    i2c = busio.I2C(board.SCL, board.SDA)
    return adafruit_ssd1306.SSD1306_I2C(128, 32, i2c)
```

9. The next block of code should be put into the `main.py` file:

```python
from screen import Screen, get_oled

MESSAGE = """\
top line %s
middle line
last line
"""

def main():
    oled = get_oled()
    screen = Screen(oled)
    screen.write('hello')

    for i in range(10):
```

```
        print(i)
        screen.write(MESSAGE % i)

main()
```

When this script gets executed, it will print out 10 multi-line blocks of text to the OLED display.

How it works...

The `screen` object takes a single argument to its constructor. This argument is the `oled` variable, which will let us interact with the display. A reference to this object is saved, and then all the pixels on the display are cleared. It also defines a method called `write`. This method receives a string, which can be a single or multi-line piece of text.

The display is then cleared and the text is broken up into a list of strings, each representing a single line of output. These lines are looped through and written each to their correct row. Once all lines have been processed, the `show` method is called on the display to render the content on the screen. The `main` function in this recipe sets up the `screen` object and then sends one simple `hello` message to the display. It then loops 10 times and generates a set of multi-line messages, which are displayed on the screen one after the other.

There's more...

The design of the `Screen` object is similar to the design of other files, such as objects, in Python. The `sys` Python module, for example, has a `stdout` object, which has a `write` method that lets you write text output to the screen. Packaging complex interactions, such as *x*, *y* positioning for text placement into a separate object, will often make the rest of the code simpler and more readable.

See also

Here are a few references for further information:

- Documentation on the `stdout` object can be found at `https://docs.python.org/3/library/sys.html#sys.stdout`.
- Documentation on file objects that expose the `write` methods can be found at `https://docs.python.org/3/glossary.html#term-file-object`.

Creating a function to show a city's weather

In this recipe, we will create a function that takes the name of a city, looks up its weather information, and then display a portion of this information on the OLED display. To achieve this, the function in this recipe will combine different pieces from the recipes covered in this chapter.

In addition to outputting to the OLED, it will also print out the same information to standard output to facilitate debugging. This recipe can be useful to you when you want to see how a project such as weather machine can be broken into separate pieces that all call one another in a structured design.

Getting ready

You will need access to the REPL on the ESP8266 to run the code presented in this recipe.

How to do it...

Let's follow the steps required in this recipe:

1. Execute the next block of code in the REPL:

```
>>> from screen import Screen, get_oled
>>> from netcheck import wait_for_networking
>>> import urequests
>>> import json
>>>
>>> CONF_PATH = 'conf.json'
>>> API_URL = 'http://api.openweathermap.org/data/2.5/weather'
>>> CITIES = ['Berlin', 'London', 'Paris', 'Tokyo', 'Rome', 'Oslo',
'Bangkok']
>>> WEATHER = """\
... City: {city}
... Temp: {temp}
... Wind: {wind}
... """
>>>
```

2. After importing the needed modules, we create a new variable called WEATHER that stores the template, which we will use to output the weather information to the display. Run the next block of code to set up the screen object and get the APPID value for the API calls:

```
>>> def get_conf():
...     content = open(CONF_PATH).read()
...     return json.loads(content)
...
...
...
>>> def get_weather(APPID, city):
...     url = API_URL + '?units=metric&APPID=' + APPID + '&q=' +
city
...     return urequests.get(url).json()
...
...
...
>>> oled = get_oled()
>>> screen = Screen(oled)
>>> wait_for_networking()
address on network: 10.0.0.38
'10.0.0.38'
>>> conf = get_conf()
>>> APPID = conf['APPID']
>>>
```

3. In the following lines of code, we define the show_weather function that takes the screen, APPID, and the city name, and weather information for that city will be fetched and displayed on the screen:

```
>>> def show_weather(screen, APPID, city):
...     weather = get_weather(APPID, city)
...     data = {}
...     data['city'] = city
...     data['temp'] = weather['main']['temp']
...     data['wind'] = weather['wind']['speed']
...     text = WEATHER.format(**data)
...     print('-------- %s --------' % city)
...     print(text)
...     screen.write(text)
...
...
...
>>>
```

4. Run the next block of code to call the `show_weather` function for the city of Tokyo. The text you see on the standard output should also be displayed on the OLED display:

```
>>> show_weather(screen, APPID, 'Tokyo')
-------- Tokyo --------
City: Tokyo
Temp: 13.67
Wind: 6.7

>>>
```

5. When we execute the following block of code, it will loop through all the cities and display their weather information on the screen:

```
>>> for city in CITIES:
...     show_weather(screen, APPID, city)
...
...
...
-------- Berlin --------
City: Berlin
Temp: 10.03
Wind: 3.6

-------- London --------
City: London
Temp: 8.56
Wind: 8.7

-------- Paris --------
City: Paris
Temp: 9.11
Wind: 5.1

-------- Tokyo --------
City: Tokyo
Temp: 13.55
Wind: 6.7

-------- Rome --------
City: Rome
Temp: 11.69
Wind: 6.2

-------- Oslo --------
City: Oslo
Temp: 10.13
```

```
Wind: 2.1

-------- Bangkok --------
City: Bangkok
Temp: 30.66
Wind: 5.1

>>>
```

6. The next block of code should be put into the main.py file:

```python
from screen import Screen, get_oled
from netcheck import wait_for_networking
import urequests
import json

CONF_PATH = 'conf.json'
API_URL = 'http://api.openweathermap.org/data/2.5/weather'
CITIES = ['Berlin', 'London', 'Paris', 'Tokyo', 'Rome', 'Oslo',
'Bangkok']
WEATHER = """\
City: {city}
Temp: {temp}
Wind: {wind}
"""

def get_conf():
    content = open(CONF_PATH).read()
    return json.loads(content)

def get_weather(APPID, city):
    url = API_URL + '?units=metric&APPID=' + APPID + '&q=' + city
    return urequests.get(url).json()

def show_weather(screen, APPID, city):
    weather = get_weather(APPID, city)
    data = {}
    data['city'] = city
    data['temp'] = weather['main']['temp']
    data['wind'] = weather['wind']['speed']
    text = WEATHER.format(**data)
    print('-------- %s --------' % city)
    print(text)
    screen.write(text)

def main():
    oled = get_oled()
    screen = Screen(oled)
```

```
wait_for_networking()
conf = get_conf()
APPID = conf['APPID']
for city in CITIES:
    show_weather(screen, APPID, city)

main()
```

When this script gets executed, it will loop through all the city names and display their weather information on the OLED display.

How it works...

The `show_weather` function does most of the heavy lifting in this recipe. When called, it first collects the weather data by calling the `get_weather` function. It then takes this information and populates a dictionary called `data` with three values. The values are the city name, its temperature, and its wind speed.

These values are then filled into the `WEATHER` template, which acts as a template to control how this information is presented on the screen. The generated text is then both outputted to the standard output display as well as being displayed on the OLED display. The main function will configure a number of variables so that the API calls can be made and the screen can be updated. Then, it loops through the list of cities and calls `show_weather` for each one.

There's more...

Python offers a lot of options when it comes to string templates. What is used in this recipe is the string formatting function that is built into both Python and MicroPython, making it an ideal choice. It's usually a good idea to keep your templates in their own variables, as was done in this recipe. This makes it easier to change labels and to visualize what the intended result will look like.

The `show_weather` function outputs the same text on both the standard output and the OLED display. One of the powerful aspects of dealing with textual output is that you can replicate the same output on many devices. You could extend this further and keep a record of every screen update in a text log file to help with debugging.

See also

Here are a few references for further information:

- Documentation on Python string formatting can be found at `https://docs.python.org/3.4/library/string.html#string-formatting`.
- Documentation on the `Template` object can be found at `https://docs.python.org/3.4/library/string.html#template-strings`.

Providing visual feedback when fetching data

In this recipe, we will enhance the code in the last recipe in such a way as to add visual feedback each time we start the operation of fetching the weather data for a particular city. The first part of this recipe is to take some measurements to find out how slow the `show_weather` function is. This will give us a sense of whether the function is slow enough that it would be visible to a user.

Then, we will use the `invert` feature on the display to provide immediate visual feedback that we have started fetching weather data. This recipe will help you as a real-life example of the performance challenges you can face with the hardware constraints of microcontrollers and how you can overcome them at times to provide some sort of feedback to the users of your application.

Getting ready

You will need access to the REPL on the ESP8266 to run the code presented in this recipe. The approach of measuring execution time and inverting colors are based on what was covered in the *Inverting colors on the display* recipe in Chapter 13, *Interacting with the Adafruit FeatherWing OLED*. It will be helpful to first review that recipe before continuing with this one.

How to do it...

Let's follow the steps required in this recipe:

1. Use the REPL to run the following lines of code:

```
>>> import time
>>>
>>> def measure_time(label, func, args=(), count=3):
...     for i in range(count):
...         start = time.monotonic()
...         func(*args)
...         total = (time.monotonic() - start) * 1000
...         print(label + ':', '%s ms' % total)
...
...
...
>>>
```

2. The `measure_time` function has now been defined. Before continuing, be sure to paste all the function definitions, module imports, and global variables from the `main.py` file in the previous recipe into the REPL. Then, run the following code block:

```
>>> oled = get_oled()
>>> screen = Screen(oled)
>>> wait_for_networking()
address on network: 10.0.0.38
'10.0.0.38'
>>> conf = get_conf()
>>> APPID = conf['APPID']
>>>
```

3. We now have everything we need to measure the execution time of the `show_weather` function. Run the next block of code to take three measurements:

```
>>> measure_time('show_weather', show_weather, [screen, APPID,
'Rome'])
-------- Rome --------
City: Rome
Temp: 9.34
Wind: 2.6

show_weather: 2047.0 ms
-------- Rome --------
City: Rome
Temp: 9.3
```

```
Wind: 2.6

show_weather: 1925.9 ms
-------- Rome --------
City: Rome
Temp: 9.36
Wind: 2.6

show_weather: 2019.04 ms
>>>
```

4. From these measurements, we can see that each call takes about 2 seconds of execution time. We will now add to calls to the `invert` method at the start and end of the `show_weather` function, as shown in the next block of code:

```
>>> def show_weather(screen, APPID, city):
...         screen.oled.invert(True)
...         weather = get_weather(APPID, city)
...         data = {}
...         data['city'] = city
...         data['temp'] = weather['main']['temp']
...         data['wind'] = weather['wind']['speed']
...         text = WEATHER.format(**data)
...         print('-------- %s --------' % city)
...         print(text)
...         screen.write(text)
...         screen.oled.invert(False)
...
...
...
>>>
```

5. The following block of code, when executed, will provide visual feedback at the start and end of the `show_weather` function's execution:

```
>>> show_weather(screen, APPID, 'Rome')
-------- Rome --------
City: Rome
Temp: 9.3
Wind: 2.6

>>>
```

6. The next block of code should be put into the `main.py` file:

```
from screen import Screen, get_oled
from netcheck import wait_for_networking
import urequests
```

```
import json
import time

CONF_PATH = 'conf.json'
API_URL = 'http://api.openweathermap.org/data/2.5/weather'
CITIES = ['Berlin', 'London', 'Paris', 'Tokyo', 'Rome', 'Oslo',
'Bangkok']
WEATHER = """\
City: {city}
Temp: {temp}
Wind: {wind}
"""

def get_conf():
    content = open(CONF_PATH).read()
    return json.loads(content)

def get_weather(APPID, city):
    url = API_URL + '?units=metric&APPID=' + APPID + '&q=' + city
    return urequests.get(url).json()

def show_weather(screen, APPID, city):
    screen.oled.invert(True)
    weather = get_weather(APPID, city)
    data = {}
    data['city'] = city
    data['temp'] = weather['main']['temp']
    data['wind'] = weather['wind']['speed']
    text = WEATHER.format(**data)
    print('-------- %s --------' % city)
    print(text)
    screen.write(text)
    screen.oled.invert(False)

def main():
    oled = get_oled()
    screen = Screen(oled)
    wait_for_networking()
    conf = get_conf()
    APPID = conf['APPID']
    for city in CITIES:
        show_weather(screen, APPID, city)
        time.sleep(1)

main()
```

When this script gets executed, it will loop through each city and call the `show_weather` function with the new inverted color visual feedback.

How it works...

The `measure_time` function helped us measure how long the execution took for the `show_weather` function. This function is fetching data from the internet, parsing it, and then performing a number of screen operations to display it. The measured execution time was around 2 seconds. Microcontrollers, compared to desktop computers, have limited computational power. Operations like these on a desktop would take a few hundred milliseconds, but on a microcontroller can take longer. Because of this noticeable execution time, we have enhanced the `show_weather` function by inverting the colors at the very start of its execution. This color inversion will be shown within a few milliseconds and will be displayed before any other processing is done. Then, at the end of the execution, the inverted colors are returned back to their normal state to indicate that the function has completed its execution.

There's more...

In a later recipe, when we connect the push button to the `show_weather` function, visual feedback will become very important. A 2 second delay in a screen update is very visible and users will lead some sort of visual feedback to indicate the machine is performing an operation as opposed to being stuck. The `invert` method shown in this recipe is perfect for this purpose and doesn't require very much additional code to achieve its result.

See also

Here are a few references for further information:

- Details on human perceptual abilities from a usability perspective can be found at `https://www.nngroup.com/articles/response-times-3-important-limits/`.
- Documentation on software usability can be found at `https://www.interaction-design.org/literature/topics/usability`.

Creating a function to display the weather for a random city

In this recipe, we will create a function that will select a random city and display its weather information on the screen each time it is called. The function will use the `choice` function from the `random` module to select a random city, and then it will use the `show_weather` function to display the weather information for that city.

This recipe can be useful to you whenever you are in a situation where you want to add some randomness to a project so that there is a greater level of unpredictability in the interaction with that device. This can create some unexpected and surprising behavior in your projects that make them more interesting to interact with.

Getting ready

You will need access to the REPL on the ESP8266 to run the code presented in this recipe.

How to do it...

Let's check for the steps required in this recipe:

1. Run the following lines of code in the REPL:

```
>>> import random
>>>
>>> def show_random_weather(screen, APPID):
...     city = random.choice(CITIES)
...     show_weather(screen, APPID, city)
...
...
...
>>>
```

2. The `show_random_weather` function has now been defined. Before continuing, be sure to paste all the function definitions, module imports, and global variables from the `main.py` file in the previous recipe into the REPL. Then, run the following code block:

```
>>> oled = get_oled()
>>> screen = Screen(oled)
>>> wait_for_networking()
```

```
address on network: 10.0.0.38
'10.0.0.38'
>>> conf = get_conf()
>>> APPID = conf['APPID']
>>>
```

3. Run the next block of code and the weather of a random city will be displayed:

```
>>> show_random_weather(screen, APPID)
-------- Bangkok --------
City: Bangkok
Temp: 30.01
Wind: 5.1

>>>
```

4. We will now loop three times and call the show_random_weather function to test its functionality:

```
>>> for i in range(3):
...         show_random_weather(screen, APPID)
...
...
...
-------- Rome --------
City: Rome
Temp: 9.08
Wind: 2.6

-------- Berlin --------
City: Berlin
Temp: 8.1
Wind: 3.6

-------- London --------
City: London
Temp: 5.41
Wind: 6.2

>>>
```

5. The next block of code should be put into the `main.py` file:

```
from screen import Screen, get_oled
from netcheck import wait_for_networking
import urequests
import json
import time
import random

CONF_PATH = 'conf.json'
API_URL = 'http://api.openweathermap.org/data/2.5/weather'
CITIES = ['Berlin', 'London', 'Paris', 'Tokyo', 'Rome', 'Oslo',
'Bangkok']
WEATHER = """\
City: {city}
Temp: {temp}
Wind: {wind}
"""

def get_conf():
    content = open(CONF_PATH).read()
    return json.loads(content)

def get_weather(APPID, city):
    url = API_URL + '?units=metric&APPID=' + APPID + '&q=' + city
    return urequests.get(url).json()

def show_weather(screen, APPID, city):
    screen.oled.invert(Truc)
    weather = get_weather(APPID, city)
    data = {}
    data['city'] = city
    data['temp'] = weather['main']['temp']
    data['wind'] = weather['wind']['speed']
    text = WEATHER.format(**data)
    print('-------- %s --------' % city)
    print(text)
    screen.write(text)
    screen.oled.invert(False)

def show_random_weather(screen, APPID):
    city = random.choice(CITIES)
    show_weather(screen, APPID, city)

def main():
    oled = get_oled()
    screen = Screen(oled)
```

```
                    wait_for_networking()
                    conf = get_conf()
                    APPID = conf['APPID']
                    for i in range(3):
                        show_random_weather(screen, APPID)

            main()
```

When this script gets executed, it will loop three times and select a random city in each iteration, which will have its weather information displayed.

How it works...

The `show_random_weather` function expects two arguments as its input. The screen and `APPID` are needed as input arguments to make the needed API calls and update the screen contents. The `choice` function of the `random` module is called on the `CITIES` list to select a random city. Once this city is selected, its weather can be fetched and displayed using the `show_weather` function. The `main` function in this recipe loops three times and calls the `show_random_weather` function in each `for` loop iteration.

There's more...

This recipe is one of the last remaining pieces of the internet-connected weather machine. We have built and tested each piece of this application to confirm that each one goes before building additional logic on the previous layer. All the code and logic of this recipe is self-contained in its own function, which improves code readability and also helps with troubleshooting. If any errors occur, it will be easier to troubleshoot by knowing exactly which function the exception was raised in.

See also

Here are a few references for further information:

- Documentation on interacting with displays on MicroPython details can be found at `https://learn.adafruit.com/micropython-displays-drawing-shapes`.
- Documentation on a microcontroller project using the Adafruit FeatherWing OLED can be found at `https://learn.adafruit.com/digital-display-badge`.

Creating an IoT button to show the weather around the world

In this recipe, we will add the final touch to our internet-connected weather machine. We will take the bulk of code introduced in the recipes throughout this chapter and add an `event` loop to our `main` function so that we can react to button press events by displaying the weather of random cities around the world. This recipe will provide you with a good example of how you can add an `event` loop to an existing code base to create user interactivity.

Getting ready

You will need access to the REPL on the ESP8266 to run the code presented in this recipe.

How to do it...

Let's follow the steps required in this recipe:

1. Execute the next block of code in the REPL:

```
>>> from machine import Pin
>>>
>>> BUTTON_A_PIN = 0
>>>
```

2. The `Pin` object is now imported so that we can interact with the board's push buttons. Before continuing, be sure to paste all the function definitions, module imports, and global variables from the `main.py` file in the previous recipe into the REPL. Then run the following code block:

```
>>> button = Pin(BUTTON_A_PIN, Pin.IN, Pin.PULL_UP)
>>>
```

3. The `button` variable can now read the state of push button A. Run the next block of code to detect whether push button A is currently being pressed:

```
>>> not button.value()
False
>>>
```

4. While pressing push button A, execute the following block of code:

```
>>> not button.value()
True
>>>
```

5. Run the next block of code to prepare the `screen` and `APPID` variables:

```
>>> oled = get_oled()
>>> screen = Screen(oled)
>>> wait_for_networking()
address on network: 10.0.0.38
'10.0.0.38'
>>> conf = get_conf()
>>> APPID = conf['APPID']
>>>
```

4. The following block of code will start an `event` loop. Each time you press push button A, the weather of a random city should be displayed:

```
>>> while True:
...     if not button.value():
...         show_random_weather(screen, APPID)
...
...
...
-------- London --------
City: London
Temp: 6.62
Wind: 4.6

-------- Paris --------
City: Paris
Temp: 4.53
Wind: 2.6

-------- Rome --------
City: Rome
Temp: 10.39
Wind: 2.6
>>>
```

5. The next block of code should be put into the `main.py` file:

```python
from screen import Screen, get_oled
from netcheck import wait_for_networking
from machine import Pin
import urequests
import json
import time
import random

BUTTON_A_PIN = 0
CONF_PATH = 'conf.json'
API_URL = 'http://api.openweathermap.org/data/2.5/weather'
CITIES = ['Berlin', 'London', 'Paris', 'Tokyo', 'Rome', 'Oslo',
'Bangkok']
WEATHER = """\
City: {city}
Temp: {temp}
Wind: {wind}
"""

def get_conf():
    content = open(CONF_PATH).read()
    return json.loads(content)

def get_weather(APPID, city):
    url = API_URL + '?units=metric&APPID=' + APPID + '&q=' + city
    return urequests.get(url).json()

def show_weather(screen, APPID, city):
    screen.oled.invert(True)
    weather = get_weather(APPID, city)
    data = {}
    data['city'] = city
    data['temp'] = weather['main']['temp']
    data['wind'] = weather['wind']['speed']
    text = WEATHER.format(**data)
    print('-------- %s --------' % city)
    print(text)
    screen.write(text)
    screen.oled.invert(False)

def show_random_weather(screen, APPID):
    city = random.choice(CITIES)
    show_weather(screen, APPID, city)

def main():
    oled = get_oled()
```

```
        screen = Screen(oled)
        wait_for_networking()
        conf = get_conf()
        APPID = conf['APPID']
        button = Pin(BUTTON_A_PIN, Pin.IN, Pin.PULL_UP)
        show_random_weather(screen, APPID)
        while True:
            if not button.value():
                show_random_weather(screen, APPID)

    main()
```

When this script gets executed, it will kick off an `event` loop that will fetch and display the weather of a random city each time push button A is pressed.

How it works...

The `main` function in this recipe creates a `Pin` object called `Button` that will be connected to push button A. We can use this `button` variable to poll the state of the push button. We then show the weather for a random city so that the starting state of the application is the weather being shown on the display. Then, an `infinite` loop is started, which will be our `event` loop to process any push button events. In each loop, we check whether push button A is pressed. If it is, then the `show_random_weather` function is called to display the weather of a random city on the screen.

There's more...

This recipe reacts to a single push button to show random weather. We could connect push button B and C to our main `event` loop and have them produce other functionalities. Push button A might change the city while B and C could let you scroll and see more weather information relating to the currently selected city. The next photograph shows what the internet-connected weather machine looks like when showing weather information on the city of Tokyo:

This recipe could also be changed to fetch and display any information from web services. You could fetch the latest news headlines and display them, or display a random joke from a RESTful joke API. The sky is the limit to what you can do with a multi-line text display and internet connectivity.

See also

Here are a few references for further information:

- Documentation on using the PULL_UP setting with buttons on MicroPython can be found at https://learn.adafruit.com/micropython-hardware-digital-i-slash-o/digital-inputs.
- Documentation on a RESTful jokes API can be found at http://www.icndb.com/api/.

15
Coding on the Adafruit HalloWing Microcontroller

In this chapter, we will create a joke-telling machine. We will use the Adafruit HalloWing M0 Express board that comes with a full color TFT display and capacitive touch sensors. Each time you press the touch button, a new joke riddle will be presented. You can try and figure out the answer to the riddle and when you are ready, touch the button to show the answer to the riddle. Pressing the touch button again randomly selects a new riddle and starts another game.

This chapter will be a useful source of information and help you build projects that let you leverage the power of a full color screen with a good enough resolution to present multi-line text and full color graphical images.

We will be covering the following recipe in this chapter:

- Discovering I2C devices
- Reading data from the accelerometer using I2C
- Detecting board-flipping with the accelerometer
- Controlling screen brightness
- Displaying a bitmap image
- Listing all image files
- Creating a joke-telling machine

The Adafruit HalloWing M0 Express

The Adafruit HalloWing is a microcontroller with a built-in 1.44 inch 128 x 128 full-color TFT display. The software for displaying images fully supports displaying full color bitmap image files. With 8 MB storage on the device, this gives you plenty of space to store and display a large number of images. The board also comes equipped with a 3-axis accelerometer, light sensor, and 4 capacitive touchpads. The following screenshot shows the TFT screen displaying a bitmap image:

The board can be powered by a portable power source. It supports both rechargeable lithium-ion polymer batteries and a USB portable power bank.

Where to buy

The Adafruit HalloWing M0 Express board can be purchased directly from Adafruit (https://www.adafruit.com/product/3900).

Technical requirements

The code files for this chapter can be found in the Chapter15 folder of this book's GitHub repository, at https://github.com/PacktPublishing/MicroPython-Cookbook.

This chapter uses the Adafruit HalloWing M0 Express board, loaded with the CircuitPython firmware. CircuitPython version 4.0.0-rc.1 was used for all the recipes in this chapter.

You may download the firmware image from `https://circuitpython.org/board/hallowing_m0_express/`.

Many of the recipes in this chapter require a set of bitmap images to be transferred to the Adafruit HalloWing device. They can all be downloaded from the `Chapter15` folder in this book's GitHub repository. They should be saved in the top-level folder, along with your `main.py` file.

Discovering I2C devices

This recipe will show you how to scan for I2C devices connected to the bus using the `i2c` object. The I2C protocol supports multiple devices being connected to a single I2C connection. One of the first steps in connecting to a device is to scan and list all detected devices. This recipe will help you troubleshoot an I2C device to confirm that it is connected and can be found in scans. It can also help you build Python scripts that can automatically scan and detect multiple devices.

Getting ready

You will need access to the REPL on the Adafruit HalloWing board to run the code presented in this recipe.

How to do it...

Follow these steps to learn how to discover I2C devices:

1. Run the following lines of code in the REPL:

   ```
   >>> import board
   >>> import busio
   ```

2. The required libraries will have been imported. Run the following line of code to create the `i2c` object that will be used for scanning:

   ```
   >>> i2c = busio.I2C(board.SCL, board.SDA)
   ```

3. The following lines of code will keep looping until a lock is acquired on the I2C bus:

```
>>> while not i2c.try_lock():
...         print('getting lock...')
...
...
...
>>>
```

4. The following block of code performs a scan and lists all detected devices:

```
>>> i2c.scan()
[24]
```

5. We can perform the scan again and convert the returned device addresses into hex format:

```
>>> [hex(x) for x in i2c.scan()]
['0x18']
```

6. The following code should be put into the main.py file:

```
import board
import busio

def main():
    i2c = busio.I2C(board.SCL, board.SDA)
    while not i2c.try_lock():
        print('getting lock...')
    devices = [hex(x) for x in i2c.scan()]
    print('devices found:', devices)

main()
```

When this script is executed, it will print out the addresses of all discovered devices.

How it works...

The main function sets up the i2c object. The try_lock method is then repeatedly called until a lock is acquired. This lock is needed to perform a scan on the I2C bus. The scan method is then called, which returns a list of device addresses. Each address is then converted into hex notation and saved as a list of strings in the device's variable. Finally, the contents of this variable are output with a message, indicating that this is the list of devices that were discovered on the bus.

There's more...

Some I2C operation, such as scanning, require a lock. If you try and perform a scan without first acquiring a lock, you will get a runtime error indicating that this function requires a lock. In the next recipe, we will see that there are other operations that don't require a lock. The addresses of I2C are frequently referred to using hex notation, and this is the reason why we converted the value from an integer into a hex value.

The Adafruit HalloWing M0 Express board comes with one I2C device—an accelerometer—which should have the address `0x18`. Our scans confirm that. If you're not sure of the specific address value for your device, you can use the scan method to detect these values.

See also

Here are a few references regarding this recipe:

- Documentation on the `scan` method can be found at `https://circuitpython.readthedocs.io/en/3.x/shared-bindings/busio/I2C.html#busio.I2C.scan`.
- Documentation on a project that uses the accelerometer on the Adafruit HalloWing board can be found at `https://learn.adafruit.com/hallowing-magic-9-ball/`.

Reading data from the accelerometer using I2C

This recipe will show you how to connect to the onboard accelerometer using the I2C protocol. Once we have an I2C object, we will use the Python `adafruit_lis3dh` library to create a `LIS3DH_I2C` object. This object will let us read live sensor data from the accelerometer. This recipe will help you whenever you want to create a project that uses board's orientation to create an interactive experience. You could, for example, create a project that reacts to the board being shaken by changing the image that's currently being displayed.

Getting ready

You will need access to the REPL on the Adafruit HalloWing device to run the code presented in this recipe.

How to do it...

Follow these steps to learn how to read data from the accelerometer using I2C:

1. Execute the following block of code in the REPL:

```
>>> from adafruit_lis3dh import LIS3DH_I2C
>>> import board
>>> import busio
>>> import time
>>>
>>> ACCEL_ADDRESS = 0x18
```

2. The required libraries have now been imported, and the accelerometer address has been defined in the ACCEL_ADDRESS constant. Run the following block of code to create an i2c object and use that object to create a LIS3DH_I2C object:

```
>>> i2c = busio.I2C(board.SCL, board.SDA)
>>> accel = LIS3DH_I2C(i2c, address=ACCEL_ADDRESS)
```

3. The following block of code will fetch accelerometer orientation data and display its values:

```
>>> accel.acceleration
acceleration(x=0.143678, y=-0.0287355, z=-9.48272)
```

4. We can also access specific information, such as the *x* axis orientation data, using the following block of code:

```
>>> accel.acceleration.x
0.124521
```

5. The following loop is used to print the live accelerometer sensor data every 0.1 seconds:

```
>>> while True:
...      print(accel.acceleration)
...      time.sleep(0.1)
...
...
```

```
. . .
acceleration(x=0.162835, y=-0.00957851, z=-9.47314)
acceleration(x=0.162835, y=-0.0478925, z=-9.52104)
acceleration(x=0.0957851, y=-0.057471, z=-9.30073)
acceleration(x=0.172413, y=-0.00957851, z=-9.51146)
acceleration(x=0.153256, y=-0.0478925, z=-9.48272)
acceleration(x=0.153256, y=-0.057471, z=-9.53062)
acceleration(x=0.162835, y=-0.057471, z=-9.53062)
```

6. The following code should be put into the `main.py` file:

```python
from adafruit_lis3dh import LIS3DH_I2C
import board
import busio
import time

ACCEL_ADDRESS = 0x18

def main():
    i2c = busio.I2C(board.SCL, board.SDA)
    accel = LIS3DH_I2C(i2c, address=ACCEL_ADDRESS)
    while True:
        print(accel.acceleration)
        time.sleep(0.1)

main()
```

When this script is executed, it will print sensor data from the accelerometer every 0.1 seconds.

How it works...

The ACCEL_ADDRESS constant contains the address for the accelerometer on the Adafruit HalloWing M0 Express board. Once we've created an i2c object, we take it and the ACCEL_ADDRESS to create a LIS3DH_I2C object, which we will save in a variable called accel. An infinite loop is started that reads the sensor data from the accelerometer on each iteration and prints them out. The loop then waits for a 0.1 second delay before starting the next iteration.

There's more...

The name of the accelerometer that's used on the Adafruit HalloWing device is called LIS3DH, which is why the Python library that knows how to speak to this device is called `adafruit_lis3dh`. This sensor can be used to detect both the orientation and acceleration of the board. In the next recipe, we will use this orientation data to detect when the board has been flipped over.

See also

Here are a few references regarding this recipe:

- Documentation on the LIS3DH accelerometer can be found at `https://www.st.com/en/mems-and-sensors/lis3dh.html`.
- Documentation on the `LIS3DH_I2C` object can be found at `https://circuitpython.readthedocs.io/projects/lis3dh/en/latest/api.html#adafruit_lis3dh.LIS3DH_I2C`.

Detecting board-flipping with the accelerometer

This recipe will show you how to create a function that detects when the board is flipped over. To achieve this, we will use the orientation data that we fetched from the accelerometer. We will focus on the z axis data as this will indicate whether the board is facing up or facing down. The approach presented in this recipe can be useful to you whenever you are creating a project and want to find a more creative way of interacting with the project than just pushing buttons. This can create a fun level of interaction when someone discovers that all they have to do is flip over your board to interact with it.

Getting ready

You will need access to the REPL on the Adafruit HalloWing device to run the code presented in this recipe.

How to do it...

Follow these steps to learn how you can detect board flipping with the accelerometer:

1. Use the REPL to run the following lines of code:

```
>>> from adafruit_lis3dh import LIS3DH_I2C
>>> import board
>>> import busio
>>> import time
>>>
>>> ACCEL_ADDRESS = 0x18
```

2. The required libraries have been imported and constantly defined. Run the following block of code to create the i2c and LIS3DH_I2C objects:

```
>>> i2c = busio.I2C(board.SCL, board.SDA)
>>> accel = LIS3DH_I2C(i2c, address=ACCEL_ADDRESS)
```

3. We can now inspect the z axis orientation data:

```
>>> accel.acceleration.z
-9.43483
```

4. Flip the board so that its display is face-down and then run the following block of code:

```
>>> accel.acceleration.z
9.50188
```

5. The orientation value of the z axis will be a positive or negative number, depending on whether the board is face-up or face-down. Execute the following block of code to calculate this value:

```
>>> face = 'up' if accel.acceleration.z < 0 else 'down'
>>> face
'up'
```

6. Run the following block of code while you flip the board between face-down and face-up:

```
>>> while True:
...         face = 'up' if accel.acceleration.z < 0 else 'down'
...         print('board is face', face)
...         time.sleep(0.1)
...
...
```

```
. . .
board is face up
board is face up
board is face up
board is face down
board is face down
board is face up
board is face up
board is face up
```

7. The following code should be put into the `main.py` file:

```python
from adafruit_lis3dh import LIS3DH_I2C
import board
import busio
import time

ACCEL_ADDRESS = 0x18

def main():
    i2c = busio.I2C(board.SCL, board.SDA)
    accel = LIS3DH_I2C(i2c, address=ACCEL_ADDRESS)
    while True:
        face = 'up' if accel.acceleration.z < 0 else 'down'
        print('board is face', face)
        time.sleep(0.1)

main()
```

When this script is executed, it will print whether the board is facing up or down every 0.1 seconds.

How it works...

Once the `i2c` and `accel` variables are set up, we can then start accessing the orientation data from the accelerometer. When the board is facing up, the z value will be a negative number, and when the board is facing down, the z value will be a positive number. We can use this piece of information to calculate whether the board is facing up or down. An infinite loop is started and the variable face has up or down values saved to it, depending on the board's current orientation. This information is then printed while the loop waits for a 0.1 second delay before starting the next iteration.

There's more...

This recipe showed you how you can use one piece of information from the accelerometer to detect a change in the physical orientation of the board. Once we've detected this change, we can make the script change its output, for example, whenever the board's face value changes. The accelerometer is also accurate enough to provide the angle the board is pointed at in reference to the z axis. We can use this information to change the behavior of our application, depending on how far the board is tilted in a certain direction.

See also

Here are a few references regarding this recipe:

- Documentation on how accelerometers detect orientation can be found at `https://ieeexplore.ieee.org/document/1241424`.
- Documentation on the `acceleration` attribute can be found at `https://circuitpython.readthedocs.io/projects/lis3dh/en/latest/api.html#adafruit_lis3dh.LIS3DH.acceleration`.

Controlling screen brightness

This recipe will show you how to control the brightness level on the TFT display that comes with the Adafruit HalloWing device. The brightness can be set to the maximum level or to lower levels by providing a fractional value between 0 and 1. The brightness setting can also be used to turn off the display by setting the brightness level to 0. This recipe can be useful to you in projects where you don't want the screen on all the time, and want to turn it on and off. It can also be helpful when you want to tweak the brightness levels of the backlight to a lower level to reduce power consumption.

Getting ready

You will need access to the REPL on the Adafruit HalloWing device to run the code presented in this recipe.

How to do it...

Follow these steps to learn how to control the Adafruit HalloWing device's screen brightness:

1. Run the following lines of code in the REPL:

```
>>> import board
>>> import time
```

2. The required libraries have been imported you can run the following block of code to set the brightness level to 50%:

```
>>> board.DISPLAY.brightness = 0.5
```

3. The following block of code will turn of the display by setting brightness to 0%:

```
>>> board.DISPLAY.brightness = 0
```

4. We can now set the brightness to the maximum level with the following block of code:

```
>>> board.DISPLAY.brightness = 1.0
```

5. The following function will take the brightness from the lowest level to the maximum level over 11 iterations:

```
>>> def fade_in():
...     for i in range(0, 11):
...         brightness = i / 10
...         print('brightness:', brightness)
...         board.DISPLAY.brightness = brightness
...         time.sleep(0.1)
...
...
...
>>>
```

6. Run the following block of code. You should see the display fade up to maximum brightness:

```
>>> fade_in()
brightness: 0.0
brightness: 0.1
brightness: 0.2
brightness: 0.3
brightness: 0.4
```

```
brightness: 0.5
brightness: 0.6
brightness: 0.7
brightness: 0.8
brightness: 0.9
brightness: 1.0
>>>
```

7. The following code should be put into the `main.py` file:

```python
import board
import time

def fade_in():
    for i in range(0, 11):
        brightness = i / 10
        print('brightness:', brightness)
        board.DISPLAY.brightness = brightness
        time.sleep(0.1)

def main():
    while True:
        fade_in()

main()
```

When this script is executed, it will fade the screen from black to full brightness, with a 0.1 second delay between each fade.

How it works...

The main function starts an infinite loop that repeatedly calls the `fade_in` function. Each call to the `fade_in` function will start a `for` loop that loops over 11 brightness values. The values vary, from the display being off to setting the display to its maximum brightness. The brightness level is calculated for each iteration and stored in the brightness variable. The value is printed and then applied to the brightness attribute on the `DISPLAY` object. A sleep of 0.1 second is then applied before the next iteration of the fade in the loop is applied.

There's more...

This recipe demonstrates how easy it is to set the brightness level of the display. It also shows you how screen effects such as fading the screen in and out can also be implemented in Python. The brightness attribute can be particularly useful when you want to turn off the display by switching the backlight of the display off. You might create a battery-operated device that can use this technique to optimize power consumption.

See also

Here are a few references regarding this recipe:

- An example of controlling screen brightness can be found at `https://circuitpython.readthedocs.io/en/latest/shared-bindings/displayio/OnDiskBitmap.html`.
- Details on the TFT display on the Adafruit HalloWing device can be found at `https://learn.adafruit.com/adafruit-hallowing?view=all#tft-2-18`.

Displaying a bitmap image

This recipe will show you how to create a function that receives the path to a bitmap image, takes this image, and displays it on the HalloWing screen. There are many different objects and options available for manipulating the contents of the screen. We will have to interact with a number of these different objects, even when we just want to show a single image. This recipe gives you an insight into what is involved in getting an image rendered on the board's screen. This recipe can be helpful if you are using the HalloWing device for projects that need to display different images and you want a straightforward way to change the currently displayed image.

Getting ready

You will need access to the REPL on the Adafruit HalloWing device to run the code presented in this recipe.

How to do it...

Follow these steps to learn how to display a bitmap image on the HalloWing device's screen:

1. Execute the following block of code in the REPL:

```
>>> import board
>>> from displayio import OnDiskBitmap, ColorConverter, TileGrid,
Group
```

2. The necessary objects from the `displayio` module have now been imported. Run the following block of code to open a file object as a binary stream:

```
>>> path = 'joke_01_question.bmp'
>>> f = open(path, 'rb')
```

3. We will use this file object to create our bitmap object and then prepare the `pixel_shader` object:

```
>>> bitmap = OnDiskBitmap(f)
>>> pixel_shader = ColorConverter()
```

4. These two objects are then used as arguments for creating a `TileGrid` object called `sprite`:

```
sprite = TileGrid(bitmap, pixel_shader=pixel_shader)
```

5. The following block of code creates a group object and appends the `sprite` to it:

```
>>> group = Group()
>>> group.append(sprite)
```

6. We can use the following block of code to show this group on the display and call `wait_for_frame` to make the block of code wait until the display has been fully updated. Now, we will close the file object as it is no longer needed:

```
>>> board.DISPLAY.show(group)
>>> board.DISPLAY.wait_for_frame()
>>> f.close()
```

7. Run the following block of code to define the `show_image` function and call it to show a different image on the display:

```
>>> def show_image(path):
...     with open(path, 'rb') as f:
...         bitmap = OnDiskBitmap(f)
...         pixel_shader = ColorConverter()
...         sprite = TileGrid(bitmap, pixel_shader=pixel_shader)
...         group = Group()
...         group.append(sprite)
...         board.DISPLAY.show(group)
...         board.DISPLAY.wait_for_frame()
...
...
...
>>> show_image('joke_01_response.bmp')
>>>
```

8. The following code should be put into the `main.py` file:

```
import board
from displayio import OnDiskBitmap, ColorConverter, TileGrid, Group

IMAGES = ['joke_01_question.bmp', 'joke_01_response.bmp']

def show_image(path):
    with open(path, 'rb') as f:
        bitmap = OnDiskBitmap(f)
        pixel_shader = ColorConverter()
        sprite = TileGrid(bitmap, pixel_shader=pixel_shader)
        group = Group()
        group.append(sprite)
        board.DISPLAY.show(group)
        board.DISPLAY.wait_for_frame()

def main():
    while True:
        for image in IMAGES:
            show_image(image)

main()
```

When this script is executed, it will repeatedly change the image being displayed between two different bitmaps.

How it works...

The `show_image` function in this recipe does all the heavy lifting of displaying the bitmap on the screen. It receives one argument, which is the path to the bitmap file. This file is opened for reading and then used to create an `OnDiskBitmap` object called bitmap.

The `ColorConverter` object is used to create the `pixel_shader` variable. A `TileGrid` object is created and requires the bitmap to be displayed, as well as the pixel shader that will be used. Both of these arguments are provided and the new `TileGrid` object is saved in the sprite variable. The sprite variable cannot be given directly to the `DISPLAY` object, so we must create a `Group` object and append the sprite to it.

We can now call the show method on the `DISPLAY` object to show the `group` variable. The `wait_for_frame` method is called to make sure that the image is fully displayed on the screen before continuing. The main function starts an infinite loop that repeatedly calls `show_image` to continuously change the currently displayed image.

There's more...

There are a lot of different types of objects that need to be employed to display a bitmap image on the HalloWing device. Part of the reason for this is that each object provides a wide variety of flexibility in terms of how the image is displayed on the screen. You can, for example, control the x and y coordinates of an image or use other bitmap objects that don't come from files.

The display can display images with a resolution of up to 128 x 128, saved in the 24-bit pixel BMP file format. You can use the open source GIMP image editor to create these images.

When you create a new image in the GIMP application, you should set the correct resolution, as shown in the following screenshot:

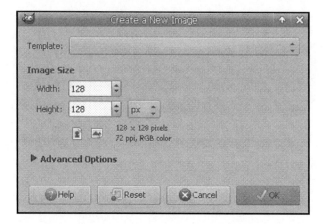

When you are ready to save the image, use the **Export** function in the file menu and save your image in BMP file format. When you do this, make sure you select the correct bits per pixel setting, as shown in the following screenshot:

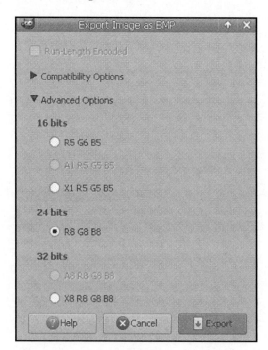

It's important to know that you can also use images of a smaller resolution, and that this will be automatically detected and correctly displayed on the screen. Smaller images also tend to be displayed on the screen faster.

See also

Here are a few references regarding this recipe:

- Downloads for the GIMP image editor can be found at `https://www.gimp.org/`.
- Documentation on the `OnDiskBitmap` object can be found at `https://circuitpython.readthedocs.io/en/latest/shared-bindings/displayio/OnDiskBitmap.html`.

Listing all image files

This recipe will show you how to list all the image files in a specific directory. In the joke-telling machine, we are creating each joke question and response as a pair of images. This recipe will allow you to list all your bitmap images on the board. We will then extend this functionality to filter the list further and have all the bitmap images of the joke questions at hand. This recipe can be useful in any project that you create where you want to retrieve a list of images to display or audio files or play in your project.

Getting ready

You will need access to the REPL on the Adafruit HalloWing device to run the code presented in this recipe.

How to do it...

Follow these steps to learn how to list image files:

1. Use the REPL to run the following lines of code:

```
>>> import os
>>> paths = sorted(os.listdir())
>>> paths
```

```
['.Trashes', '.fseventsd', '.metadata_never_index', 'boot_out.txt',
'joke_01_question.bmp', 'joke_01_response.bmp',
'joke_02_question.bmp', 'joke_02_response.bmp',
'joke_03_question.bmp', 'joke_03_response.bmp',
'joke_04_question.bmp', 'joke_04_response.bmp', 'main.py']
```

2. We have now retrieved and output a sorted list of all the paths on the board's root directory. We will use the following block of code to list only bitmap image files:

```
>>> images = [i for i in paths if i.endswith('.bmp')]
>>> images
['joke_01_question.bmp', 'joke_01_response.bmp',
'joke_02_question.bmp', 'joke_02_response.bmp',
'joke_03_question.bmp', 'joke_03_response.bmp',
'joke_04_question.bmp', 'joke_04_response.bmp']
```

3. We can extend this further and only list joke question image files, as shown in the following block of code:

```
>>> questions = [i for i in paths if i.endswith('question.bmp')]
>>> questions
['joke_01_question.bmp', 'joke_02_question.bmp',
'joke_03_question.bmp', 'joke_04_question.bmp']
>>>
```

4. The following block of code will select the first question image and save it to a variable:

```
>>> question = questions[0]
>>> question
'joke_01_question.bmp'
```

5. The following block of code can be used to calculate the name of a joke's response image based on the question image:

```
>>> response = question.replace('question.bmp', 'response.bmp')
>>> response
'joke_01_response.bmp'
```

6. We will use the following block of code to confirm that the calculated response image exists as a file:

```
>>> response in paths
True
```

7. The following code should be put into the `main.py` file:

```python
import os

def get_questions():
    paths = sorted(os.listdir())
    return [i for i in paths if i.endswith('question.bmp')]

def main():
    questions = get_questions()
    for question in questions:
        response = question.replace('question.bmp', 'response.bmp')
        print(question, response)

main()
```

When this script is executed, it will list all question images and calculate their related response images.

How it works...

The `get_questions` function in this recipe saves a sorted list of filenames in the `paths` variable. It then filters the listing to only include the question images by checking whether the `question.bmp` string appears in the filename. This filtered list is then returned by the function.

The main function calls the `get_questions` function and saves its results to the `questions` variable. Each question is looped through and has its response image calculated when we replace the `question.bmp` value with `response.bmp` in the filename. Both the question and response filenames are then printed before the next iteration of the loop commences.

There's more...

A number of images will be used to create the joke-telling machine. We could have saved the names of the necessary images in the script itself, instead of directly listing them in the filesystem. But the approach taken in this recipe is better because it avoids us having to hardcode the image list directly in our application. This means that we can have 5 jokes or even 50 on the board without us having to change our application's code.

Each time we start the joke-telling machine, it will automatically grab the latest listing of joke images. The following screenshot shows the joke question and the responses that will be used in the next recipe to create the joke-telling machine:

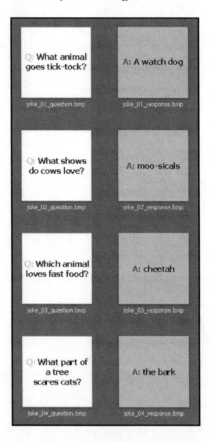

You can see that the filenames follow a simple naming convention to make it easy for you to see each question and response when they're viewed in an image viewer. This naming convention also makes it an easy process to calculate the related response image for a specific question image.

See also

Here are a few references regarding this recipe:

- Documentation on the BMP file format can be found at `https://www.fileformat.info/format/bmp/egff.htm`.

- Details on using bitmap images on the HalloWing device can be found at `https://learn.adafruit.com/hallowing-badge/hallowing-badge-and-image-player`.

Creating a joke-telling machine

This recipe will show you how to list all the image files in a specific directory. In the joke-telling machine we are creating, each joke question and response will be provided as a pair of images. This recipe will show us how to list all our bitmap images on the board.

We will then extend this functionality to further filter the list so that we have all the bitmap images of the joke questions at hand. This recipe will help you if you want to create a project where you want to retrieve a list of images or audio files so that you can display or play them in your project.

Getting ready

You will need access to the REPL on the Adafruit HalloWing device to run the code presented in this recipe.

How to do it...

Follow these steps to learn how to create a joke-telling machine:

1. Run the following lines of code in the REPL:

```
>>> from displayio import OnDiskBitmap, ColorConverter, TileGrid,
Group
>>> import board
>>> import random
>>> import time
>>> import touchio
>>> import os
```

2. We have now imported all the necessary modules. The following block of code will create a `TouchIn` object:

```
>>> touch = touchio.TouchIn(board.TOUCH1)
>>>
```

3. In the following block of code, we will check the status of the touchpad:

```
>>> touch.value
False
```

4. Touch the pad while executing the following block of code:

```
>>> touch.value
True
```

5. The following block of code will define the `wait_for_touch` function, which will keep looping until a touch event is detected:

```
>>> def wait_for_touch(touch):
...         while not touch.value:
...             print('waiting...')
...             time.sleep(0.1)
...
...
...
>>>
```

6. We will use the following block of code to call `wait_for_touch`. After executing this function, wait a few moments before touching the pad to confirm that the function returns from its `while` loop once it detects the touch event:

```
>>> wait_for_touch(touch)
waiting...
waiting...
waiting...
waiting...
>>>
```

7. The following block of code will save the list of question images in the `questions` variable:

```
>>> def get_questions():
...         paths = sorted(os.listdir())
...         return [i for i in paths if i.endswith('question.bmp')]
...
...
...
>>>
>>> questions = get_questions()
>>> questions
['joke_01_question.bmp', 'joke_02_question.bmp',
'joke_03_question.bmp', 'joke_04_question.bmp']
```

8. We will use the following block of code to randomly select a question from the questions list:

```
>>> question = random.choice(questions)
>>> question
'joke_04_question.bmp'
```

9. The following code should be put into the `main.py` file:

```python
from displayio import OnDiskBitmap, ColorConverter, TileGrid, Group
import board
import random
import time
import touchio
import os

def show_image(path):
    print('showing image', path)
    with open(path, 'rb') as f:
        bitmap = OnDiskBitmap(f)
        pixel_shader = ColorConverter()
        sprite = TileGrid(bitmap, pixel_shader=pixel_shader)
        group = Group()
        group.append(sprite)
        board.DISPLAY.show(group)
        board.DISPLAY.wait_for_frame()

def wait_for_touch(touch):
    while not touch.value:
        print('waiting...')
        time.sleep(0.1)

def get_questions():
    paths = sorted(os.listdir())
    return [i for i in paths if i.endswith('question.bmp')]

def main():
    touch = touchio.TouchIn(board.TOUCH1)
    questions = get_questions()
    while True:
        question = random.choice(questions)
        response = question.replace('question.bmp', 'response.bmp')
        show_image(question)
        wait_for_touch(touch)
        show_image(response)
        wait_for_touch(touch)

main()
```

When this script is executed, it will start the joke-telling machine and let you see joke questions and responses on the display each time you press the touchpad.

How it works...

The `main` function creates a `TouchIn` object that's connected to the first touchpad connector on the board. The list of question images is retrieved by calling the `get_questions()` function and saving the returned list in the `questions` variable.

An infinite event loop is then started, which first selects a random question and calculates the associated response image for that question. The question image is then displayed on the screen by calling the `show_image` function. The `wait_for_touch` function is then called, which loops and checks for a touch event every 100 milliseconds.

Once a touch event is detected, the function is returned, and then the `show_image` function is called to show the response image. The `wait_for_touch` function is called again so that the user can see the response before deciding to load another question by pressing the touchpad. Once the touchpad is pressed, the current loop iteration ends and the process starts again with a new, randomly selected question.

There's more...

The joke-telling machine is a fun way to use the input and output potential of this board. It uses the board's graphical display to show the different joke questions and responses, as well as the capacitive touch sensors as input to make the application load the next question or show the answer to a loaded question.

This base recipe can be extended in many ways. Since the board comes with four touchpads, you could create a simple menu system where people can choose from different categories of jokes. You could even create a project for digital dice by having images of the six sides of a die and showing a random side each time the touchpad is pressed.

See also

Here are a few references regarding this recipe:

- Documentation on the `ColorConverter` object can be found at `https://circuitpython.readthedocs.io/en/latest/shared-bindings/displayio/ColorConverter.html`.
- Documentation on the `TileGrid` object can be found at `https://circuitpython.readthedocs.io/en/latest/shared-bindings/displayio/TileGrid.html`.

Other Books You May Enjoy

If you enjoyed this book, you may be interested in these other books by Packt:

Artificial Intelligence for Robotics
Francis X. Govers

ISBN: 978-1-78883-544-2

- Get started with robotics and artificial intelligence
- Apply simulation techniques to give your robot an artificial personality
- Understand object recognition using neural networks and supervised learning techniques
- Pick up objects using genetic algorithms for manipulation
- Teach your robot to listen using NLP via an expert system
- Use machine learning and computer vision to teach your robot how to avoid obstacles
- Understand path planning, decision trees, and search algorithms in order to enhance your robot

Learn Robotics Programming
Danny Staple

ISBN: 978-1-78934-074-7

- Configure a Raspberry Pi for use in a robot
- Interface motors and sensors with a Raspberry Pi
- Implement code to make interesting and intelligent robot behaviors
- Understand the first steps in AI behavior like speech recognition visual processing
- Control AI robots using Wi-Fi
- Plan the budget for requirements of robots while choosing parts

Leave a review - let other readers know what you think

Please share your thoughts on this book with others by leaving a review on the site that you bought it from. If you purchased the book from Amazon, please leave us an honest review on this book's Amazon page. This is vital so that other potential readers can see and use your unbiased opinion to make purchasing decisions, we can understand what our customers think about our products, and our authors can see your feedback on the title that they have worked with Packt to create. It will only take a few minutes of your time, but is valuable to other potential customers, our authors, and Packt. Thank you!

Index

B

C

setting, to same color 41, 42

O

octave notation
  reference link 60
OLED display, CircuitPython
  reference link 348
OLED display
  clearing 328, 329, 330
  colors, inverting on 345, 346, 348
  filling 328, 329, 330
  lines, drawing on 336, 338, 339, 340
  pixels, setting on 331, 332, 333, 334, 335
  rectangles, drawing on 336, 338, 339, 340
  reference link 348
  text, writing on 341, 342, 343, 344
OLED watch, MicroPython
  reference link 345
OnDiskBitmap object
  reference link 403
open function
  reference link 271
operating system (OS) 8

P

parse_url function 291
PC Mag, microcontroller
  reference link 11
phototransistors
  reference link 107
picocom command
  reference link 238
pin 13 LED
  turning on 28, 29, 30
Pin object, machine module
  reference link 325
pins, general-purpose input/output (GPIO)
  reference link 256
pitch
  reference link 59
pixel color
  obtaining, by creating generator 132, 134
  obtaining, to create generator 133
pixel features
  reference link 158

pixels attribute, CircuitPython
  reference link 35
pixels
  controlling, NeoPixel object used 156, 157
  lighting up, by creating touch handler 161, 163, 164
  settings, on OLED display 331, 332, 333, 334, 335
play_file method
  references 67
play_tone method
  reference link 56, 66
pprint module
  reference link 354
PrinceTronics
  reference link 63
PULL_UP setting, with MicroPython
  reference link 383
pulse width
  correcting, by tuning servos 180, 181, 182
push button presses
  detecting 77, 78
push button
  active LEDs, moving with 86, 87, 88
  LEDs, controlling with 79, 81
  reference link 79, 81, 229
push buttons, servos
  reference link 197
Python classes
  reference link 127
Python library
  reference link 117
Python module
  creating 127, 128, 129
  references 129
Python range function
  reference link 59
Python string formatting
  reference link 370
Python string slicing
  reference link 44
Python-based software synthesizer
  reference link 60

R

rainbow animation
  reference link 52
rainbow colors
  LED animations, creating with 49, 50, 51
  reference link 52
random colors
  LED animations, creating with 46, 48
random library, Circuit Playground Express
  reference link 46
random method
  used, for selecting cities 358, 359, 360
random module 360
random NeoPixel LED colors
  generating 44, 45
range of motion of servos
  reference link 186
raw sockets
  used, for performing HTTP request 288, 289, 290, 291
Read-Eval-Print Loop (REPL), MicroPython
  reference link 18
Read-Eval-Print Loop (REPL)
  accessing, Mu used 19, 20
  accessing, screen used 17, 18
  commands, executing in 21, 22
  reference link 18, 24
  using, over serial connection 236, 237
rectangles
  drawing, on OLED display 336, 338, 339, 340
recv method, MicroPython socket
  reference link 292
red LEDs
  controlling 254, 255
red_led property
  reference link 30
remove function
  reference link 266
repeat key action 79
RESTful API
  developing, to control LEDs 314, 316, 317
  reference link 318
RESTful jokes API
  reference link 383

RESTful web service
  JSON data, fetching from 296, 298
RGB code
  used, for displaying LED color 35, 37, 38
rmdir function
  reference link 266
running_time function
  reference link 231

S

scan method
  reference link 240, 389
scientific pitch notation (SPN) 60
ScoreBoard class
  adding, to event loop 140, 141
  scores, displaying with 135, 136
  winners, detecting with 137, 139
screen brightness
  controlling 395, 396, 397
  reference link 398
Screen object
  about 360
  creating, for text handling 360, 361, 362, 364
screen
  used, for accessing Read-Eval-Print Loop (REPL) 17, 18
scroll method
  references 226
scrolling text
  displaying 224, 225, 226
seed function
  reference link 360
send method, MicroPython socket
  reference link 292
Service Set Identifier (SSID) 240
servos and DC motors, CRICKIT board
  reference link 207
servos components
  reference link 182
servos motion
  reference link 189
servos objects
  reference link 197
servos, inner working
  reference link 182

Printed in Great Britain
by Amazon